Tyrel grew up in central Canada in the Prairie town of Rosetown Saskatchewan. Since 2017, he has been working for Hokkaido University's Faculty of Education where he currently holds a DX Fellowship. He lives in the city of Sapporo, Japan, where he splits his time between his family and reading and writing history and travel.

Dedicated to C, J, & L. Your love and support give me life.

And to Paul Theroux and Colin Thubron—titans of travel; boundless sources of inspiration and pleasure. Your stories are alive in my imagination and this, too, gives me life.

Thank you for each and every one of them.

Tyrel Cameron Eskelson

THE ISLAND OF MORA MORA: A JOURNEY INTO MADAGASCAR

AUSTIN MACAULEY PUBLISHERS™
LONDON * CAMBRIDGE * NEW YORK * SHARJAH

Copyright © Tyrel Cameron Eskelson 2023

The right of Tyrel Cameron Eskelson to be identified as author of this work has been asserted by the author in accordance with sections 77 and 78 of the Copyright, Designs and Patents Act 1988.

All rights reserved. No part of this publication may be reproduced, stored in a retrieval system, or transmitted in any form or by any means, electronic, mechanical, photocopying, recording, or otherwise, without the prior permission of the publishers.

Any person who commits any unauthorised act in relation to this publication may be liable to criminal prosecution and civil claims for damages.

The story, experiences, and words are the author's alone.

A CIP catalogue record for this title is available from the British Library.

ISBN 9781398486164 (Paperback)
ISBN 9781398486171 (ePub e-book)

www.austinmacauley.com

First Published 2023
Austin Macauley Publishers Ltd®
1 Canada Square
Canary Wharf
London
E14 5AA

Special gratitude to four men who give far more than they take from this world. Dr Erik Patel, a great scientist, humanitarian, and friend.

Rabary Desire whose knowledge and actions are an inspiration those in this world who prefer to build rather than tear down.

Dr Steve Goodman for your thirty plus years of work in Madagascar building institutions and advancing knowledge, and for taking the time to talk to me.

And to Floris Saula, a husband, father, and man who represents a more prosperous and resilient future for the people of Madagascar.

This book would not be without your generosity and hospitality.

Table of Contents

Preface	11
Chapter One: Antananarivo	13
Chapter Two: Diego Suarez	39
Chapter Three: Diego to Ambanja	58
Chapter Four: Night Bus to Mahajanga	77
Chapter Five: Camp Indri	91
Chapter Six: Sambava to Maroantsetra	118
Chapter Seven: The Train to Tana: Maroantsetra to Antananarivo	134
Chapter Eight: The Land of the Invincible Multitude: Antsirabe, Fianarantsoa and Manakara	153
Chapter Nine: Goat, Circumcision and a Crayon Fence: The Last Road to Toliara	185

Preface

Madagascar is a big island where things happen slowly. This was something that I had to learn, and gradually absorb, until it became a habit of travel. It is fitting to write about Madagascar in a travel narrative because it is an island inhabited by the descendants of ancient and enigmatic travellers who left their home for unknown reasons. These people eventually found their way to the shores of Madagascar and stayed for good.

The island of Madagascar was part of the ancient landmass of Gondwanaland, which broke apart millions of years ago and sent the Indian landmass hurling into the Asian continent, forming the Himalayas, while Madagascar drifted down to its current coordinates where it made up the eastern coastline of the Mozambique Channel. Its natural history has left the island with an overabundance of endemic species of flora and fauna.

Though Madagascar is an island geopolitically grouped with the continent of Africa, it is more fitting to see it as belonging to the Indian Ocean. The Malay trading networks over a thousand years ago created a trans-oceanic system that ran from Eastern Africa to India and down to the archipelagos of the South Pacific. Historically, human beings were a recent addition to Madagascar and this trading network was what brought them to the island.

With these curiosities of natural and human history, Madagascar holds many distinct experiences for the traveller. My aim was to visit as many regions as possible and to talk with people to get a glimpse into their lives. I had traversed half the world, leaving from Japan, overnighting in Hong Kong, a night in the Doha airport, and then a flight to Paris. In Paris, I had the feeling of being on the other side of the world, but I was not yet in the correct hemisphere. From Orly airport in southern Paris, via the island of Reunion, I flew to the capital city, Antananarivo. After several days of travel, I was ready to begin my journey into Madagascar.

Chapter One
Antananarivo

I arrived at my hotel late in the afternoon after a long day. I took a room downtown in the former French Colonial section called Avenue de L'Independence. It was a wide street of pre-war colonial buildings that stood three-stories-high, with exterior arcades partly enclosing the sidewalk. Each building was shingled in hues of either badious, ochre, umber, or russet browns. The road had a thin adornment of trees and a grassy walkway running down the centre lane. I estimated the distance from one side of the street to the other to be about eighty meters across. The sun was setting and I decided to get settled into my room, take a shower, and get some sleep.

The next morning, at breakfast, the waitress's eyes widened when I asked her for yet another cup of coffee, my third.

'You want more?'

I had just eaten an omelette with fruit juice for breakfast, and other than scratching a fresh mosquito bump on my arm, was now enjoying a peaceful morning in a large colourful room with lots of natural light flowing through the many windows along the back wall of the hotel's bar and restaurant.

The waitress, a woman of about forty, had black hair down to her shoulders and a lightly bronzed skin colour. This light tone of brown skin was representative of the Malagasy whose ancestors arrived here from Borneo over a thousand years ago. Her hair and her facial features could have belonged to the Philippines or Indonesia. When she smiled, it showed a hesitant reluctance, before she could no longer contain it and gave into the mirth, while shaking her head like a girl giggling at a misbehaving boy. I had seen this side of her, but now I could see surprise, even disapproval, as though she might be restraining mothing instincts to tell me that two cups of coffee were more than enough. She brought me the coffee and when she saw my satisfaction, the smile returned to her face.

A man in his forties walked into the room and over to the bar where he uttered something in French to the waitress. He was still standing there drinking a glass of thick frothy juice when I went to pay my bill. This man was not Malagasy; I placed his features as Indian or perhaps Middle Eastern. He told me his name was Sal, short for Salman, and that he had grown up in London, which was evident in his accent.

'I've had the hotel for two years,' he told me in a soft spoken voice.

'Do you want to try this juice? It's avocado, we're testing it out.'

The waitress brought me a cup and after sampling it, I indicated that I liked it.

'The fruits and vegetables grown here are excellent. Full of anti-oxidants.'

He lit a cigarette and we chatted about life and business in Tana.

'It's hard to find long term staff in this city. I've had trouble with workers taking money. They don't think about employment in the future. They had a chance to take money now, and took it.' He then pointed to another waitress who had been working behind the bar counter while I was eating my breakfast. She was a petite woman in her early twenties.

'She started this week and has been great so far.'

Sal told me that he was married and had children, but he and his wife were separated and she and their children were living in Mauritius.

'I miss them a lot, but my wife and I needed to take a break. We had some problems. We still talk every day though and will probably work things out.'

Though his voice was low and calm, and his manner gentle, open, and genuine, there was also a sombre aura to his demeanour and I judged that he carried a lot of weight on his shoulders. I was not certain if it was his character to reveal personal information readily, or if in this moment he saw an opportunity with me to unburden himself, but I was glad to listen. Just then, as if he sensed what was on my mind, he told me:

'It can be hard making a true friend in this city. I run a casino upstairs and have lost a lot of good friends who borrow money and never return. How long are you in Madagascar for? Three months; that's good. You should come to the bar tonight. We have a company party here tonight that should be fun.'

I walked outside to Independence Avenue where a waiting throng of pestiferous men implored me to buy vanilla, sapphires, marijuana or change money. Others were touting poorly-made instruments and one had a large wooden model ship. They were the quintessential 'anything-everything-man'. I was reminded of a conversation I had had in Jaipur with a taxi driver who asked me: 'Do you know what is impossible or forbidden to do in India? Nothing!' There were also the 'anything-everything-men' on the streets of Kathmandu, who uttered in a low aggressive desperate tone: 'something?' Among the impoverished of the world, there were always those willing to do anything and everything if it meant a bit of money.

Independence Avenue was lined with a row of identical moonlight-coloured Citroen taxis, which were small cars with beady eyes and bubble butts. Many of the cars looked to be from the 1950s, and were perhaps like the cars Norman Lewis depicted in his book *Dragon Apparent,* in which he travelled around Southeast Asia in the early 1950s. I later found a photography piece done by Clare Spencer of the BBC, who had written that these taxis were cheap and easy to repair, but they don't go very fast. They have been a favourite of taxi drivers in the capital for over fifty years.

If there was a garbage service in this part of the city, it had yet to arrive that morning. There was garbage sitting in piles, litter strewn around, and the air was thick with smog from all sizes of vehicles that looked like they had never run smoothly. They coughed out plumes of blue and black smoke whenever the strain on the engine was anything but a downward frictionless plane.

Tana was built on and around a large hill which gave the city a pseudo-grandeur, but for the most part it was a low-built city with structures that reached no higher than four-stories. Some of the winding streets up the side of a hill were cobbled with paving stones. I watched a man hopping onto a taxi-brousse that was crammed full of people presumably commuting to their place of work. The taxi-brousse was the ubiquitous form of travel for the Malagasy, both in cities and for transport between cities. Each of them was a large cargo van, equipped with ten to fifteen seats that usually had a minimum of twenty itinerant passengers.

This area of Tana had a mixture of people moving with something to do, others sitting around waiting for something to do, and a third scattering of people who had nothing and had long ago given up looking for something to do. It was late April so the Southern Hemisphere was in the middle of Autumn. Many Malagasy I passed were wearing light jackets and scarves in the cool sunny morning.

For the destitute who were lying around, the winter months at this altitude subjected them to several weeks of freezing in the evenings and thawing throughout the day. This, combined with malnourishment, was enough to drain them of energy and strength. They looked defeated and I could not imagine how they survived being homeless and destitute in a place where everyone else was impoverished.

Though this was my first morning in the city, I had limited time to look around because I had somewhere to be. I was fortunate enough, after inquiring, to be invited to the University of Antananarivo campus where Dr Steven M. Goodman helped run Vahatra, a program that supplemented the education of local scientists with graduate degrees recognisable around the world. Through email, I asked him if I could come and ask some question about his involvement in the institution and his work in the country, and he was nice enough to offer me some of his time.

During my taxi ride to the university, through the busy morning traffic, I talked with my driver who told me his name was Ando and that he was forty-two years old. He had a beaky face with a smoky complexion and he often smiled when chatting. He rested his right hand on the steering wheel when it wasn't needed to shift gears. He asked me where I was from.

'How cold does it get in Canada? Whooa, I think Malagasy would die.'

I told him Malagasy people study in Quebec and Ontario every year and we send them back alive. Traffic was moving slowly enough that hawkers could walk among the cars trying to sell things. A man was determined to sell me sunglasses even though I was wearing a pair. Ando and I had to talk over the chatter coming from just outside my car window.

Ando told me he had lived in Tana all his life, he had a wife and son, and had been driving a taxi for the past twelve years. As we were pulling in to the university campus, I asked Ando: 'what do you think of living in Tana?'

'People here are very poor, but I like Malagasy people and I like this city.'

After about fifteen minutes of traveling southeast from Avenue de L'Independence, Ando left me outside a large brick wall that had a small picture of the Vahatra symbol beside a black steel door. The symbol appeared to be the lower part of a black tree trunk with tree roots. I knocked at the gate and waited until a security guard came to the door. He showed me to one of the two dark red concrete buildings. The one I entered had two floors built on the side of a hill, and the entrance was split between the first and second level. A secretary on the top floor came down wooden steps to the entry-way and directed me downstairs.

At the end of a short dark hall, I came to the entrance of an office where I saw Dr Goodman sitting at a desk with his face partially obscured by a large computer monitor. He looked over top and then stood, welcomed me in, shook my hand, and offered me a seat across from him. He was tall, wore glasses, and had streaks of black remaining in his greying beard.

He said in a friendly voice: 'I couldn't remember if you were coming today or tomorrow,' and then added, 'but now is fine.'

A window on the far wall from the entrance provided the room with natural light. The walls were lined with tables and cabinets of books, stacks of papers, and specimens from the field, spread and scattered in a professorial order.

Dr Goodman held the chair as a field biologist at the Field Museum of Natural History in Chicago. He grew up in the countryside of Michigan where, as a child, he became interested in understanding the nature around him.

'In my heart, I'm a Victorian naturalist and it became abundantly clear to me after a few weeks in Madagascar in 1989, there were few places in the world that were better for a Victorian naturalist than Madagascar.'

After field work in Egypt and Pakistan, Dr Goodman came to Madagascar with a project sent to examine the environmental impact of forest removal at an illuminate mining site in South Eastern Madagascar.

'I realised very quickly there are some interesting discoveries you can make here. It was very enticing for me to stay.'

Over twenty-five years ago, there were still many species of flora and fauna in Madagascar that had yet to be scientifically classified. When Dr Goodman began his work here in the 1990s, the possibility for discovering new species was wide open.

'The rate of discovery is slowing down now, but if you turn to organisms such as frogs, the estimate now is three-hundred species of frogs described in Madagascar but from vocalisation and genetics we think there could be six or seven hundred, perhaps eight-hundred.'

He explained how the President of Vahatra, Sheila Rasomanala had been responsible for the discovery of over one hundred species of frogs.

'It's kind of a joke, but it gives a real sense. Years ago we would have missions where Sheila would come back and we'd say: *how many new species of reptiles*, and they'd have ten or fifteen. A couple years ago, I asked the same question and she said: *uhh, only three or four.*'

He drew my attention to a table behind me and said: 'on the table there are specimens of new species discovered in just the past month. The new species accumulation curve certainly isn't reaching a plateau. On the one hand it shows how spoiled we are but on the other, the rate of discovery is no longer exponential in growth.'

Nearly every book written about Madagascar in the past forty years mentioned the words *biodiversity hotspot, conservation, slash and burn, and poverty*—and the purpose of many of these books was to examine the relationship between these topics. Alison Jolly's book *A World Like Our Own*, published in 1980, was written with love for the flora and fauna of Madagascar, but also described the problems for the conservation of nature, which could have been written last year. In the introduction, she stated that this book "is about the conflict between the short-term urgency of rice for today and the long-term hope of rice for tomorrow. It is about the quality of life for the Malagasy if they choose to save or to destroy their natural heritage."

These lines still describe the problems faced in the country today. I mentioned to Dr Goodman that I had been reading some books about conservation in Madagascar. That it seemed to me a nearly impossible task to slow the trend that was wiping out the plants and animals on this island. I said: 'one of the questions I had was over the repeated figure of ninety percent of the natural forests being cleared. I saw this figure numerous times but also read a recent book that dispelled the figure as too high.'

He said 'there is very good evidence that when humans first arrived in Madagascar there was natural ecological formations from coast to coast, but a problem is with the language. Implicit in the argument is that there was coast to coast closed-canopy forest, which wasn't the case. If you say ninety percent of the natural formations on the island have been destroyed that is probably correct. Here's a good example. Madagascar is rich in fossil remains of animals that were alive a few thousand years ago. You can find animals at certain sites that based on their pelvis and forearms, they were clearly closed canopy forest dwellers. They physically couldn't walk on the ground. In those same deposits we find animals that were very baboon-like and terrestrial, and further you find animals that were aquatic such as the pygmy hippopotamus. Carbon dates are more or less the same period, so the only way to interpret the ecology of that zone is heterogeneous, running from marsh habitats with fresh water, to wooded savannah, to closed canopy. The actual figures are not so important; what is important is that the natural formations have disappeared. A whole range of different formations. There is virtually no wooded savannah that remains in Madagascar.'

One of the specific considerations with conservation projects in Madagascar was the drastic changes in elevation and how this affected what species of flora and fauna lived in that region.

'If you compare Madagascar with the Amazon basin, the Amazon basin is basically lowland forest; or the Congo basin; you can move one or two hundred kilometres and as long as you don't change much in elevation, things remain relatively the same. In Madagascar, what you might conserve in a block of forest, twenty kilometres away in another block, there is significant change. It's notably more heterogeneous.'

Madagascar was large enough to have a number of distinct biomes and the conservation policies were determined primarily by biotic richness. One of the most important factors was the human element when it came to protecting an area of land. When it came to conservation, Dr Goodman explained that there were two ways of looking at it.

'There is science pure on the one side and conservation science on the other. It gets at the philosophy of—why conserve? There is a bifurcation of human needs and biodiversity. If it is for human use, such as medicinal plants or forest resources, small parcels of conserved land are just fine. They can be managed by communities. Ecosystems are a whole other ball of wax. Once you start talking about ecosystems—what is the minimum space needed to conserve ecosystems? So, what do you want to conserve and why do you want to conserve it?'

We sat and chatted a little longer about the challenges associated with conservation efforts in Madagascar. I then asked him about the pedagogical aspects of Vahatra. Thirty years ago, people here knew very little about the unique biological diversity on the island. Part of the mission of Vahatra was to train Malagasy students so that they could become engaged with their own research projects. Dr Goodman created an ecology training program that took Malagasy graduate students in the field to demonstrate techniques, sent them to overseas labs, and had them work with a whole variety of people to develop a tool set that eventually led to the completion of PhDs.

'Nine years ago, the Ecology Training Program was passed over to Vahatra and this still remains the mandate. Many of the people from the first ETP are now university professors. They've been integrated into the governmental or non-governmental sectors and the idea is to create something that can approach or achieve exponential growth. We are pretty close to there now. Our goal is to advance the Malagasy people and when they're given a chance to make a decision for their country, they'll be able to do it.'

Through the course of our conversation, he asked me if I have seen the book he published called *Extinct Madagascar*. When I expressed an interest to buy the book, he said, 'I think we have a few copies of it here.' With that we stood up and I followed him to go find a copy of the book. We used the occasion for a brief tour around the building. Along the wall downstairs were small framed pictures with species that Vahatra scientists had discovered. We walked back down the hall to a room at the bottom of the stairs, where inside several students were working on laptop computers.

'Those two over there are working on their masters,' and he then turned to the girl sitting to the left of the entrance and said 'she just finished her PhD.'

When we turned around from the entrance, Dr Goodman pointed to an adjacent room: 'We have a kitchen over here where the students can get something to eat while they are here working.' He then turned around and pointed to some contraption under the stairs while saying 'the entire building runs on solar panels.'

We went upstairs to a lab room where on the counters I saw jars with various indiscernible things floating inside. He walked over to a filing cabinet where he pulled open fossil shelves.

'The university of Michigan gave me these when they got new ones.' He took out a small jaw bone which he said was from a pygmy hippo and handed it to me to hold. I was reminded of a program that I had watched on George Washington, who had teeth constructed from a set of hippo tusks.

'As you can see, it wasn't very big. Maybe twice the size of that table,' he said, referring to a small wooden coffee table that looked like one built in high school shop class.

When I asked Dr Goodman how much the book cost, I told him that I would have to come back because I wasn't carrying that much cash on me.

'It's not a problem. You can take the book now and come back any time you want to pay for it.' I thanked him for his time and he offered me the opportunity to return should I have further questions.

Later that afternoon, while lying in my hotel room reading and dozing, I heard music playing from the bar and restaurant downstairs and remembered Sal's invitation. When I entered ten minutes later, I found ten people with their hands on the hips of the person ahead of them, laughing and dancing in a Cuban Conga line. A foreign man and woman, perhaps forty and thirty-five respectively, stood out among the eight Malagasy men and women that formed the dancing procession.

The atmosphere had changed from the peaceful breakfast I had had that morning. The lights were dimmed and three surrounding televisions showed the music videos of the songs being played. When the song ended, the marching dancers dispersed like a football huddle that had just received a play-call to take a drink. A song called *I Took a Pill in Ibiza* by Mike Posner came on the sound system and televisions.

'Glad you could make it.' It was Sal greeting me warmly, smiling, and offering me his hand to shake. This handshake was not like our one of introduction that morning. This was a handshake done for the rest of the people in the room. It told them that some level of familiarity existed between those two people.

'That man over there,' he was referring to the European man standing by a table sipping a drink. 'He runs an I.T. business in several countries. He recently opened an office in Tana. They're having a company party to reward the employees.'

I stepped over to the bar counter, which was close enough that I could maintain my conversation with Sal, and ordered a beer and asked for a menu.

'Do you like Indian food?' Sal asked me.

'Yes, I love it,' I said.

'We are testing some new dishes this week; do you want to try one?'

Sal and I were chatting when a woman in her early thirties approached him. Sal's reaction told me they were friends, and when they embraced, they exchanged a kiss on the cheek. She had the light brown complexion of a Merina, long straight black hair that extended below her shoulders, and dark red lipstick. She wore a nice dress that wrapped tightly to a buxom frame which revealed a sensual figure. Her style and appearance gave the impression of someone who often dressed well, and when Sal introduced us, she offered me a warm smile.

'This is Tiana; she is a travel agent and does some work for clients at the hotel. If you need any help arranging a trip she can help you.'

'How do you spell your name?' she asked me after I repeated it one time for her. She asked me some questions about why I was in Madagascar and how long I planned to stay. She told me that she was thirty-one years old and had one daughter. Tia was not able to stay and chat. She asked me: 'do you play poker? I will play poker upstairs tonight; do you want to come?'

I was not interested to play but I told her that I will come up and watch after I finish eating my Indian food. Tia left the room and I joined Sal, who altered his stance to include me into the conversation he was having with the European man he had pointed out to me earlier. The European man's name was Martin and he was from Brussels. Martin's co-worker, Anna, stopped by to get another drink from the bar, and I learned that she had recently moved to South Africa to work in the office there. She said: 'last year we opened an office in Tana. This is my first time coming here. It's a good place to start a business and the salary for the employees is cheap. Those workers earn fifty dollars and month which is ok in Madagascar.'

'Doesn't sound like much to me,' I said, and just as I was asking her the name of the company, another lady called her.

'Okay, I'm coming.' Anna turned back to me, 'sorry, I have to go.'

The casino room upstairs looked like two former hotel rooms had been partly re-designed into what was now a makeshift professional poker room. There was a small bar, two dealers dressed in uniforms, and three men in their twenties sat at the table playing with Tia. She invited me to sit beside her and said 'do you want a drink? You don't have to pay for them in this room.'

They played on a professional table with a green top and cushioned edge. The room was thick with smoke and they all talked and laughed with each other with some measure of familiarity. The man at the end of the table, closest to the entrance, received his cards, peeked at them, then spent the rest of the hand texting on his phone, almost looking indifferent to the game in which he was a part. Across from him to my left, by the bar, was a gregarious man who spoke like a semi-automatic rifle. He wore a uniform and changed money for chips, but he was also in on the action. Across from me, near the dealer, another man of about twenty-five years old, smoked cigarettes, fiddled with his chips the way gamblers manage the pressure of high-stakes, and said nothing but the occasional smile to acknowledge he was following the table's conversation. They usually spoke French, but mixed it frequently with Malagasy. When they spoke English, they had French accents. They looked like they were having fun but I grew bored watching the game, and I also felt I was cheating the hotel by drinking beer for free in the casino.

Back down in the bar, much of the party were gathering their things and people were saying their goodbyes to one another. Sal invited me to grab a chair and come and sit in a small gathering on the dance floor. Two young men had acoustic guitars and began playing a Bob Marley song, then the French song *Formidable*, and some others. It was a relaxed way to finish the evening. We sang, we drank, and we enjoyed each other's company.

The next morning, I spent a couple hours walking around the bustling neighbourhoods near my hotel. Not far from Independence Avenue, I turned to ascend a narrow road that wound up a hill. After about one-hundred meters of climbing I had to turn around and come back down. The air was hard to breathe because there were plumes of exhaust lingering in the air like a blue acid-fog. Many of the buildings looked precarious and poorly constructed. The cyclist and author Dervla Murphey wrote of Antananarivo in the 1980s that it was poor, but not Third World poor. As I looked out at the buildings and people of Tana that morning I felt Mrs Murphey's observation to be too generous. I judged the city to be thoroughly Third World poor; it looked scarcely better than a slum for most inhabitants, at least for those with a roof over their heads. Notwithstanding, I enjoyed Dervla Murphey's *Muddling through Madagascar* with her daughter in which they both demonstrated wit, self-deprecation, and equanimity as they faced the vicissitudes of travel. The two main narratives of travel that I had read about Madagascar occurred in the 1980s, so I was curious to see how, if at all, travel here had changed.

I found a market to walk through where people were selling fruits, clothes, and other various goods. Two shirtless boys followed me through the market imploring me to give them something. They were barefooted and grimy, but more animated than the impecunious people I had seen lying on the side of the road the day before. Today's market was lively and full of pedestrian foot traffic, scooters, and other vehicles.

At a small market crossroads without vehicle traffic, I came upon two young men who were playing a game of hacky-sack with a round dried piece of fruit the size of a ping pong ball. When they saw that I had stood to watch them play, the invited me in to give it a go. We had several tries together and managed to keep the fruit in the air for six times at best. This event was not so noteworthy but when I looked up from the game, I was startled to see upwards of one-hundred people staring at me from all corners of the tight intersection. Feeling too conspicuous, I left, and the young boys continued to follow me. After about ninety minutes of wondering around the markets and shops, I returned to my hotel and found Ando, who took me back to the university campus so that I could pay for the book at Vahatra, and afterwards, I planned to find my way back to Independence Avenue on foot.

A little later, I left Vahatra and walked down a narrow descending street in the direction of the main road connecting the campus to the city streets. There were many students walking to and from the university which stood across a small valley-like dip from the Vahatra offices. I walked over to the hilltop campus and from there, had a nice view of the Queen's Palace atop another hill in the distance, but my gaze was averted when I noticed two young men walking and holding hands, and was curious whether this indicated a romantic relationship, or just an expression of Malagasy friendship.

The young energetic and chattering faces made me feel old like the brick buildings on campus. I walked to a spot where an elevated walkway wrapped around a ground level square pond. In the distance, many kilometres to the south, I could see a horizon filled with overlapping hills and the sprawling remnants of the city as they gave way to countryside. My overall impression of Tana was slightly improved after taking in the campus. It was austere, and the attempts at landscaping and architecture were not sophisticated, yet the atmosphere had a comfortable and optimistic feeling that contrasted with my earlier negative impressions of the other neighbourhoods I had explored in Tana.

As I approached two young women, I could see they were talking about me, so I said hello to them and we introduced ourselves. Their names were Marie and Andry. They were both short, in their early twenties and dressed well. Both girls had long black hair; Andry had a thin face and Marie had rounder cheeks. Marie spoke to me with a slightly sideways glance, her eyes fixed on me, but her face looked more towards Andry beside her than directly at me. Marie, who did the talking, because Andry was too shy to say anything, told me that she had just finished her master's degree in biology and was from Mahajanga. She asked me why I was at the university, how long I planned to stay in Tana, and what I did for a living.

'I'm a teacher,' I said to her.

Marie said: 'I belong to an English club. We meet and practice English, sometimes talk about books. Do you want to come? Maybe you can give a lesson about English?'

'I would love to,' I said. 'When is your next meeting?'

'We are meeting tomorrow morning.'

Marie and I made a plan to meet in the lobby of my hotel the following morning, and just like that, I had something to do the next day. I bid them adieu, and then at a casual pace walked down the streets, keeping an eye out for various building landmarks that I had made a mental note of earlier. When I reached a long tunnel, I knew I had navigated my way back, and that Independence Avenue would be on my left after reaching the other side.

Back in my hotel room, after a trip to the bathroom, I noticed in the mirror that I had black smudges in my nostrils. Alarmed, I rubbed at them and when the black smeared off, I realised that I must have acquired this soot when transiting the tunnel fifteen minutes earlier. To suppress thinking of what sorts of particulate matter had entered my lungs, I resolved to avoid walking through that tunnel again in the future.

While looking at the dinner menu that evening, I heard the words 'are you coming to watch poker tonight?' It was Tia, who had approached my table. She was smiling with big red lips that matched her fingernails. I invited her to join me for dinner. I knew why I was at this hotel for several nights in a row, but why did this woman come here so much? She told me her work is not too busy at this time of year and she loved to play poker.

'What do you think of life in Tana?' I asked her.

'Tana is a good city. I have my mother and my daughter. If I have a bad time or bad day, I can phone my friends and they can help me to forget and have fun.'

Our food came and I was just about to scoop some off my plate into my gaping mouth when I paused, because I noticed that Tia had scrunched into a new position with her eyes closed. She was saying a prayer. I apologised to her but she smiled and seemed to have no issue forgiving my heathen table manners. After we had a couple bites of our food, I asked for more details of the topic she was discussing a couple minutes earlier.

'There are many things in life I can't control. I need Jesus and God in my life to help me. I'm raising my daughter to believe in God. For example, my birthday is on the Pentecost. My friends say to me, *come on! Let's go celebrate.* But I have dinner with my mother, then I took my daughter to church. I think god is good.'

I said 'tsara ny tompo,' meaning the lord is good. It was a phrase I had picked up somewhere in my reading. Her eyes brightened in appreciation that I knew this phrase. The momentum of this success led my mind and mouth to move faster than my self-control and good judgement, and before I knew it, the next words coming out of my mouth were 'Allahu Akbar.' Thankfully, I had little time to feel embarrassed at my awkward attempt at humour, because Tia immediately responded 'Alakbar is the Jesus of Sal.' The strangeness of this phrase made me burst out into laughter and when she saw my reaction she joined me.

Tia seemed like a grounded and honest woman. I judged her to be someone with a big heart that could be empathetic to a fault. But, in addition to these qualities she was also a woman who was addicted to evenings of drinking, gambling, and late nights; a lifestyle that I did not associate with a mother in her thirties. In all, I enjoyed her company and I would have been glad to spend another dinner or evening the same way; as long as I could skip the poker.

The next morning, I found Marie waiting for me in the hotel lobby and we walked to the end of Independence Avenue and got into a taxi-brousse. We left early as a precaution, but the Saturday morning traffic was light and didn't take us long to get to our destination. Though brief in duration, the ride was rather cramped and noisy, and wasn't conducive to chatting, so we mainly waited until we arrived at the destination.

'I ride these buses every day,' Marie said to me after we were out onto the street and near our destination. 'The cost is only ten percent of taking a taxi.'

The ICE Club met in a large public area with a series of buildings and a big dirt courtyard, all of which, was across the street from the Tana zoo. I had read before coming to Madagascar that, somewhere in the zoo, there was a museum that housed the skeletal remains of an Aepyornis, or in common English, an elephant bird. The elephant bird belonged to the ratite family along with the ostrich, moa, emu, and rhea. Scientists believed that ratites dated back prior to the breakup of Gondwanaland, and after the landmass split into the southern hemispheric continents, the ratites diverged into different species in South

America, Africa, Australia, New Zealand, and Madagascar. Madagascar's elephant bird was not as tall as New Zealand's extinct giant moa, but the elephant bird had greater mass, at around eight-hundred pounds, making it the largest bird of the group.

Marie and I walked down the road a short distance and found the entrance to the museum. A man on the grounds told us the museum was closed, but when I offered him ten-thousand Ariary, he was able to help us sneak into a side entrance of the building. Our entrance was a fire escape and upon entering we found ourselves on the wrong side of the museum exhibits. We carefully walked around the skeleton of a large extinct species of dolphin and then lifted our legs over a rope.

To my right, I spotted the Aepyornis skeleton and walked over to it at the back of the room along a wall. The leg bones were as thick as both the meat and bones on my legs and I estimated its height to be about seven feet. I found the thought of meeting such a bird as frightening as crossing paths with an apex predator and was becalmed only by the certainty of this massive bird's unfortunate extinction.

'I want to take your picture,' Marie said. She had her phone in her hand and was holding it up to frame when we heard the man say something.

'He said it is five-thousand Ariary more to take a picture.'

I had no problem with paying the man to let us in here, but this was insolent. I walked over to the man, who now seemed racketeering, smiled, gave him some money and said 'you're a scoundrel aren't ya.' He smiled, pocketed the money, and Marie took my picture.

We had a few more minutes to look at other exhibits and then had to go back across the street to our lesson. I had not planned to do much in Antananarivo other than talk with Dr Goodman and see the skeleton of this bird, with its melon-sized egg that looked like an elongated moon. After just three days in Tana, I achieved what I had wanted to do, but I still planned to stay for a few more days.

The large public compound across the street was busy with people. Off to one side, a group of thirty people surrounded a band and eight teenagers who were performing a cultural dance. The musicians used accordions, horns, and drums to play a lightly measured rhythm and the dancing appeared conservative and formal in its movements. Elsewhere in the courtyard, men played a game called petanque, which used heavy silver balls thrown at another on the ground forty-five feet distant. The name petanque was Occitan from the southwestern

Mediterranean, and meant *to plant your foot*; more than likely a French importation during the colonial period of the early twentieth century.

Marie and I waited at the back of the compound near one of the entrances to the large building. Another member of the ICE English group, Hery, arrived, and seeing us waiting said to me 'we have to wait for the staff to return. The door is locked.' When I asked Hery questions, he scrunched up his face behind his black-rimmed glasses, as though to say '*what a ridiculous thing to ask*.' He became awkward and was reluctant to respond, and I took this as a sign to leave him alone. As new arrivals joined the group, they exchanged handshakes with those already present. True to their club's purpose, they all greeted each other speaking English, and I could not remember hearing any of them using French or Malagasy during the whole time we were together.

We entered the building and walked a short distance to an open room with chairs stacked one atop the other. After we all had grabbed a chair and were seated in a circle, I counted fifteen young men and women in total. The leader of the group, Jean, said a few words and then introduced me. I had recently read Robert McCrum's *Globish,* and the day before prepared some talking points about how English became a world language and some other anecdotes I hoped would interest them. Then I told them a little about some of my travels and what it was like teaching English in China, Japan, and Russia. After fifteen minutes, I realised that I had forgotten to tell them to please interrupt and ask me as many questions as they wanted. The second I mentioned this, they asked me questions for the rest of the time we spent there. The first questioner had been reading *Animal Farm*, and so had Orwell on his mind.

'Do you like George Orwell? What is his best novel?'

We discussed Orwell's novels and journalism, and since no one had read it, I was able to recommend to them *Politics and the English Language* for its clear-minded maxims and rules for writing concise sentences.

'How many countries have you visited?'

'How many international children have you fathered?'

'Do you like Donald Trump? Who will win between Trump and Clinton?'

'Does Japan have good trains?'

'What do you think of Vladimir Putin?'

'Who is your favourite writer?'

I enjoyed talking with them and answering their questions. These young men and women were educated, fashion conscious, curious about the world, and asked me about Claude Levi-Strauss, Jean Jacques Rousseau, and because I had brought him up, they asked questions about the journalist Christopher Hitchens.

They told me that they were in need of books.

'Our goal is to start a collection of English books. It's hard to find English books.'

They were friendly, humorous, encouraged each other, and seemed to enjoy each other's company. They had formed an informal institution of education and each took the group seriously. Jean said a few words to close the meeting and then after putting the chairs back in their stacks and saying goodbye to everyone, Marie suggested we go for a walk around Lake Anosy.

Lake Anosy lied directly south of Independence Avenue at a low spot among the Tana hills. To the southeast from Lake Anosy, atop the city's large hill, was the Queen's palace, the seat of the Imerina monarchy from the seventeenth century to the nineteenth century, until the island became a colony of France. From the lake's edge, I saw a thin walkway that extended into the centre of Lake Anosy, and at the end of it stood a light brown and bronze obelisk commemorating Malagasy service members in the French army during the First World War.

Researchers from the University of Antananarivo published a paper in 2013 entitled *Malagasy Volunteers and Conscripts in the French Army during World War I*, in which they found, from records, that over forty-thousand Malagasy served in some capacity in the French troops during the First World War. Also, reprinted in this paper from the *Tribune de Madagascar* in October 1915, were the following lines:

'They were gone, the soldiers,

They left Tananarive;

Under their fez flowers fell;

They went far away, on the other side of the river.'

I asked Marie some questions about her family. She told me: 'My parents are separated. I have one brother, three sisters and many stepsisters.'

'Did your father remarry?' I asked.

'Yes, both my mother and father remarried and had more children.'

'What do you plan to do after university?' I asked.

'I want to go to university in Canada, but it is difficult. I am applying to go to an exchange program in Finland next year.'

As Marie and I circled the lake, certain locations framed a decent view of the water and its hilly backdrop. At other spots around the lake, I was reminded that this location was swamp land until the missionary James Cameron oversaw its conversion to an artificial lake. The area stilled smelled like a swamp and certain parkland areas surrounding the lake had people sleeping under trees and garbage scattered everywhere. For the most part, it was an area of the city that, for its nice qualities, attracted the abundance of homeless people and their squatter tents. But who could blame them when they had nothing and nowhere else to go?

I asked Marie what she did in her leisure time.

'I like to invite my friends to my house and make pizza. We like cooking and watching movies. I have a duck at home today.'

I told her Canadians love eating pizza and watching movies as well. We followed a path around the water where we approached three children playing a game with a bottle cap. Just off the path, I saw a group of teens playing a game of billiards on a miniature table.

'I go to church every Sunday. I will go tomorrow morning. Are you a Christian?'

I said 'I don't go to church like you but I enjoy studying the history of Christianity. I would really enjoy going tomorrow,' I said.

She laughed and said 'you want to come?' She was not mocking, but instead reacting to the unexpectedness of my interest in joining her. 'Yes, of course you can come.'

The Sunday morning church service was somewhere on the main hill in the city but I had an impossible time maintaining my bearings after twenty minutes of driving up and around the hilly streets. As we drove over the cobblestone streets, the car doors rattled and the tires made rubbery thuds almost as though we had descended down stairs rather than over paving stone.

Marie was a member of the FJKM which means The Church of Jesus Christ in Madagascar, a Protestant, Presbyterian denomination that was the most popular affiliation in the country. The former President of Madagascar, Marc Ravalomanana, was a member, and served as the vice-president of the church in Madagascar before he was ousted from government in 2009 and forced into exile. The fact that a Protestant denomination was the most popular in Madagascar, despite its French colonial history for over sixty years, reflected the historical presence of the London Missionary Society who arrived in the early nineteenth century.

Up a steep set of steps we reached a long and wide concrete hall, which inside had seating in three columns with twelve seats to a row. We sat in the middle of a crowd of roughly five-hundred people, with an age demographic that skewed to the young. From my seat, I could see a band on the right side of the stage and on the far left side a choir. From the ends moving inwards, were two rows of chairs facing each other, leaving their occupants in profile to the audience. These chairs were filled with people wearing white robes. In the centre was the pulpit.

A small television screen hung above the aisle before the stage, and throughout the service it had the scriptures listed to help people follow along, but it was little help to me. I struggled to keep up with the service, yet, nonetheless was grateful to be there and appreciated that everyone looked at me as if I belonged. Two things made a religion go viral: an alphabet and the acceptance of anyone and everyone. I felt welcome.

There was lots of singing and throughout the preacher's service we stood up and sat back down numerous times. The austere wooden pew was tighter than an airplane seat and the pain of sitting in it gave it an overwhelming sense of authenticity. There was no flash or pomp in the leader or the crowd; no eyes closed with hands in the air; it was a tidy, subdued, well-behaved service that lasted an hour and a half. 'Poverty is well dressed in churches and everyone is approachable,' says Paul Theroux in his travels in *Deep South*. The pastor said something that made everyone laugh as people brought collection baskets around the room.

'What did the pastor say?' I asked Marie.

'He said, we opened our doors to you, now it is time to open your wallets. Earlier when people were laughing, the pastor...' Marie paused because it was our turn to put money in the collection basket. I put some money in and saw that everyone must have put in what they could, because it was full of bills.

Marie continued: 'Earlier when people were laughing, the pastor said something about,' she hesitated a moment and whispered 'circumcision.'

We held hands in a final prayer and then the service was finished. I thanked Marie for letting me tag along with her, and offered to take her for an afternoon meal, but she said that she had family plans for the rest of the day. So, I had some pasta in the restaurant of a hotel near my own. Then, I went to a *Shoprite* grocery store and bought some snacks and bottles of beer to take to my room.

There were two large mendicant families, absent fathers, sitting on a blanket outside the shop. One of the women was nursing a baby. Other little ones ran around without footwear or much clothing. The sight of the nursing child, and the thought of malnourishment inhibiting the cognitive growth of all of these children, made me turn around and go back into the store and buy a bag of groceries for them. Because the street and intersection were busy with people, and I had my own food to get back to the hotel, I decided to walk among the crowd and let the children come to me, which they did. In an inconspicuous manner in the middle of a crowd, I extended my hand enough that the boy understood. He grabbed the bag and I kept walking.

The next evening there was another party and concert at the bar and restaurant in my hotel. The room was filled with about sixty people who had come to see the performer. I had seen Tia when I first came in, but she had since ventured upstairs to play poker with some others. Sal walked around the room and played host, shaking people's hands and joking with them. When he had come by my way, he introduced me to Luk, a man in his late thirties. I grabbed us both a beer and then we sat down at a table. Luk, an investigative journalist, was thirty-seven-years-old and a single father of a son. I asked him how long he had been a journalist and he told me about fifteen years. After some banal small talk, I asked Luk what the newspaper business was like in Tana. He told me that he wrote stories about politics.

'Can you print what you want?' I asked him.

'Yes.'

I repeated the question to press the issue: 'you're free to print whatever you want? Scandals, corruption, exposes?'

'Yes, it is free, but, there is a danger to print everything you want. Sometimes journalists get arrested.'

Where was I going with this? Did I expect him to say anything different? When I asked Luk if he had ever had any trouble with this, he said that he hadn't.

I asked him if he could remember when the Queen's Rova (Palace) burned on 6th November 1995. I had seen it earlier that day, so it was on my mind. I was sure that he would, considering that he would have been around eleven years old at the time. The fire destroyed many monuments in the Palace but what was devastating for most Malagasy was the destruction of the royal tombs. According to the director of the University Museum, Jean-Aime Rakotoarisoa, in a piece called *Fire of the Rova, the Queen's Palace, in Antananarivo*, the official investigation that occurred after this fire swiftly concluded that it was an accident, raising suspicion among many people, who then were led to believe various conspiracy stories. According to the same article, that night of the fire, the remains of Queen Ranavalona III were found in the centre of the city.

Many people still believed that the fire was the result of deliberate arson, and the conclusion of the fire as an accident was evidence of a cover-up. I guess I had hoped that since Luk was a journalist, he might have some insight into a story with conflicting narratives.

'That is our culture,' Luk said, raising his voice and becoming animated. 'They burned our palace; it's our culture.' Then without explicit connection, he said 'and in 2009, the coup d'état; it was French supported. The French control this country's business interests. Marc Ravanaloa tried to open our country to new investment and this created competition on the French monopoly.'

'Do you believe all of that?' I asked him.

'Yes, we have evidence of it,' he said. He dug into his bag and retrieved a book which he handed to me. It was called *Madagascar une culture en peril?* and written by a man named Sylvain Urfer. 'This man helped Malagasy people,' Luk said to me. 'This book has evidence.'

I wanted to ask Luk more questions but decided to let off since the topic became a little heavier than I expected. Since he had shown me a book, I used that as a prompt to change to a lighter topic and asked Luk about books, since he was a writer.

I have a question for you,' he said as a way of reply. 'I have written a novel in French. How can I translate it into English? I want to publish it in English.'

'Why don't you try to publish it in French and then later a publisher can arrange to have it translated into English,' I replied.

'No, I want to publish the book in English. Do you know how I can get it translated into English?'

It was clear at this point that he just wanted help publishing the book, but what was not clear was why he thought I could help him publish it. Furthermore, he was a journalist, well-educated, and trilingual. He knew how to use the internet. Why did he not look this up on the internet?

'Why don't you submit the manuscript to a publishing house in Paris or Montreal, and if they print it in French, it may later get translated into English,' I said one more time, but none of this satisfied him.

'I have one more question for you,' he said to me, seeing that the conversation about book publishing was going nowhere.

'I want to know your advice about getting a girl,' he said.

'Luk,' I said, lightly smiling, 'you have a son. You know how to get a girl.' But Luk told me that he wanted a new woman and wanted advice on how to get one. Perhaps he was just curious to see what I would say, so I gave it a shot. I told him:

'Luk, most woman want someone who is patient, sober, and can carry things for her. If you want to get a girl, I suggest you first define what exactly you would like to do with your life, then aim at this vision, and work extremely hard to get it. The right woman will appreciate that you have things figured out and are aiming at some vision. You also need to be as responsible and as dependable as possible.'

He seemed to approve of this answer and then said, 'Tia likes you.'

'You know Tia?' I asked.

'Yes, she is here all the time. What do you think of her?'

I said, 'Tia is very beautiful and nice to talk to.'

Our conversation ended because the performance began and was much too loud to allow us to continue. The last thing Luk said was 'this woman is famous in Madagascar.' She wore a red costume, a light brown fedora hat, and black high-heeled boots which looked like a Canadian Mountie. Four young woman wearing matching black outfits danced behind the lead singer. When she began playing, several people started dancing. Among them Sal had a large smile on his face as he joined the dancing group. I left the bar and retired back to my room where I had a shower and then worked on writing some notes for an hour or so, then I went to bed.

Something woke me up, but I did not know what it was or what time it was. I could hear the muffled sound of music. I lied in bed under the blankets and in the mosquito net, and listened. It was a knock on the door. I got out of bed and went over and opened the door a crack. It was Tia.

'Is everything alright,' I asked. 'Do you want something?'

She leaned in a little and in a loud whisper to remain audible over the loud music, she said. 'I want to suck you.'

Was I awake? My stomach turned upside-down and my arms and legs felt weak. And then, as though returning to consciousness, I realised that the door had already gently swung open, and I had stepped aside as she entered my room. 'Tsara ny Tompo and Allahu Akbar.'

The next two days passed with some kind of party with the regulars and Sal at the hotel. I took Marie to the Pirate Museum which was underwhelming in content, but I was impressed with the fact that it existed and was well-maintained. On a Wednesday afternoon, I met a man who claimed to be a local historian who said his name was Eric. I told him that I needed to get away from the hotel for a day and wanted to see some of the local Merina culture. He told me that he could arrange a trip into the countryside and would show me some local village life and cultural history. I accepted his offer and gave him some money and left the details in his hands. He said, 'let's meet at six-thirty tomorrow morning. If we leave early, we can beat the morning traffic.'

The next morning, Eric had a durable SUV and a driver waiting for us outside the hotel in the chilly morning air. On our way out of the city, we stopped at a roadside shop that sold fried bread, coffee, and tea. Eric said 'Malagasy workers who do not have enough time to make rice in the morning stop at a shop like this and eat this fried bread.' The bread was oily and tasted like a donut. Eric said this kind of breakfast restaurant could be found everywhere in the country. We stood outside next to the shop and wolfed it down, then jumped back into the vehicle and proceeded north out of the city.

Eric explained to me that the monarchy and capital city established its seat of power among twelve important hills throughout this geography.

'Later today we will visit a place called Ambohimanga. This was a palace observation point for the king to defend his territory.'

We were too early to visit this place, so Eric first planned for us to visit some site where he could teach me about Malagasy shamanism.

Somewhere to the northeast of the capital, we parked our SUV and made a light climb up a hill, down the other side, then up an adjacent hill about three-hundred meters. We walked up a dry bumpy trail through tall porcupine-looking grass. At the top of this little climb was a white building, with a fence, a red roof, and what I counted to be four national flags flapping in the breeze. The sky was cloudy above us and the mild sweat from the climb was now exaggerating the chill of the breeze. Eric told me that this hill comprised a sacred area where the king's shaman prophesised and sacrificed animals. With the help of UNESCO funds, a new red and white building now preserved the tradition of shamanism.

A fence of thin red iron strips surrounded the one-roomed building and premises. The fence was supported by white rectangular pillars that had statues of white eagles on top. In this small complex, we found the leader of the nearby village standing next to a large pile of boulders that were about the size of a car and together looked like a tortoise. There was a green and white symbol painted on the largest of the rocks. The man was cleaning the dried wax out of a candle holder. He wore a baggy blue jacket, white pants, and as we walked up to join him, I saw that he had left his sandals down at ground level. Eric said 'we must remove our shoes. Shoes are dirty and not allowed in the ritual area.'

Next to the steps that ascended to this platform, there was a rock that had an angled surface. It looked like a tombstone missing one of its corners. The rock and the white wall behind it were both covered in black stains from the many sacrifices that had occurred there. Eric greeted this man, shook his hand, and conferred with him for a moment. I saw him slip him some cash in a discreet manner. Eric then looked at me and said 'We are lucky; a family is coming to do a ritual and this man said it is ok if we watch.' I was not sure if perhaps some of this was staged for my benefit, or if my guide had done a good job and we happened upon this place at an opportune time. While we waited for the family to arrive, Eric said a few things to me.

'People here do not ask for many things. They pray for health and that their family will be healthy. They ask for good agriculture so that they can feed their families. They ask for many healthy children for the next generation. Malagasy people respect the power of shamanism. Even the president, during the election, will ask a shaman *how is my chance?* If a villager has a nightmare, he will tell the leader of his village about the nightmare. The leader will consult the shaman for an interpretation of the dream. If a fady (taboo) is broken, perhaps he will recommend a sacrifice. He will say something like—go to the market and find a cock with the colours of red and brown. They will make a speech and sacrifice to purify life and spirit. People here continue the power and memory of their tradition.'

The concrete steps were cold against my socked feet as we ascended to a small building. The inside looked like the attic of a house. I sat next to the wall where I would be out of the way as an observer. Across the room, on a gable, there were many clocks above a small wooden cabinet resembling a cupboard. The clocks were all within twenty minutes of the correct time. The only light entering from the entrance seemed to get trapped by the dark red walls. On the wall, among the clocks, hung a picture of the historic king wielding a spear and wearing a lamba over one shoulder. Another picture depicted a bearded man who was the king's shaman.

A family of six entered; two older women, a man, his son, and daughters. They were all wearing torn winter clothing. I could see no indication of which lady was the mother of these three children. They lit the candles. Eric whispered to me 'the candles are a symbol of a pure heart when they ask for something from their ancestors.' They poured a glass of rum and put it in the cupboard. Eric whispered 'when they return in two days, that rum will be gone. The ancestors will drink it.'

The six kneeled on the ground before the leader, who sat on the upper level in a casual pose. Wind rustling in the entrance made loud gusting noises. The leader began calling the ancestors. Eric whispered 'you gave us the earth for living. We can do nothing without you. We are ready to receive your benediction. Show us a good way.' This continued in this manner but I could not keep up with the writing and began watching the family's reaction instead. They raised their supine hands, slightly extended, to head level, and in low voices, they each made individual prayers. They placed money inside a bowl, then each drank a glass of rum. The leader said a prayer over each member of the family and then spooned some honey into their mouths. They each caught any drippings that fell, and in a ritualistic manner, rubbed it into their hair. The leader said something that seemed offhand. I looked at Eric, and he said 'try not to get any on the floor.'

They poured more rum and took another drink. The leader found a small rag and wiped up some spots where rum or honey had spilled. He then moved to another part of the room and peeled the bark off chunks of wood. Eric said 'they will take it home and keep it in their rooms.' Just as I thought we were finished, three teenagers popped into the entrance and began playing music. One had an accordion, another a drum, and a third a type of maraca. Their playing indicated our cue to leave the room, and the music accompanied our exit.

Eric and I then walked down the hill and up another hill, and from there, I could see Tana many kilometres in the distance. We soon arrived at an important site for Malagasy history and culture called Ambohimanga. I learned that UNESCO had designated this place a World Heritage site in 2001, and according to their website, this fortified royal city and burial site was called the 'Royal Hill of Ambohimanga.' After poking around this site for fifteen minutes or so, we went back to the vehicle and drove to a village to buy some food at a market. We then drove to the outskirts of the village, where we made a charcoal fire at the side of the road, and cooked a lunch of potatoes, rice, tomatoes, and onions. After this strange, cold, and dusty picnic, Eric and the driver took me back to Tana. I thanked him for an enjoyable day outside the city.

There was another party in the restaurant that evening, but I chose to stay in my room and get a good night's sleep, and to my satisfaction, woke up the next morning having done just that. I spent the next day making some onward plans. I had to be in Tana in ten days for a meeting that I had pre-arranged before coming to the island. I decided that the best course of action would be to fly to Diego Suarez the next day, and then travel over land and be back here in ten days to make my meeting. This planning went well and the following day I left the *city of a thousand* on an early morning flight.

Chapter Two
Diego Suarez

The morning was bright and warm; the sun parched and stung the skin on my open shoulders, only partially relieved at intermittent breezes from the Indian Ocean. Winter in the southern hemisphere was near, but it posed no threat to the northern-most tip of the island. In a small, biscuit-coloured Renault taxi, windows down, no radio, and weak suspension, the car rattled over a pockmarked paved road, absorbing metallic thumps as it passed over the potholes. Out the driver's window the sunlight shimmered on the Bay of Diego Suarez, and on my side was Montagne de Francais, a rocky, tree-covered rise in the land which extended south several kilometres.

The car window was so small I had to put my arm outside the way a sofa is rotated through a door frame, and upon performing this contortion, my hand was able to rest on the mirror in comfort. The driver, having won his fare over other drivers with some temerity, was busy with his console stick, shifting gears in and out as we navigated the cratered pavement, moving counter-clockwise in a north-eastern direction. We did not attain any comfortable cruising speed, but instead, shifted forward and back in accelerations, stops, and swerves.

The roadside was adorned in copses of tropical green vegetation, which in its pleasing tones, contrasted with the asperity of sparse housing and patches of red soil occasionally visible along the surface. At the Northern tip of Madagascar, the city of Diego Suarez was built on the southern edge of one of the world's great natural harbours, third largest by most accounts, which penetrated deep inland and nearly severed the Northern Cape, its amoeba-like shape connected by a narrow strip of land.

Though most people today called it Diego, its Malagasy name is Antsiranana, which means 'to the port/sea', a reference for where inland people were walking. The names of cities and villages reflected a relationship between the people and their geography; the cultural ways of expressing proximity and orientation; of understanding your surroundings. The name Diego Suarez had other origins.

When Vasco de Gama made his way around the Cape of Good Hope at the end of the fifteenth century, he sailed up the Mozambique Channel and came within a couple hundred kilometres of Madagascar. De Gama established a port of call in the Kenyan cities of Mombasa and Malindi, where traces of the Portuguese checkpoints still stand.

One subsequent Portuguese Indian Armada, commanded by Pero Lopes da Sousa, left Lisbon in the Spring of 1539, and after rounding the Cape of Good Hope and making it up to Mombasa by August, caught the favourable Indian Ocean trade winds to Goa by September. His return voyage, however ended up shipwrecked somewhere near Diego Suarez in February 1540.

The Portuguese governor of India, who was da Sousa's brother, sent Capt. Diogo Soares to Madagascar to look for da Sousa. Diogo Soares sailed into the bay that I was currently driving around. He didn't find da Sousa, but did make it back to India the same year with silver and slaves that he had plundered from this region.

The Indian Ocean entered the mouth of the Bay on the eastern-side of Madagascar, and our direction of travel was towards this point, the equivalent of Watsons Bay to the Sydney Harbour. The resemblance, however, ends there. The Bay of Diego Suarez, after passing through a narrow mouth, opened into four large amorphous quadrants.

My driver was taking me to a small fishing village called Ramena near the mouth of the bay on the western side. As we drove the thirty kilometres around the south-eastern quadrant of the bay along a remote road, my driver, Alan, pressed for further work tomorrow. He had dark skin, a clipped head, and scheming eyebrows. Along the road we passed villagers in small groups walking to some unknown destination, perhaps one of the few houses we had passed earlier.

Some of the women were cloaked at the waist in earthy red- and orange-patterned lambas, and others wore them around their body and head. The lamba was the traditional dress for most of the country, though most men today opted for the cheap clothes sewn in China or second-hand things sent from North America. The men carried machetes, the ubiquitous tool used for work in the fields and forests. Each time we passed a woman walking on the road, the driver honked or hissed out the window in a lewd manner. The Malagasy noise for getting attention was like a shady man on the street corner trying to sell something illegal. Alan slowed the car alongside a young woman, her torso cloaked in blue and black, hair braided for convenience. He stuck his head out the window—'PSSST.' There was a licentious glaze in his eyes that made me distrust him. Showing good taste, she ignored him and we continued.

Zebu were munching in the grass next to the road, and on one occasion blocked our path as they crossed it. The roadside was well represented in cow turds, and from the relaxed pace of our movement, I could easily identify which ones were fresh and which ones were dried and faded from the sun. Among the grass alongside the road, patches of soil lay bare. I found myself staring at it out the window in near disbelief that this dry, red earth could sustain such deep tropical greens.

My eyes were used to the earthy tones of the North American Prairies with big light-blue skies, deciduous greens, and the yellows and greens of the wheat fields and grasslands growing in the rich black soil. In Madagascar, mother earth played a trick on the eyes, clashing fiery red soil with beautiful greens so vibrant that amongst this dry scorching morning they stood as a promise that a rain cloud was on the horizon.

The taxi took me to a place outside Ramena called Lakana Hotel. This sleepy resort was nestled among tall trees that enclosed the premises and blocked a view of the bay. This was still low season so I didn't bother with reservations nor did I plan to for my future arrivals; my plan, if there was one, was to just show up, pack slung on my shoulder, and find a place to stay.

I followed a lady along a crushed white rock path to where she showed me one of several thatched-roof bungalows.

'Is it ok for you?' she asked as I was inspecting it. A large pole in the centre of the room supported a high ceiling. It had a bed and mosquito net, desk, and adjacent shower room.

'How many nights do you want?'

'Just one,' I replied, and with that she left me the key.

The room had a low wattage bulb that offered little added light in the day, but the wooden shutter on the window near the end of the bed was open and allowed adequate light to brighten the dusky room. Gusts of wind blew in through the window, lifting a thin curtain and momentarily revealing red hourglass bars on the outside of the window frame. I heard a low chirp from a bird, which sounded as though it was coming from inside the hut. I glanced around the layers of brown thatched ceiling supported by ascending columns of thick bamboo, and found the noise was coming from the ballooning throat of a small lizard or gecko; I wasn't sure what it was.

Feeling hungry from my journey, I went to the restaurant at the front desk—a tile-patterned concrete slab with tables under an awning roof, built on the side of a wall-enclosed kitchen. Overall, the premises appeared secluded and cosy which made me feel on edge. Places like this resort were built to offer foreign guests a chance to enjoy the sea and sun behind a barrier from the native people who lived here. I resolved these thoughts by saying to myself that I was only here for one evening. I ordered soup and fries because I did not know what the other dishes on the menu were, then took a seat in the wicker furniture on the sand adjacent to the main dining area. I started reading the first pages of a book called *People of the Sea*, an account of an anthropologist who lived among the Vezo people of South Western Madagascar.

I had just finished a few pages, which was off to a jargon-filled start, when a wrinkle-faced man wearing nothing but a pair of tight briefs came over to where I was sitting, and saying nothing, offered his hirsute hand for me to shake. Across a small glass table between us, he sunk into the sofa at such an angle that he struggled with his weak torso to prop himself upright. He exhaled through his nose as he smiled at nothing. He was drunk enough that he had little control over his features; his face scrunched up in inebriated bliss which gave the impression of a simple and stress-free mind. A harmless oaf.

He was obscenely hairy, and his lack of teeth left his tongue absent a reference to flick when producing words; he just emitted drunk, gummy noises. After trying a line that I didn't get, he mumbled the line in English 'eef I breeng my wife, I can't say hello,' which was a euphemism meaning: *If I bring my wife, I can't enjoy the inexpensive prostitution.* The waitress brought him a plate of seafood baked in half a shell, which he must have ordered ahead of time.

I pointed at his dish and said 'crab?'

'Oui.'

He pulled the fork from his toothless mouth, scooped some more and held it across the table for me to try.

'It's good,' I said. 'thank you.'

Tasting this *crab farci*, I regretted my poor choice of order. It was delicious. I saw the waitress exit the kitchen with my food and I left my seat to go sit alone in the shaded dining area.

At the table, I finished my soup and picked at the remaining fries while continuing the book. I felt a slight jarring thump on my chair and turned my head around. I was face to face with a lemur hanging on the back. It was the size of a cat and had a black nose and white trimmed ears protruding from an otherwise round head. It jumped over my shoulder on to the table and then leapt to the next one. Under its grey back and tail it had a white bottom and underside. And she had friends.

Four more leapt across other tables following the first through the dining area, causing the waitress to come out and chase after them. Lemurs, I later learned, are naturally shy of humans unless they get used to people feeding them. Later in the day I noticed a lady from the kitchen give them each a banana. Lemurs, like people, will give up self-sufficiency and resort to dependency if allowed. I asked the waitress how far the village was and she told me just a couple kilometres down the beach.

I walked a couple minutes through the trees and reached the packed white-sand beach. I could see the land across the bay that formed the northernmost tip of the island, and in the sky, thin clouds hung above the dark blue water. I started walking towards the village along the beach which extended north-ward with no-one in sight. The surface of the packed sand was perforated with thousands of tiny holes that kernel-sized white crabs scuttled into as I passed. A small blue fishing boat that had the name *Piscou* in red letters sat on shore at the water's edge. Along the edge of the beach, opposite the water, small, colourless, concrete houses stood among trees.

I reached the beachfront of the village where a couple sea shacks stood. Ramena was small and only a portion of it was visible from the beach. I stopped to watch some children who had gathered to begin a soccer game. A man walked over to me and said: 'do you want to go kite surfing? No, something?'

'I just want to have a look around. Is this a team?'

'I am their trainer' he said, and abruptly left.

Other than the kids, there were few people around. Some men were on a boat at shore fixing something. Another, I saw tending to his zebu. Things looked quiet and sleepy which reminded me that I too felt weary from the early morning flight, so I decided to retire back to my room. I wandered back the way I came and returned to my book for the rest of the afternoon. Though the weather was excellent and area relaxing, my notebook only contained the sarcastic phrase: *hairy French guy gave me crabs.* The next morning, I returned to Diego Suarez.

While driving back to Diego I observed the landscape while Alan drove and hissed at women. All of Madagascar laid before me in this direction. As we rounded the water in a south-western direction three small peaks on French Mountain were visible in jagged waves running southward. On the horizon to the south west I saw the bigger of the two, Montagne d'Ambre (Amber Mountain). The bay was enclosed in low green hills which sloped gently down to the water's edge.

I asked the driver to take me downtown and was dropped off at the Concord Hotel along Rue de Colbert, a paved street of hotels, banks, and restaurants. The hotel was a vertical structure with a maze of stairs in different corners. The concrete walls were pink with teal edging. Like my shower room in Ramena, this room's shower had a sunken, square floor, a bucket and a scoop, and a telephone shower head tethered to the faucet.

I went to the grocery store across the road from my hotel to get some things. *Score* was a foreign company from France that imported common things like packages of sandwich meat or yogurt cups. The prices looked too expensive for most locals to shop here. I got some things to make a sandwich, peanuts, a few beers and bottles of water for my room, and took the goods back across the street. The afternoon heat felt above thirty, but I was fed, hydrated, and went to have a look around.

I walked south along Colbert Street among pillared, two-storied colonial buildings which looked old and uncared for. These French-built constructions stood in cities around the country but as in other colonised cities in Africa, there was little or no tradition left for preserving these buildings. All of Diego was horizontal. The trees rose up above the roof tops in most neighbourhoods. I came upon a bar named Libertalia nestled among the French designs and across from a large building that said *Administration*.

The name Libertalia came from the island's once being a haven for pirates, who created a settlement on the east coast of the country. The history of pirate settlements on Madagascar attracted the attention of William S. Burroughs near the end of his career. According to his biographer, Ted Morgan, Burroughs, in old age, had few relationships left in his life and so spent the remainder of his affection on his five cats, and learning about the lemurs of Madagascar. His short story, *Ghost of Chance* was about a pirate settlement on the coast of Madagascar. Though Burroughs's books such as *Junkie,* or *Naked Lunch,* were revered Beatnik literature, none of these books were as engaging as the life of Burroughs itself, told in straightforward prose by Morgan. Burroughs's method of cut-up mashing paragraphs together inspired the likes of David Bowie, the hippies, and counter-culture in general, but its style did not suit my taste. I did, however, share his fascination with the lemurs and pirate history of this island.

Libertalia in Diego had a small black brick bar and service window facing the street. The entrance looked like a hole in the wall but it opened up into an outdoor courtyard of red concrete. I sat with a beer, the only patron, and watched a man in a yellow shirt, with tied up hair and narrow eyes, complain in a raised emotional voice about some grievance. His female co-worker stood behind the bar, near the entrance, and listened in silence. He ranted and we all had no choice but to listen. Amid this soap opera my attention was rescued by a rabbit and lemur scuttling around the bar floor in play.

The lemur, having longer limbs and hands, had the advantage, but the rabbit appeared to be a willing or at least passive playmate. The rabbit stood in place and the lemur nipped and rolled over him in agile gestures of mammalian play. The rabbit hopped across the room and the lemur leapt across the tables in the same direction. He stopped, aimed at his now sedentary target, and pounced from above. The sheer strangeness of this occurrence made me laugh. This sleepy bay city had so far offered me few personal experiences, but little moments and chance observations like this coloured and characterised the subjective experience of travel.

On the wall there was a painting of a pirate in a hammock with the inscription *Utopic Republic of Libertalia.* The back wall had two pictures of a Malagasy man and woman, and a third of a bearded face chomping a cigar. A man and two women entered and placed a boom box on the floor opposite the bar. They played music and started rehearsing dance steps which I presumed to be tonight's performance. The ranting yellow-shirt walked over to them and chatted, while dabbing his lips in a feminine way with a cloth. My thoughts of him were that he enjoyed being the centre of attention, and after the dancers had entered for their rehearsal, the gravity pulled him over to the other side of the bar to pout and complain.

I paid for the beer and went back to the street, where now cars, Indian tuk-tuks and small yellow taxis passed by in steadier numbers. One yellow tuk-tuk carried the inscription *Jesus is my God*. I continued south, and in the distance ahead, I could see a group of about forty people gathered at a property that divided the road into a 'Y.' This commotion easily caught my eye considering my first impressions of the sleepy city centre.

As I approached, I could make out that the music came from a large truck parked to the left side of the crowd. I entered the crowd and at first felt exposed, standing half a foot above everyone, but all eyes were on the centre of the group, where young men and women entered into the open space to take a turn at dancing. They moved with expert seduction to the rhythm, their joints popped and rears shook to the beat. It seemed to infuse a style of American hip hop stepping with a local flavour of shaking their hips and bending their arms and waist forward into the music. I came on the scene, watched and left, without drawing any notice. They were too busy enjoying themselves. I was far from inconspicuous throughout my trip in Madagascar and there were many times later that I wished for this anonymity.

As I retraced my earlier steps, now moving north towards the bay shore, more people were moving around than before, yet this increase was far from hectic. City traffic was light and slow and the pedestrian movement had the step of a small town. The blue sky had light plumes of puffy clouds that ambled in laziness and appeared to mirror the pace of life on the street.

I felt uplifted from the sea, sun, and air, and the alcohol in my head had my cheeks and mood glowing in heightened pleasure. A palatial building called Grand Hotel stood in dissimilarity from the aged colonial street. What caught my interest was a sign indicating that I could use a cash machine to get some money, which I needed before leaving the city. I kept moving north along Colbert which sloped downward until it reached the water a few hundred yards ahead. Another bar down the road interested me so I went in to have another beer on its street-level terrace that extended from an open wall with a few seats inside the building.

I sat down and ordered a beer. The bar was full with young women and older French expats, but my attention fell to an old man and woman approaching a nearby table, he French and she Malagasy. I judged them to be in their seventies and watched as he doted on her with gentle affection. He tucked her into a chair then sat perpendicular to her, and they seemed to be discussing what drinks or snacks to order from the menu. There was something genuine about these two that stood in palpable contrast to other tables of pot-bellied pensioners with red-lipped local teenaged girls. I imagined a fictionalised history of this man's background:

'His father was a colonial bureaucrat on the island where this man was born. After Madagascar gained its independence, his mother, father, and sister returned to France. He decided to stay because he had fallen in love with a local girl. They got married and he vowed to live with her in sunny Diego for the rest of his days…'

'Do you want another beer?' It was the waitress who noticed I had drunk much of the first.

She walked back into the bar where a band was preparing their equipment. Moments later, she returned with my beer and then took a bottle of cola over to a young man sitting at a table adjacent to mine. He took the bottle of cola, poured a little in his glass, walked to the edge of the terrace, lifted his glass over the railing and dumped its contents on the ground. My first thought was that he did not trust the cleanliness of the cup and wanted to rinse it. Was my glass dirty as well? I spent the next minute inspecting my glass, looking at the man's glass, and re-examining mine, scrutinising the little bubbles forming at the sides, and looking for signs of dirt. This neurotic inspecting went on until the band started their first song.

Satisfied the glass was clean, I leaned back in my chair, enjoyed my beer and the live music. I was relaxed, nobody bothered me, and I was quite content to sit and drink until the sun dropped below the low buildings. Satisfied and light-headed, I bumped through the plastic chairs on my way into the bar, paid my tab, and walked back to my hotel as the city street darkened. It was six o'clock, the sun was down, and I had a quiet dinner at my hotel and then went up to my room for the night.

After an early bedtime, I beat the sun up the next morning and walked up to the flat roof of my hotel to watch the city wake. The roof had a tin canopy and under it there were clothes hanging on a line. A bell rang from a plaque-coloured church tower in the direction of the harbour, and as the tintinnabulation rang over the city, the sun's crown appeared from behind a long stretch of ocean clouds that formed like an army about to march on to shore with the wind at its back.

To the north, the bay had a silvery shimmer and the more immediate trees in the city were still tenebrous in the morning dawn. I could see French Mountain to the south-east. It looked like a giant alp with its top blown off, leaving a rocky and green thousand-foot base, with narrow jagged escarpments that tapered southward beyond visibility into the horizon. Rotating my gaze clockwise to the south, by southwest direction, Amber Mountain remained obscure in a glaucous haze where the grainy dark resolution of dawn had yet to disperse.

Despite the tranquillity of the previous two days, they were companionless, and I felt determined to look for someone who could show me around the city. I also wanted to arrange some transportation for tomorrow to Amber Mountain where I could do some hiking. I found a guy at the Grand Hotel who spoke English well and offered to show me around for a small fee. His name was Claudio.

'People call me Claude,' he told me after introducing himself. 'It will be better if we hire a car to take us around Diego.'

I agreed to this and after a phone call, an SUV soon arrived and we departed.

Claude was slight in stature, his body lean except a small belly which rolled out from his ribs. He had a dark skin tone and features that looked of African ancestry. He spoke in a polite friendly manner and I was eager to ask him lots of questions. I asked him where he was from but he only said 'my hometown is far from here. People from all over Madagascar migrate here for work.'

'Why do the migrants come here?'

'Most people want to work for themselves. Vendors enjoy being involved in a variety of sales to make their work activities interesting.'

'A city of small businesses is good,' I said.

After a couple turns we arrived at a small grass park with a black obelisk in the centre. A four-foot wall ran around the perimeter of the park, and at its entrance, a woman was sifting rice in a large woven disk, looking for any small stones camouflaged among the grains. As I walked past the wall I noticed a young boy standing at the woman's feet. He looked up at me and said 'Vahaza' (pronounced Vaza meaning roughly white foreigner).

Vahaza was similar to the Chinese *lao wai* or Japanese *gaijin*. In North America or other multi-ethnic societies, it was not really possible for a child to have this equivalent experience. It was not as plain as it was for this young boy who innocently and instantly could recognise me as an outsider. He knew my name: white stranger.

The obelisk, Claude explained, was remembrance for those who died in the independence movement.

'Each June 26th people bring flowers here to celebrate Independence Day and remember the past.'

Though this was two months away, I was happy that I would be in the country for the celebration. On top of the pillar was a thin arch with a rifle and axe forming an 'X.' A man sat on a bench in the corner and appeared to be resting from his morning stroll. A park was perhaps not the right word to describe this little corner; it was just a small lot with unkempt grass and a monument; a meagre city gesture of maintaining nationalistic pride. After about ten minutes, we left the park past the smiling woman and boy who again said 'Vahaza, Vahaza.' I said veloma (velooma-goodbye), returning the smile.

'Can you speak Malagasy?' Claude asked me. I had learned a few words before coming but it would not get me far. I replied in the negative.

We walked for a few minutes down commercial streets and arrived at the hospital, which was off-set from the road on which we came. We hooked around to a path strewn with garbage and sewage and walked a few meters. In a shaded musty corner behind buildings was an eight-hundred-year-old Ficus tree standing in smooth cratered earth.

It was not remarkable in height, but it had a series of grey sinewy trunks and a wide berth of branches which gave the tree volume. The relic was older than the city, which built around it and forgot it in a secluded rubbish pile. The tree gave me the feeling of leaving my mother in a lousy and corrupt senior's home.

'This tree is sacred,' Claude explained. 'People believe the ancestors dwell in this tree. The Ficus is sacred, the Tamarin is sacred, but not the mango'

'Why do people throw garbage here if it is sacred?' I asked.

'Yes, it is a shame people don't care for it more. Let's walk over to the pier,' he said changing the subject.

We walked west towards the pier but made a stop along the way at the ruins of a large building. A blue sign near the sidewalk said the building owed its dereliction and abandonment to Cyclone Kamisy which hit the city in 1984.

'People here used to call it the hotel of the navy,' Claude said.

'Now it is nothing more than the splendid memories of its glorious past,' I said reading the last sentence on the sign.

'I wish someone would fix this building.' Claude said 'It could be a nice place.'

Diego had the natural endowment to have a much stronger economy yet it seemed to lack the strength of institutions to do this. Its oldest sacred tree and grandest old building lied in garbage and ruin. Whether this was a harbinger I was not sure, but I was having conflicting feelings about the potential of the city after visiting these sites.

'Hopefully someone will restore it,' I said. 'It's the best location in the entire city.' The ruined hotel rooms once looked out onto a beautiful view of the harbour.

I later learned that this bay was the intended rendezvous point for Admiral Rozhestvensky, who was commanding the Russian 2nd Pacific Squadron from St Petersburg to Port Arthur and the rest of the Eastern front, where the Russian ground troops and navy were at war with the Japanese. The squadron first anchored at the port of Tangiers, late in 1904, from which Rozhestvensky sent some of his boats east across the Mediterranean to pass through the Suez Canal, while he took the rest down the Western coast of Africa and around the Cape of Good Hope.

Their plan was to meet in the Bay of Diego Suarez, but due to conflicting commands, the Suez team re-routed to the North-Western coast of Madagascar and put in at a little island called Nosy-Be. After reunification, they spent over two months at anchorage, impatiently heeding their superiors back in Russia, and waiting for a 3rd squadron to come and join them. The presence of thousands of naval crewman and officers created an entire pop-up economy on the island of Nosy-Be, attracting merchants, importers, and every prostitute that could make the journey arrived and hung up a shingle.

What I knew at this time was that Nosy-Be was a popular tourist spot for European visitors and I intended to avoid this location when I left Diego Suarez tomorrow to travel down the Western coast of the country.

Claude and I walked to the pier on the west side of Diego, where a limb of water channelled its way along the west side of the city peninsula and then widened into the south-western quadrant of the bay called *cul-de-sac Gallois*. The port was small and had a few dozen containers, but it looked of good standing and well kept. South of the port I could see the plant where the company *LSM Salinair* made salt to supply the country. I remembered seeing a bag of the stuff in the supermarket. Near the salt factory was another business called Pfefoi which made canned tuna.

Our vehicle was waiting for us nearby at a monument of Marshall Joffre, a French man who designed the city into a naval base. The monument was a white tiered structure more than ten-feet tall, and atop it sat a bust of a brown head on a limbless body. A variety of trees enclosed the spot from the city buildings behind them, and towards the water a rounded fence skirted the edge of a steep descent down to the port. After taking in the view of the harbour we returned to the SUV and continued.

I did not know where we were headed next but our path drove through an army training barracks as we moved in a southern direction through the city. The conditions of the camp looked dreadful from the street. The dark yellow buildings had stains and decay, and the ground looked dry and dusty. Without prompt Claude said 'all over Madagascar there is corruption.' The army barracks must have triggered the comment. Further on, we passed a small government building: 'this is the anti-corruption office but we don't know what they do in there,' Claude said with a laugh.

We drove south past the colonial part of town to a market spot where many people also lived in the surrounding area. I saw a mixture of housing ranging from small concrete structures to many tin roofed slum dwellings. A few middle-aged women were outside these huts cooking their meals on charcoal-heated woks.

"People from the country bring their food to this market every day but Sunday."

The market was a series of old wooden kiosks with displays of vegetables, fruit, and fly specked meat. The aisles were busy with shoppers but most vendors looked defeated from the sun and only rose when a customer stopped to look at their stall. As I approached one stall, the man behind the display used a stick with thick ribbons on the end to stir the flies that had been crawling all over the meat he was selling. The flies started buzzing around my head causing me to tighten my lips and lightly swat around my face. I was finally relieved when they resettled back down to the cuts of red zebu meat.

Moving on, there were kiosk tables selling cucumbers, tomatoes, carrots, oranges, and bananas, which, though scant, their colours brightened an otherwise dull-coloured market. The next stalls had rice sold in bulk, with a measuring cup resting on top. Claude said 'this cup is called a kapoka. It is used to measure rice in Madagascar.' This market was a typical primitive market that had no unusual features. Walking amongst these stalls made me cognisant that this little bazaar could be repositioned anywhere in the world, and the locals would instinctually be fluent in bartering and know how to navigate this agrarian-supplied marketplace.

Our last stop was a British cemetery where three-hundred of his majesty's soldiers were buried after a battle in 1942 between the British and Vichy French. Nearly forgotten in accounts of the Second World War was this interesting battle called *Operation Ironclad* and subsequent British invasion of Madagascar.

The British were concerned the Japanese Army would take control of the Bay of Diego Suarez, endangering the British ability to provide support to North Africa, South Africa, and Burma. Over several assaults at different points, the British took control of the island without difficulty, and after the war, returned Madagascar to the French. Fifteen years later, Madagascar's path to independence was mild compared to the Vietnamese and Algerians, though not completely without bloodshed.

I found an interesting account of the British assault on Madagascar from a member of No5 Commando whose diaries were published online. His account ended with him returning home and surprising his family at Christmas where he said with a touching tone of British character: "My mother dropped the teapot and my father (a Great War veteran) came out with his usual remark whenever he saw me, 'I don't believe it! The bad penny survives once again'." Three-hundred of his mates didn't make it home though.

The cemetery was well maintained with rows of clean, handsome-looking headstones in precise rows, and green grass, flowers, and bushes. The groundskeeper was a short, gaunt looking man about fifty-five years of age. He wore only a pair of shorts and sandals leaving exposed the wiry muscles in his arms and back, doubtless formed over a lifetime of strenuous labour. His name was Arilova and he said he has been looking after the place for six years. With Claude translating I asked 'do you like your job?'

'The pay is not enough but it is always on time.'

'Does the British Government fund this place?'

He said a representative came twice a year to check how things are. 'I never suffer to get money but I must do a second job to have enough to live. I work very hard.'

It was indeed well-kept. Green trees and hedges enclosed the perimeter, blocking views of the city and giving it the appearance a tropical garden. Walking back to the entrance I noted some names on the headstones: 'Moses Steamer, Abdulla Kasembo, Ali Muhammad,' and another only said 'A soldier of the 1939-1945 war.' Reflecting on these imperial names, my final thought in leaving was that this was *truly a graveyard of the British Empire.*

I avoided the afternoon heat in my room with a couple beers and the remainder of my book. *People of the Sea* was written by Dr Rita Astuti who spent eighteen months along the west coast of southern Madagascar with the Vezo people. Her study was of the difference between Vezo as an active identity and of one inherited through cultural lineage. The Vezo were a littoral people expert in fishing and paddling. Their villages and livelihoods revolved around catching fish from dugout canoes to feed their families and sell at market. Overall the book had interesting anecdotes and observations, with other contrived equivocations about identity that only meant something to an academic, but nonetheless, the book left me interested in visiting these people when I made it to that part of the island later in my journey.

I was contemplating the differences between her work as an anthropologist and my own endeavours in writing a travel narrative when my thoughts were interrupted by a man outside the window, who was putting a new coat of pink paint on the walls. When returning to my room earlier, I had seen this painter standing on a thin railing, above a three-story fall, painting a section of wall above the balcony. This vertiginous feat was done with no precautions to safety other than confident balance. I could now, once again, see him standing on another railing, performing a similar dangerous feat, while painting the hard-to-reach sections of the hotel walls.

Roused from my train of thought, I took a shower, which, due to the design of the bathroom, resulted in water on the floor, mirror, and toilet. I moved my sandals over by the door for future trips to the head. I had another beer and ate some peanuts while updating my notes on the day, making asides to look into the Battle of Madagascar when I returned home, and jotting down a few lines from *People of the Sea*. I could feel the beer flooding my head and remembered I had not eaten an actual meal since breakfast, so went back out to Colbert Street to look for a restaurant.

The sidewalks were busy with people and the street had more traffic than yesterday, but it was free flowing and uncongested. I walked towards the water past the terrace where I had listened to music the previous evening, and found an attractive looking joint with tall dining tables and chairs. Two people sat at a table on the sidewalk and two more were playing pool inside. A wall divided the dining area into two sections and I chose the seat in the initial room beside the divide. The walls were painted in nautical themes and next to my head was a large likeness of Capt. Jack Sparrow. Beside my shoulder was the name of the artist—*Olive Desire*—along with a phone number. I ordered some pasta from a pretty young waitress and then took out my notebook for something to read.

As I was writing down *Olive Desire,* a honeyed female voice said 'she did all of these.' I looked up following the voice and saw a woman, who having seen my notes, spoke to me in decent English as she referred to the paintings. She told me her name was Arielle. She had short wavy black hair and a brown dress. Her right hand was tightly wrapped in brown tensor bandage from her forearm up to her middle finger.

'May I sit with you to eat?'

I smiled and gestured, and she sat down across from me. She and her French husband owned the bar. The waitress who took my order arrived with her plate of meat and rice, which she managed to get into her mouth with her left hand the way a drunk driver touches his nose at a police roadblock.

'Did you fight,' I smiled pointing to the cast. After a generous chuckle she explained that one of the bar stools fell over and the edge of the seat landed on her fingers.

'Are you right-handed?'

'It's a problem for me. I asked the chef to cut my food for me. Even when I went to the bank and I signed my name they said "this is not your signature." I had to explain that this was my writing hand.'

She held up the forearm as she did at the bank.

'I showed them my identification and they finally said ok.'

The bar had the usual sights and sounds of a watering hole. Neon signs, a mirror, and a top shelf of spirits. Light music played in the bar accompanied with the occasional sharp crack of pool balls coming from the table near the entrance. I was suddenly aware that the waitress was standing not far behind me; her bright red dress had caught the corner of my eye.

'Where did you study English?' I asked Arielle, as she was munching her food.

The British travel writer, Christina McDowell, who had visited Madagascar several times, told me that few people on the island spoke English. She travelled the country in the 1990s, so I was interested to learn if the youth of the country were incorporating English into their education.

'We learned some English in high school. I studied French from baby school and English in high school. I can only speak English and French a little. Italian is my best language. Often Italian expats come here for lunch and I speak with them.'

'How many Italians live here?'

'Italian, maybe twenty-three and French,' she paused to consider, 'three-hundred.'

She finished her meal, stood and said, 'We have a—how do you say serveuse? —yes, waitress. We have a waitress who speaks English very well.'

Without another word, she went around to the other room, and a moment later a lissom young woman, tall and elegant looking, popped back around. She wore a black dress which drew little contrast on her beautiful raven skin. 'You requested to see me?'

I wouldn't put it exactly like that. Arielle said there is another waitress who speaks English and left and while I am interested in speaking to you, I didn't exactly request per say.

'Umm yes,' I managed to fumble out of my mouth. 'I'm Ty, nice to meet you, care to join me?'

'My name is Erika,' she said in a gentle voice while sliding up on the chair. Her eyes and teeth shined brightly in her dark complexion. She had the aura of shy innocence and youth and through conversation revealed some bookish interests. Erika was a waitress at the bar during the day and tutored students in the evenings. Before when I had gone to the bathroom, I noticed her with a girl in the back room, but took them to be patrons.

'Are you from Diego?'

'Yes, I live here with my mother and brother.'

She told me that her grandmother had passed away a couple years ago.

'My grandmother lived in France. She was going to pay for my university but she died before I finished high school.' This implied that whatever revenue stream was to pay for Erika's studies, perhaps a pension, had voided at the unfortunate death of her grandmother.

'Now, I want to study in Canada, but getting a visa is very difficult and the study costs too much money.'

This had to be true, I thought, because I too could not afford it.

'What about starting at the University of Tana and then applying for some kind of transfer? I was just at that university last week; it looked quite good.' I offered this thinking maybe it held more promise.

'Even moving to Tana and getting a place is too expensive.'

I thought to myself what a shame it was that a bright young mind, eager to improve her education and social standing through merit, felt stuck here with few options to pursue.

'Who is your student?' I asked changing the subject.

'She is Arielle's daughter. I tutor her in French, English, history, and literature. I'm sorry, I must get back to her lesson. She is writing a test so it is ok that I was gone for a little while.'

'Come back when you are finished if you like.'

'I can stay until 8:10pm but if I stay any longer, my mother will worry.'

With that she returned to her lesson, and I, having finished my pasta, turned my attention to the red-dressed waitress still standing behind my left shoulder where I could still sense her attractive presence. Angelica was twenty-two years old, short, curvy, and her smile, if any more beautiful, I would not have been able to stand it. She told me that she had been working at the restaurant for more than a year, and that she was interested in getting married and having a family.

'Do you have a wife?' she asked in limited English

When I asked her if she was married, she said 'not yet.' A customer called her, and as she walked away, I was left fixated on the final exchange of words we shared: 'I am chastity before marriage,' to which my reply was 'you're very strong.' The truth was, I found this principle honourable, and more than I was capable of personally upholding.

I sat in silence for just a moment and then Erika returned, followed by the adolescent she was teaching. Her features were European but her hair and body shape Malagasy. She moved with the awkward gait and mannerisms of a growing teen in an environment that was routine, but her recently lengthened limbs lacked a mature grace as she dragged a chair over to the table in an ungainly manner and began eating a meal. Erika and I chatted some more until we were shyly interrupted by Arielle's daughter, who said something, hardly looking up from her plate.

'She said she likes hearing us speak English,' Erika translated.

I asked the girl her name and in a mouse squeak she said, 'My name is Tina.'

'Nice to meet you Tina,' I said and then told her mine.

Erika tried to encourage Tina to say 'nice to meet you too,' giving her wide eyes that said: *we practiced this,* but she was too timid to utter another peep.

I walked back to my hotel in an empty, dark street, tipsy from drink, and wondering how firm a principle 'chastity before marriage' might be? I next thought it is best I would be moving on tomorrow, or else I feared I would become that old French man who, in his youth, fell for the local girl, and remained in sunny Diego for the rest of his days.

Chapter Three
Diego to Ambanja

I was in a crepuscular routine of stirring before dawn, which did not feel unusual, because the late-autumn hours of sunlight in Madagascar plunged the island into darkness every twelve hours. After a shower, I packed my things and went down to the restaurant for breakfast where I had an omelette and coffee before checking out of the Concord. I was ready to leave the city and explore the country side.

I wanted to go hiking at Amber Mountain which was around forty kilometres to the south. Not far beyond Amber Mountain was the Tsingy Limestone National Park called Ankarana, and since a guide is mandatory to visit both of them, I hired a guide and driver for the next three days.

At the desk downstairs, I met the owner of the hotel. 'Did you enjoy?' he asked swiping his arm back through the air to indicate the hotel. He looked of Arab ancestry, with olive skin, a black beard, and large bald spot on the top of his head. He grabbed my hand to shake and said 'Please tell your friends to come here.' I thanked him and walked out to the street where a car and driver were parked, and another man stood outside the vehicle waiting to greet me. The street was busy with weekday traffic and the weather looked favourable for our journey.

'How do you spell your name?' I asked the man not catching it.

'You know a florist? Drop the "T" and you have my name.'

Floris was a local scientist and English teacher in the Antakarana region and he lived in Diego when he wasn't out working in the forest. His hair was clipped down to stubble with sparse strands of greying at the temples. He had a broad nose and jowls, and his right eye remained closed as though injured from an amateur boxing career. He walked upright despite a problem with his hip or leg which did not move in perfect parallel with the other.

'It's great you are alone, we can do anything we want,' he said after we introduced ourselves. I got into the backseat feeling I was in good hands as we departed south on Route Nationale 6.

'If it's alright with you, I'd like to show you where I grew up. It's a town called Joffreville not far from here.' Floris and I liked each other right away and spent the next three days yakking about everything and nothing.

The outskirts of Diego were full of slum-like suburbs, buzzing with people and yellow tuk-tuks which Floris told me had recently arrived from India. As we left the city, we met oncoming traffic of all kinds.

'People from the countryside bring their vegetables to the market,' Floris explained, 'it's busy like this most mornings.'

From the back seat, I had a full-range view of the well-trodden, brick coloured landscape around the main road leading us out of the city. Wooden carts yoked to one or two zebu carried people and their goods, slightly obscuring traffic on the narrow road. Taxi-brousses carried baskets of fruit strapped to the roofs, and weaved around pot-holes, carts, and pedestrians. And those without transportation, walked; the roadside was full of pedestrians moving in both directions.

As vehicles passed carts or people they honked their horns, which was used for more than an expression of anger or frustration. Drivers honked to say 'I'm going to pass,' and even 'thanks for letting me pass,' and 'you're welcome' often came in response if it was another vehicle.

French Mountain to the east ran over twenty kilometres in a southerly direction. It remained visible until we turned off RN6 and continued west down a country road towards the small town of Joffreville. As we progressed south away from Diego, the air thinned and the temperature dropped a few degrees as the land rose up towards Amber Mountain. This old volcanic mountain provided fertile soil for agriculture and a source of fresh water for the surrounding regions. The second half of the journey to Joffreville went slower on the country road.

Floris told me he had a wife and two kids that lived with him in Diego. In his spare time, he helped run an English school and also maintained a tree nursery of endemic species.

'When I was at home in Diego my wife told me about some student protests against the headmaster.'

'Why did they protest?' I asked.

'It was for political reasons. The police came and threatened the protesting kids with guns. There are gangs in Diego, groups of ten or twenty kids who beat people and rob them. Some of these kids even broke the trees in my tree nursery. These gangs need to be stopped. The police do nothing about these gangs. Why do they threaten school kids with guns but don't shoot at this gang? Our mentality needs to change.' If Madagascar was to have a better future, Floris seemed to be an example of that path forward. He was a well-educated man, trilingual, and spent his time concerned with nature and the education of others.

We travelled along a section of road where I had only glimpses of the country savannah. Much of the road felt like driving through a tunnel with its high banks and tall bushes with sunset-coloured flowers. We met fewer people walking, though there were signs of a farming population. Looking over the banks, I could see rectangular country houses, no bigger than a garden shed, with thatched roofs and walls built of tree branches. Some were near the road and others visible from it.

The way of life here was like a window into the past. The farm houses had no electricity, running water, nor any other sign of modernisation. Some properties had several houses built together with a stick fence marking the perimeter. In one such property, I saw children playing and chickens foraging near the road. They all scuttled in a panic to avoid our car as we passed. An old country school stood alone. It was a concrete structure with one room, and I imagined it served the same purpose as country schools did in North America a hundred years ago, when farm kids trudged to school in the morning from miles around.

The agricultural land surrounding Amber Mountain was among the most important for supporting the northern economy. Ancient lava-forged suppressions in the land provided excellent growing conditions for fruit and vegetables, and rice farther on in the basins below. The Malagasy boasted of eating more rice per capita than any other nation. To them, it was more than a staple; the people of Madagascar ate rice at least three times a day. Having lived in Japan, I was used to eating rice once a day, but three times seemed a bit monotonous. For many in Madagascar, the alternative calories came from cassava (manioc), a starchy, stringy tuber, soaked in sugar water for flavour.

The most important harvest in this area, besides food, was the cultivation of khat, a bushy plant that reached seven or eight feet when fully mature. The leaves, when chewed, provided a mild amphetamine stimulant akin to several cups of coffee. The plant was introduced to Northern Madagascar by Yemeni dock workers at the beginning of the twentieth century. During the island's time as a French colony, creoles took up the practice of growing the leaves as a cash crop. Khat was traditionally grown in Ethiopia, Kenya, and Yemen, and was popular in Muslim teetotaller countries as a social alternative to alcohol.

The chewing of the leaves gained popularity among the Malagasy, first among laborers, and then drivers, and later among youth and adults alike. Couples chewed it as an aphrodisiac, people chewed it with friends in social gatherings to help stimulate conversation, and drivers chomped on the leaves to stay awake at night.

Prof. Lisa Gezon's book, *Drug Effects,* an excellent study of khat in this region, found that the plant provided significant income to small scale farmers and has even become 'central to local identity.' The leaves are best chewed within forty-eight hours of harvest, before the cathinone breaks down and reduced the strength of its stimulating effects. The town Floris was taking me to, was an important hub in the khat economy of Madagascar.

Joffreville derived its name from Marshall Joffre, who began construction of the town as part of a military base because the elevation offered a good vantage of the harbour. The last third of the journey was uphill. We stopped at an open area to have a look at the landscape, and could see Diego and the harbour in the distance. As we entered the town Floris pointed to his childhood home, a concrete house with two entrances. It looked big enough to have two rooms and had a small surrounding dirt yard.

'My cousin still lives in the house,' he said as we moved into town.

Joffreville's architecture looked like a nascent boom-town, half-finished, and then abandoned to entropy, though there were some other signs of normal life. School-children, wearing sky-blue uniforms, walked to what was left of their dilapidating school. Other French colonial buildings, stained and falling apart, lined the road into the town. A two-storied, yellow building, operating as a bar and shop, stood alone in bringing any colour to the town.

At the top of the hill we turned left and approached the main intersection of town. The intersection was a large square with two stacked tires denoting the centre. A car sat at the side of the road with a couple young men working under the hood.

'The Malagasy way of life is expert in improvisation,' Floris said prompted from the sight of these two.

'Things break, transport is slow, and life gradual, so we must be laid back and take things slowly. In Madagascar you only have stress for two days, the day you arrive and the day you leave. Here the pace of life is the spice of life,' he said chuckling at his use of the English idiom.

'We call it *Mora Mora* (moora). Mora mora means slowly slowly.'

This made sense to me without any further explanation. It was an attitude adopted to cope with the slow progression of things. I liked this phrase for its simplicity, and over the next two months of travel throughout Madagascar, I found occasion many times to internally repeat this phrase as a mantra to patience. Travel in Madagascar became intertwined with this laid back approach to delay, to hardship, to inefficiency, to the way things were and would be for a long time. Madagascar became for me *The Island of Mora Mora*.

The buildings surrounding the main intersection were within shouting distance of each other. This junction served as a pickup point for shipping khat into Diego, where it was sold to merchants. It didn't look like much, but this muddy, quiet intersection was one of the most important distribution points in the northern economy. From this region of Madagascar, khat was supplied to the entire island. It would serve as our point of reference for the day as well. We packed some water and bananas to spend the rest of the afternoon hiking on the mountain, after which we would return to Joffreville to meet Floris's brother in the evening.

Amber Mountain's forests were a refuge to many species of plants and animals. The forest had lots of annual rainfall which replenished the lakes and underground rivers. The runoff supplied much of the surrounding countryside to the north and west of the mountain with fresh water. The land was fashioned in volcanic eruptions from which black lava rock was still present everywhere.

We entered the forest at an elevation of eight-hundred-and-five meters and began our climb on a well-worn trail that gently coiled up the mountain. In the forest, the earth was moist and russet coloured, and leaf litter covered the ground beside the walking trail. Large trees formed a canopy fifteen to twenty meters above, which overhead reached across the trail, and allowed some light to dapple the forest floor. All of this filled the air with a cool and mossy atmosphere that was earthy and pleasant to the senses. There was little sound; I could hear no buzzing insects or rustling of animals, nor was a breeze detectable. Best of all there was no throng of chattering *Homo sapiens*. In a forest of more than a thousand species of plants and animals, the only movement was that of hundreds of butterflies that were blue, orange, white and black in colour. These travellers of the forest fluttered around doing their daily business as though it all was theirs alone. Our eyes remained vigilant in the forest canopy, pausing now and again to scan carefully.

At one moment we stopped, and pointing to a branch on a tree, Floris said, 'there is an animal on that tree, can you see it?' I looked the branch over several times before the vague etchings of a head revealed itself. The leaf-tailed gecko was an expert in camouflage, which in addition to being a perfect match to the tree branch in colour, had skirting around its body that prevented the cast of its shadow. Even with us near, it sat motionless on the branch, because its defence mechanism was an evolutionary confidence in its ability to hide in plain sight. Its head looked like an illusion of pareidolia, the pattern recognition that allowed us to see faces in clouds and cliff sides.

At the peak of our journey, we reached a secluded lake called Petite Lac. It had dark green trees around the perimeter and I estimated the diameter of the lake to be about seventy meters. The water was light blue and calm enough to see blurred pictures of trees reflected on its pellucid surface. Though annually a well visited spot, that day it was isolated with only me to enjoy it, and I felt like I had stumbled upon a secret swimming hole.

Our afternoon culminated in a visit to the Sacred Cascade, a small amphitheatre-like drop in the mountain side. In some spots water trickled over the cliff face's crescent edge, and to the left it burst out in consistent volume, which sustained a pool of water below. From here, this water flowed down the mountain and emptied into a network of rivers that sustained life in the countryside. Many rural people lacked running water and some even a decent well to get drinking water, so they relied on the river systems for washing, for laundry, and for life in general.

In total, Floris and I spent four hours on the mountain hiking or relaxing and chatting. The peace and quiet of the hike was soothing and the mild exertion revitalising. On the way to our rendezvous point with the driver, we were fortunate enough to spot a small family of Brown Sanford Lemurs in the tree canopy. They darted across our path, twenty meters ahead in the branches stretching over the trail. The height was too great to see the lemur's features in detail, but I could see enough to appreciate their mobility in the treetop. The agile group leapt from branch to branch with such speed that we were lucky to happen upon them. For a moment one remained, but then in an instant, it followed the others and disappeared into the forest.

'A complete day,' said my companion.

Our lodging for the evening was a couple of bungalows in Joffreville. My particular bungalow, constructed in a tree, impressed me because it had running water and toilet facilities. After a meal of rice and zebu meat, Floris and I grabbed our torches and walked up to the tire intersection where we met his brother. Floris's younger brother was a short laconic man who only smiled. I forgot to write down his name in my journal later that evening, and it was not until I was back at home, that I discovered that I had committed this careless error.

Towns and cities lacked adequate lighting, so the Malagasy relied on flashlights to walk at night. Those without flashlights seemed to rely on a feline ability acquired over a lifetime without electricity. Or maybe acquired is the wrong way to put it. Perhaps, instead, most people have lost this ability because they have had artificial light their entire lives. The stars made for a beautiful sky but this offered no aid to vision along this country road. Had I not been next to these two locals, I would have been apprehensive in this remote dark place, but next to them, I felt excitement at what we may find.

The three of us headed out of town, in a direction that I believed to be west, and walked along a trail with three narrow beams of light leading the way. We reached a spot and stopped to scan the tree branches in search of chameleons, and if we were lucky, a mouse lemur. As we beamed our light across the tangled branches, I reflected on where I was and what I was doing. In the black of night outside a country village in northern Madagascar, I was searching for chameleons by flashlight. An uncanny feeling accompanied the excitement of this unfamiliar experience.

Of all the unique creatures in Madagascar, chameleons and lemurs seemed to be the most well-known among the world. Chameleons, for their ability to change colour, catch prey with their tongue, as well as the ability to look both forward and backward at the same time. Their legs extended underneath their bodies, which gave them better balance along narrow tree branches. If they came across another chameleon on their tree branch, they were willing to fight to defend the real estate. James Sibree, a man who spent most of his nineteenth-century life in Madagascar with the London Missionary Society, recounted in a book for children:

"I saw that a pretty little snake, very common in the country, had caught a chameleon, and had coiled round it two or three times, and was evidently just preparing to swallow it, although it seemed impossible for so small a throat to take so bulky a mouthful. As we all pity the weaker side, I uncoiled the snake with the point of my sun-umbrella and drove it away. But it was this fact that struck me as very curious; the chameleon was perfectly white! White evidently with terror in the clutch of its enemy. I carefully placed it on a bush, and in a few minutes it gradually regained its usual colouring of green and yellow and black, as its fears passed away."

In an hour of walking through trails we managed to spot a few small ones. In the torchlight Floris used a bent knuckle to point at a small chameleon on the tree and then explained that 'it is fady (taboo) to point with you finger at a chameleon.'

The Malagasy people have many different fadys that govern their lives. Chameleons tended to be feared among most tribes and their unique abilities have lent themselves to metaphors such as 'keep an eye on the future and one on the past,' or an opportunistic politician who changed his opinion could be called a chameleon in a negative connotation.

To most Malagasy, it had taken years of adjustment to understand the value or interest of the flora and fauna of their island to the foreigner. To the locals, a chameleon was an uninteresting run-of-the-mill part of the landscape. It was peculiar when foreigners arrived in car loads to take pictures of the creature. Such an occasion happened to us when driving earlier today: Floris told the driver to stop as we were approaching a village because he had spotted a chameleon. The sight of a foreigner looking in the ditch prompted curiosity from the villagers who were heard saying 'what are they looking at over there?'

Our walk that evening was brief, and before long, I was back in the tree house, shrouded in a mosquito net and falling asleep to the sound of a light breeze rustling the shaky dwelling.

A rooster misfired an hour or so before dawn, but the rest of the birds took their duties more seriously and waited for the right moment to announce the morning. There were strong gusts of wind during the night which made the curtains hanging on the windows move in and out as though the tree house had taken a breath and exhaled.

Floris and I had a baguette with honey, coffee, and juice for breakfast. A litter of black and orange puppies wandered under the table and were playing on my feet until a man walked over with a branch and callously chased them away from us, managing to whip one as they scattered. In the time it took to eat, a lemon slug had moved about one inch across a nearby clothes line. We had a few hours of driving to do in the morning, so after breakfast, we prepared our vehicle. As we were getting into the SUV, school children walked up the dirt path on their way to morning classes. We drove by them up the hill as we retraced yesterday's trail back to RN6.

The main highway extended south through savannah hills where some areas were used for agriculture, but most of the countryside rolled in gentle ripples of high and low landscape, absent notable life. The land was sparsely populated with a few small villages and farm houses along the road. Every once in a while we passed one or two locals who walked along the roadside.

I saw people bathing in rivers and others times women washing clothes. Each river we reached had a narrow bridge that permitted one vehicle to pass at a time. And of course, the pervasive pot holes that shook me in the back like a cinderblock thrown into a spinning washing machine. At one point I had an itch near my eye but did not dare scratch it for fear of losing it.

One of the villages was memorable for the length of its name, Ankitsakalaninaom, which meant 'to the rice field eaten by zebu.' Village markets were the main social gathering for commerce among the rural Malagasy. Small villages had a certain day of the week when people brought their goods to sell, and then to another village on a different day. It also looked like a good opportunity to socialise and meet people, perhaps even look for a potential mate.

There was meat, fruits and vegetables, clothes, sandals, and other cheap plastic goods like flashlights, radios, or tools. Some sold their goods from a kiosk and others had laid a blanket on the ground and displayed their wares on top. They were usually set up right along the highway, so each village we passed offered a glimpse of their weekly markets as we idled through.

There was little continuity in the land. In many areas it was hilly, others had patches of tropical trees or sun-baked flaxen scrub and savannah, and others still had introduced trees like Eucalyptus, which was hearty enough to survive in the depleted soil. The soil here was closer to a pastel orange than the rusted red I had associated with the island. We passed a series of hills, and again new sights and life were waiting in the next basin.

After three hours of driving we took a break to stretch our legs at a village called Anivorano. This village also had a market just off the main highway running through town. To the south east of the village there was a large crater lake that was sacred among the people. The crocodiles there were believed to be in possession of ancestors, so the villagers fed them a sacrifice during an annual ceremony. At the market most people appeared to be socialising and we asked a man if he had been to the lake with the crocodiles, but he replied that he hadn't and that he was not from here and walked away. The town had a large administration building on the road with an open space in front of it. People sat at the base of a small statue at its centre and chatted.

With little time to waste, we returned to the vehicle and continued for another hour. While on the road, Floris asked me a question about English phrasal verbs, 'When do I use the phrase *fed up*? Ahh, ok. At first I thought it was something to do with food. When I finished a meal I would say: *I'm fed up.*' There was a harmless chuckle from us both and I helped him clarify the different uses of 'fed.' His next question was over the status of the word *environmentally-friendly*. We arrived in the town outside Ankarana at 11:30 and had some lunch at a restaurant across from the village school. The nearby park was the location for our next trek.

A sign at the entrance to the park warned that the following were forbidden:

'Introduction of ravinala (traveller's tree leaf), wicker basket; the consumption of pork;' and lastly, 'it is forbidden in the caves to be tempted by sexual acts or for menstruating women to enter.'

These were part of the local taboos and forbidden in the park. None an issue for me.

After four hours in the car it felt good to be hiking again. Ankarana was a National Park of tropical deciduous rainforest which existed alongside a massive network of kharst limestone called Tsingy. Tsingy, in Malagasy, meant tip toe, a reference to when people without shoes walked through the sharp limestone, they had to do it carefully. I had once seen kharst limestone in Slovakia's Tatra Mountains and was interested to make comparisons to Madagascar's Tsingy.

The adjacent forest was shaded and cool, offering cover from the sunny midday. Not long into the hike we spotted a nocturnal species of lepilemur. She was only visible because of the oversized paedomorphic eyes, which were lazily looking down at us and wondering why we had disturbed her sleep. She had dark shades of grey and brown fur, and her body was folded on the branch in a way that made her look much smaller than her actual medium size. Not wanting to disturb her any longer, we continued.

The hike was a level trail and required little exertion to navigate. After twenty minutes through forest we turned out to the limestone rock and walked out onto the sharp grey pinnacles. The landscape opened in the periphery and extended in both directions well beyond the sightline from my vantage point. Its width to the other end, opposite my entry point, was eight kilometres, and its total length stretched over thirty kilometres.

In its entirety, it was a field of limestone stacked in sedimentary layers and rows, spires, and points. Water had eroded its edges into arrow heads and blades, nature's primitive weapons. Each step required careful attention because the rocks underfoot were jagged, wobbly, and uneven. Using your hands to break a fall would slice into the skin. I had brought a large pair of hiking boots for occasions just like this one and was glad because I could feel the sharp points digging into the soles of the boots. They held up well and the high ankles and tightened strings provided me adequate stability.

We walked twenty meters over the rock, hopping from stone to stone, balancing across vertiginous narrows, and squeezing through interstices and corridors where the rock rubbed against my chest and thighs. We reached a suspended bridge, perhaps thirty meters in length, that spanned a gap between two ledges of the rock. The view across the chasm revealed a surprising amount of green trees among the grey columns underneath. The bridge trembled as I stepped across its planks. The ledge on the other side was terraced in rows with plants growing among the levels. These ledges were high enough that they blocked what lay beyond, except for some tree tops sticking up to the horizon line.

From the other side I climbed up the layers of rock to a spot that looked out onto the wide expanse of elephant grey stone. I found a place to sit and take in the landscape below. I looked out at the rock and felt my appreciation at the Earth's magnificent diversity widen into new levels of awareness. My gaze fell from the distant to immediate where a prickly brown rupestrine bush grew from the rock. The plant was below my waist in height and had brown rope-shaped shoots that forked like a cactus. This Ephobia, endemic to the park, had odd intricate stems where red buds formed. The bush was one example of how evolution took its many courses in the shaping of life. Today, this bush, the limestone, and the forest, belonged to me alone and I felt as if this remarkable piece of landscape justified every thought that compelled me to make the long journey to this island on the other side of the world.

We retraced our steps back across the bridge and walked through the forest to a different vantage point of the Tsingy. Near the edge of the forest we met a family of crowned lemurs who jumped at a low elevation through the trees and on to the ground right in front of us. There were six of them, the females grey, and males brown. They were the same species that interrupted my lunch at Ramena, though these ones today were completely wild.

They were on the ground licking at the soil near a tree, which Floris explained helped them digest their food. I stood motionless, six feet away from them, because the slightest move made the lemurs jump in skittish reaction. They kept a cautious eye on us, and in between licking the soil they emitted light throaty grunts, and one gave an affectionate mew. Our observation followed them out to the Tsingy where we watched them scuttle across it with nimble ease. They looked just as able on the sharp rocks as they did in the tree tops.

These crowned lemurs in Ankarana were not studied until the British doctor Jane Wilson brought a team here in the late 1980s. Thinking of her book, *Lemurs of the Lost World*, I was reminded of the bureaucracy Dr Wilson had to navigate during the socialist days, and I was glad that Madagascar National Parks (MNP) today made it easy to buy a permit and enter the park. Like other countries of the twentieth century who tried socialist governments, Madagascar's experiment only increased the layers of crushing corrupt bureaucracy which led to negative economic growth and halted progress. North Korea was one of their main allies in those days.

Stephen Ellis's recent history of the country recorded that the days of socialism left money scarce and began the neglected withering of the French Colonial buildings. The socialist President Didier Ritsiraka dug Madagascar into a perpetual hole of poverty and torpid growth. Current times were also a difficult period for most Malagasy following the 2009 *coup d'état* which ousted President Marc Ravalomanana.

The problem with political instability in Madagascar was not so much with who was in charge, it was the occurrence of political crisis itself. After the coup, tourism halted, foreign aid and more importantly foreign investment fled, and the people fell on harder times. Seven years later, they were still trying to recover from the blow.

I had sympathy for the view that foreign aid was debilitating to the innovation and psychology of a country. Over the past seventy years, Madagascar had received much of its aid from France, which actually worked in their favour, because French companies held a monopoly on major businesses and industry in the country. The flow of foreign aid and foreign investment into Madagascar in recent decades had not grown the Malagasy economy in a way that has provided better economic opportunities for the local people.

The Chinese have gradually increased their presence in Madagascar, where they have bought companies and mining rights. My own thoughts were that if this trend intensified, Madagascar would be re-colonised by the Chinese under some euphemistic title of aid and land purchases. But, for now, the forest and Tsingy were protected and I was more than pleased with my experience here.

I spent the evening in a bungalow without electricity which felt quaint as I wrote by candlelight at a desk. The main room of the guesthouse premises was well stocked with warm *Three Horses Beer,* the local island-brewed beer, and I had a couple bottles before dinner. Dinner was *poulet coco*, a common dish of rice and a small tin bowl of broth with a chicken wing. The room had a comfortable bed and I awoke the next morning to a magpie robin chirping outside my window and chickens clucking around the yard. Today the plan was to drive to Ambilobe and then Ambanja, where I would say goodbye to Floris and continue without him.

As we continued south, I saw several different individual enterprises. Some farm yards had fifty-kilogram rice bags, full of charcoal, for sale at the edge of the road near their property. I also saw women and men in many places hard at work crushing rocks with a hammer. They sat next to piles of grey stone and hammered it into pieces that they then sold as gravel or for other construction purposes. The work looked monotonous, dusty and probably noisy, sitting there pounding all day. On more than one occasion, we passed children shovelling dirt into potholes and imploring passing vehicles to pay them for their efforts.

We ascended a network of hills in the land, and after going over and around them, the horizon retreated and opened upon farmland used to grow sugar cane and bananas. I also saw a larger frequency of the national tree, the Traveller's Palm, which was a type of palm tree that had a rainbow of green branches, each with one big leaf, and formed the shape of an oriental fan. They were a healthy green with shades of yellow on the other side and stood over ten feet in the air. They grew in plenty and I enjoyed them for their irregular but attractive features.

Ambilobe was an important city in terms of population and large agricultural production of sugar cane. While passing through the city, Floris said 'the sugar cane factory Siramamy was recently sold to a Chinese company. They bring

Chinese workers here and take everything back to China so it doesn't benefit Malagasy people at all.' Ambilobe was the first city we reached since leaving Diego two days ago. It had several paved streets, brick and mortar businesses, and petrol stations. I saw boutiques with windows, and the nicest looking school I had seen thus far. With no lights or stop signs, we passed through and kept moving.

The final stretch to Ambanja had a further change in the landscape. A spine of mountainous rainforests ran the length of the east coast of the island, and tapered North West towards Madagascar's largest mountain, Tsaratanana, which I could see on the horizon to the south. The valleys and basins around the city of Ambanja trapped warm air and allowed tropical vegetation to grow. Traveller's palms did not grow in dense clusters but were visible everywhere. The region produced a lot of vanilla, coffee, rice, cocoa, and spices.

After seeing variations of the same villages and landscapes, interacting with people in the city and countryside, I was feeling a new level of comfort with my surroundings as we reached the edge of Antakarana and were near the end point of the northern territory.

Ambanja was a small city with slow-moving vehicles due to an overabundance of bicycle rickshaws, which clogged the streets and slowed the pace of traffic. It was around noon when we arrived to a dusty parking area outside a series of restaurants and market activity. Hordes of uniformed children were walking home for their midday break and would return to school later to continue in the cooler afternoon temperatures.

Floris suggested I stay at the Nord Inn Hotel, a pink three-story hotel, and so I took a room there for fourteen bucks a night. It had a bed, shower, and electric fan, and seemed more than adequate for the price. I put my bags down and joined Floris at a restaurant to have a drink together before leaving.

Upon entering the restaurant, he said 'the food here is ok and it is fairly clean.' For him to have said this about this particular restaurant betokened an ominous feel to the city. The premises were outdoors and open, but had a canopy to provide shade, and was next to a small outdoor market that had several umbrellas to block the sun. We sat at the wooden tables and ordered a big bottle of cola to share. There was a biblical swarm of flies gathered here for the food, the shade, the sweat, and the sheer sadism of pestering the locals. They buzzed around my head and landed on my arms and legs giving me no relief in my attempts to swat at them.

'In Madagascar, it is common to put some drink in your glass and then dump it on the ground for the ancestors,' Floris explained. I told him about my seeing this in Diego and mistaking it for a dirty glass, which made him laugh.

'Do you know why we clink glasses before drinking? We see and touch the cold glass, smell the liquid, taste the beverage; the clink is to complete the full range of senses.'

'I like the sound of that,' I told him before we drank to our new friendship.

Before leaving he asked me to take a picture with him and said with a laugh: 'my brother asked me if you were my bodyguard so I want to get a picture of us together.'

Floris and I discussed my future visit to Diego and my helping him teach at his English school. Now in addition to the beautiful waitresses in the pirate bar in Diego, I had a job and friend as well. More compelling reasons to return. We exchanged contacts and I thanked him for his enjoyable company. Floris left and I felt saddened that my arrival in this city meant his departure.

I went to the back of the room to pay, where I noticed a young European man sitting at the table nearest the register. He was working at a laptop computer and eating from a plate of greasy fries and tomato stewed zebu meat. At an exchange of glances, we said hello, and he said 'have a seat if you like.'

His told me his name was Emile, he was twenty-two years old, and came from France. He had dark hair, was thin and bony, and there was a wisp of moustache above a set of tobacco stained teeth. This restaurant was not on the main tourist circuit, so I asked him 'what do you do here?'

'I have lived here for two years. I have a boat and crab business and in my free time I fix computers.' He finished his last bite of zebu, lit a cigarette and then sizing me up said, 'Madagascar is a hard country for backpackers. You always have to pay Vahaza prices.' By this he meant that when foreigners buy something, the Malagasy often charge more than what the locals pay.

'I can speak Malagasy so when they hear me speak their language, they realise that I know normal prices.'

'How's business here?' I asked.

'I have several employees that work for me. It is hard to work here but it's an adventure. I'm a computer guy, I can work on computers, but sitting at a desk all day at the computer is not a life I want. A virtual life is not a life. Are you going to Nosy Be?'

I told him that I planned to go to Mahajanga.

'It's a pity, it is a beautiful island.'

'It is more interesting for me to talk with someone like you in this restaurant. Tell me more about your work.'

'My competition here are the Chinese and they are not good people that come here.'

'Why is that?' I asked.

'In China sometimes they give a small criminal or crook the option, you can go to jail or you can go work for us in Madagascar.'

'I heard they bought the sugar company near Ambilobe,' I said passing on my new information, 'but I have not seen any Chinese people around here yet.'

He seemed ready for this—his expression and voice became conspiratorial, and he leaned towards me slightly.

'You never see them around, but they are here, and they're dangerous.'

This was the kind of generalised statement I was always suspicious of, but there seemed to be genuine fear in his voice and I was interested to hear more.

'I sleep with a cut; how do you say machete? Ahh, yes, machete. I sleep with a machete every night. You know, maybe I will die tomorrow but at least I am living an adventure. When I was nineteen, I went to university for computers but it was not my way. What do you do?'

'Ahh a teacher, it is great. Both my parents are teachers. When I was a child, I spent four years in Comoros. Later we came to Madagascar more than once for a vacation. I promised a friend here I would return and I did!'

'How long do you plan to live here?'

'For life,' he replied without hesitation. 'My life here is busy. I sleep four hours a night, but I like it.'

'Where do you live?'

'I sleep at our crab shack and so does my staff. There are ten of us and sometimes two tons of crab all in the same room at night.' While making a pincer with his hand he said smiling, 'all night we hear click, click, click. And if one gets loose.' He made the gesture of pinching himself between his legs and laughed as though it happened to another and not him. Two people approached the table. Emile said 'we are supposed to have a business meeting now.'

I left them to it, thinking maybe I will return here for dinner later. The road outside was busy with market activity and congested with slow moving vehicles. A steady walking pace was just as fast as the vehicle progress. In the market I saw hats and clothes made in China, though the people were wearing used clothes shipped from North America in equal number. My eyes were drawn to a red shirt that said the words *Canada* across the chest.

The afternoon drove me indoors to my room where I sat with a couple beers I had bought in the lobby. I updated my notes and wrote down my conversation with Emile while it was still fresh. From outside the window I heard two people talking in a small courtyard that was only accessible from one of the buildings that surrounded it. The chatter that had drawn my curiosity to the window seemed to be about a bicycle. In the background beyond the city there was a tree-covered peak in the landscape.

Three hours later, the flies were still tormenting the diners at the restaurant and Emile and his team were still conducting their business. Three Malagasy men and one woman sat at the table and the five of them were chewing khat with a wad of bubble-gum. I didn't interrupt their meeting but sat near them and ordered rice and chicken from a teenage girl with long braided hair. I could see through the opening to the back of the restaurant where they had charcoal fires cooking food.

'You are back' Emile had noticed me.

'Hungry,' I said smiling.

When their meeting finished, he grabbed a motorcycle helmet and walked outside to a red street bike and took off.

I defended my meal against the flies as I ate a bowl of rice and scrawny leg of chicken. I was in the mood to drink beer, so I sat for about an hour, watching traffic and writing a little, when the lady behind the counter said something to me. It was in Malagasy and I didn't understand her. She pointed outside to the sun, which had sunk enough to be beaming late-afternoon light in through the open side, and then pointed to my back where the rays were hitting. She was suggesting I change my seat to across the table to get out of the sunlight. The waitress earlier did not speak French, so as I moved my seat, I said 'Thank you.' A man behind her, who I did not notice before said 'you're welcome.' I was surprised by the response. 'you can speak English?' I asked him.

Jean had studied English in his spare time and was interested in practicing it. I invited him to sit with me and ordered two more beers which he seemed happy to accept. The lady who invited me to move out of the sun was his wife, and they had a daughter who was six years old. We began exchanging words in English and Malagasy. I woke up the next day with three pages of Malagasy phrases and

I couldn't remember how some related to our conversation. Others such as *misotra be tsaka*, meaning 'to drink a lot,' were easy to understand.

Jean asked me about the Canadian flag so I drew a picture of it in my notebook to show him, and then he drew the tri-colour Malagasy flag and explained its red, green and white colours. A little later I asked him about a toilet, and was sent through the kitchen into the back yard, which was fenced in and shared by the buildings on either side of the restaurant. I walked past ducks and chickens to the toilet, which was a toxic mound of dirt and sewage, piled with garbage and used needles. Suddenly, I was conscious of my open-toed sandals. I relieved myself to the hoots and laughs of the staff cooking in the back who watched me. I laughed and wobbled, zipped and returned to the session of language and beer.

While having an enjoyable time with Jean and his family, I was thankful that I had stuck it out among the flies and was rewarded with an evening with Ambanja locals. We drank together long past sundown and were all drunk. Jean's wife wanted to know if I was married, to which I replied that I was not. In my drunken state, I did not see where this was going soon enough to avoid it. Jean and his wife began suggesting to their waitress, who had joined the three of us, to go back to the hotel with me. She was medium height and build, and I believed about sixteen years old. At the posing of this question, she looked at me, smiled, and shook her head at Jean's wife to indicate yes.

When Jean communicated this to me, I tried with as much tact as possible to decline this suggestion. I said to Jean, in not so many words, that it was taboo in my culture for an adult to have sexual relations with someone who was not yet an adult. I guessed that this would not have made any sense to them had I not used the term 'fady' to explain why I did not want to do this, but it worked. Thankfully, we moved on from this topic without awkwardness, and we continued to drink together until we were thoroughly drunk.

Jean and I stumbled back to my hotel through the dark streets. Jean insisted that he saw me safely back to the hotel since it was after sundown. I thanked him for a nice time with his family, and he told me to please come back again sometime.

The electricity was out when I awoke the next day, but sunlight poured through the window heating the room to a stifling temperature. My mouth and throat were dry. I could feel sweat had dampened the bed sheet under my back.

My head was heavy and tired from the countless bottles of beer consumed the night previous. I showered and went down to find some coffee.

While at breakfast, I wrote some more notes about what had happened the previous twenty-four hours. As far as this city went, I felt like I had accomplished a decent afternoon and evening. I had a revealing conversation with Emile and an enjoyable evening with Jean and his wife and daughter. With my notes updated, my thoughts turned to departure. I planned to take the taxi-brousse to Mahajanga but it didn't leave until two o'clock in the afternoon. After breakfast, I returned to my room and tried to sleep for the rest of the morning.

Chapter Four
Night Bus to Mahajanga

At the bus station, in a small room buzzing with flies, I waited for my taxi-brousse to make its departure. In the afternoon sun, the air was dusty and stifling. I slouched in my chair and kept my mouth wet with frequent sips of water. Every so often, I felt a bead of sweat trickle down my stomach or my lower back.

I had tried eating a plate of rice earlier, but the heat and hangover allowed me three bites before pushing it away. Two men sat on a thin bench beside me, one of them reading a newspaper. He chuckled and showed the other a cartoon, which soon had them both laughing. It was too hot to laugh. A man sat at a desk receiving customers and listening to the radio on the shelf beside his head.

After an hour, a lady looked at me and said, 'Tulear?'

'No, Mahajanga,' I replied.

In French, she said, 'Are you Tulear?' She was trying to pronounce my name and I had misunderstood.

'Yes,' I stood up. I took my bag around the corner and handed it to a man on the roof of the large, blue, taxi-brousse. I watched the bag disappear into a chaotic pile of luggage and started to feel anxious that it was not up there at all.

I walked around the bus slowly, looking at the luggage from every angle trying to see the orange rain cover on my bag. I couldn't spot it. Was it passed over the other side to another person? I subdued this paranoia with a defeated nihilism. I had my money and passport in my pocket, if the bag was gone, so be it. I mopped the sweat from my brow.

A lady arrived in a tuk-tuk and ordered the driver to move her basket over on to the ground. The basket was larger in circumference than a barrel and was heaping with a small green fruit. The tiny driver pulled on the basket and managed to keep it level as it fell to the ground, and he then proceeded to drag the basket over to the van. The woman pulled out two rice bags, transferred the fruit into the bags, and then, under the effort of two men, they were hoisted up to the roof.

It took an hour to ready the vehicle, and I stood and watched the busy intersection, which had a large centre and a road that cut through diagonally across the main route through town. The taxi-brousse station had vehicles preparing to go in all directions. City trucks passed by, leaving clouds of dust in the air. Across the intersection, not far from where I was standing, was a red building called *Bazar Be* which was a market. It had umbrellas, tables and stools sitting in front of it on the street. The area was a frenzy of pedestrians; students in school uniforms, women with mud caked on their faces, some men moved with purpose and others who looked as though they had nothing to do but stand in superfluity. Everyone, I felt, was staring at me.

From one direction I thought I saw a foreign man approaching from fifty meters up the street, but as he neared I realised he was not a foreigner, he was albino. He wore a dusty old suit and hat, and walked through the crowd of people almost as an invisible ghost. He walked slowly, with his eyes focused on the ground in front of him, but when he neared my position, he stopped, and then looked up and into my eyes which gave me an eerie shudder. I watched the wraith until he disappeared into the distant crowd.

A car arrived with a hatch full of khat and people crowded around it buying a bundle of the fresh leaves. I watched this for a while until the roll call for our vehicle began. An hour behind schedule, we embarked—destination, the west coast city of Mahajanga.

Taxi-brousses are the transport of the people. They are cheap and packed to capacity. Twenty of us sat bone touching bone, our flesh mashed and contorted in whichever direction was available. A man and woman sat in the front seat with their child, who they handed off to the back seat to sit on the people in the second row. The vehicle was full with young, old, men, women, children, and me. Loud music filled the remaining air in the van, and the young lady next to me sang along without inhibition. The initial hours were spent in quick bursts along good stretches of road, and then careful creeping around craters, over bridges, and through the numerous villages. I saw little out the window and just sat with zen concentration to endure the cramped space, motion sickness, and sweating.

We stopped frequently and were assailed at the windows by vendors selling fruit, fried bread, and fish. The smell of food mixed in the air with the body odour of the twenty souls crammed together. On one occasion, we stopped and the passengers jumped out to relieve themselves in gender segregated groups. The men stood along the side of the road, abreast of each other in a line, from where parallel streams of urine arced or piddled into the grassy ditch, while the woman walked a few paces farther, separated themselves a safe distance apart, and squatted bare-bottomed over the ground. With the passengers now relieved, we jumped back in and continued.

The man from the front seat tore the plastic off a package of cigarettes and discarded the old package and new plastic in the ditch. He had a thin moustache, a large T-shirt and pants hung off his medium frame, and his gaze and demeanour seemed an overcompensated bravado. His face wore a permanent expression of superiority but I couldn't imagine anyone took it seriously.

After six hours, long past night fall, we stopped in a small city, the name of which I wasn't sure. In what seemed the driver's habit on this route, he pulled up to a large restaurant, which stood like a large concrete skeleton. The area looked like a truck stop of sorts, and had several vehicles and restaurants in the form of a large square.

As the passengers filed out of the van, an Indian woman rounded them up with a caustic, raspy voice, and aggressively guided people into her restaurant. I jumped out of the car and turned to go up the steps but the presence of a dog stopped me. This tired, old, flea-tortured dog stood up in the commotion and panted from the effort. It stood on three legs, using a hind leg to scratch its belly incessantly, but it found no relief. My own breathing felt heavy watching it, and the thought of fleas changing hosts froze my feet in place.

A young girl and her younger brother wandered among the vehicle passengers asking for food or money. She was so thin and frail I thought her to be starving. I gave her some money and walked by the pitiful pair and the flea-ridden mutt into the restaurant. I ate *poulet demi* which looked and tasted much better than the environment in which it was prepared. It cost less than a dollar. Our stop was brief, perhaps forty minutes and soon we continued our course, the passenger's bellies now full and eyes closed. Mine too.

Around midnight I awoke. We were sitting at the side of the road and the hood of the van was open. I got out of the vehicle and joined a group of men standing in front of the van, watching two others who were looking under the hood with the light from their phones.

A young man approached me and asked, 'you speak English? We are having problems with the alternator belt.' He was a young man, around twenty-five, and said his name was Olivier.

'Can we fix it?' I asked.

'We fixed it but we lost an important piece, so they are trying to find it.' I guess I was late to the party because I took their searching by light to be looking for the original source of the problem.

'We may be here until sunrise,' he said.

'Mora mora,' I said with a light smile, but the use of my new Malagasy idiom had no effect on him.

I returned to my seat and tried to get a little more sleep, waking periodically to let people by me. I must have slept more because I woke at 4:00am to the sound of the engine firing, and then we started moving again. We would go for ten minutes then stop, and three or four of us got out and pushed the van to start it. This happened so frequently, I held my breath every time we slowed for a pothole, silently hoping the driver didn't kill the engine. But each time, he did.

While out there pushing on the fourth or fifth occasion in the dark countryside, I recalled looking left and seeing long thin strips of silhouetted clouds above the horizon, and behind the clouds was a small but fierce orange ember of sunlight which had not reached our dark road yet. The whole scene had me recall some words from Blake's poem:

Tiger, Tiger, burning bright.

In the forest of the night.

The sky was dark to the west where the village huts were still a silhouette. In the silent stillness, it all looked like the paintings I had seen in hotels and markets. For a brief moment the asperity of life was masked and everything looked beautiful.

Some villagers were jogging in the dawn morning along the road, a couple zebu carts pulled farmers, and others were walking to some place I could not imagine. Presumably, most or all were going to the field for work. The one consistency was that they all stopped to have a long look at the tall, blonde, vahaza, pushing the van down the dark road in the countryside at five in the morning. Other taxi-brousses slowed and chatted with our driver and then continued.

Outside, on one occasion, Olivier said to me: 'these situations are a habit of Malagasy people. We are very poor, so can't afford to travel another way. I have never been on an airplane.'

'What do you do?'

'I work with my father,' was all he said.

'Did you study English at school?'

'I learned with Mormon missionaries. It was a great chance to speak English with North Americans.'

As Olivier and I were chatting, frustrations with our slow progress led to an argument between two men. The man from the front seat climbed to the top of the van and was about to start untying the luggage when another passenger yelled at him to stop it. They argued with each other and the man from the roof jumped down. They did not go near each other and the situation remained without violence, but the temperature had warmed slightly.

All of this fighting was pointless because we were now awaiting a rescue operation. The driver had phoned and asked another taxi-brousse to come get us. We waited another hour and a new van arrived. We transferred the luggage from one van to the next. It was then I remembered my anxiety; was my bag up there? I asked Olivier to ask the driver about an orange bag. He said something, of which the two words, 'orange,' and 'vahaza,' I comprehended. The bag was up there and I dismissed the paranoia to a hungover error in judgement.

We piled into the smaller vehicle and continued down the RN6. I asked Olivier where we were, but he had no idea. It turned out we were thirty minutes from the west turn on to RN4 at the junction city of Ambondromany. We stopped in a village before Mahajanga and parked near a small warehouse that had stacks of rice in large bags. We waited while a team of three transferred a few of the bags onto our van, and then we continued.

From the point of our rescue, in took five hours to reach the outskirts of Mahajanga, and then forty minutes more to get through the morning traffic. After twenty-two hours we were clammy, weary, and deserving of freedom, but we had reached our destination. I wanted to find a hotel and try a get a little more sleep. I found a nice place called the Coco Lodge just five minutes from the station.

I ended up doing little for the entire day: I rested, ate a nice meal, did laundry, updated my journal, read, and went to bed early. I felt pleased with how the trip was progressing, and perhaps, just a little pride at enduring such an uncomfortable journey.

The next day after breakfast, I walked fifteen minutes to the supermarket to get some bottles of water and beer, because they were much cheaper than the same bottles at the hotel. At the sight of me, a group of children sprinted across the street and asked me to give them something; anything. One child grabbed at my wrist, which I gently pulled from his grasp, but then I stopped, realising he wanted the elastic band I had around it. I had a few of my clothes bunched in elastic bands and I must have put one on my wrist after unbundling a fresh batch. I took off the elastic and handed it to him, and for whatever reason, he was pleased to have it.

While in the store I bought a bag of small chocolates to give the kids on my return, but they were not around when I emerged from the shop. Rickshaw pullers slept in their carts under the shade of a tree and they didn't stir as I passed. I walked by a team of three youths who were at a coconut tree. Two were on the ground and a third had clambered up the twenty-foot trunk to knock coconuts down to the awaiting partners.

I improvised a new route back to the hotel and stopped at a series of restaurants. On the menu displayed outside one restaurant I saw the dish crab farci. I had wanted the dish since Ramena and went in and ordered a plate. The place was empty except for a waitress, Koulina. After asking her to spell her name, I found out that she came from the central highlands near Tana. I asked her why the restaurant was called 'Loch Ness?' She was not sure, so I explained the legend to her while I waited for my food. Koulina told me the restaurant owner was from Poland. I ate the crab farci with some crusty bread and a glass of fruit juice and felt satisfied. I wished Koulina a good afternoon and continued on my way.

I took my bag from the supermarket back to my hotel room and then walked towards the water, which was just a couple blocks down the road. The road came to a perpendicular intersection that the town fashioned into a round-about centring on a baobab tree. I could see the water not far beyond the other side of the intersection. It was not like the baobabs I had seen in pictures, but was unmistakably a shorter member of the family. It had a fubsy trunk and a large dome of complex branches from which fruit grew.

As I stood looking at the tree, I caught the attention of a young man, who approached me, and introduced himself as Henri. He was in his early twenties, thin, and appeared to have a mixture of Arab and African ancestry.

'Where are you from?' he asked. 'Canada, whoo it is very cold there.'

'Only in the winter,' was my usual grumble to this presumption. He told me that this baobab tree was one of two species not endemic to Madagascar. 'This one also grows in Mozambique.'

He was saying something about it being fire resistant, but my attention wavered at the sight of a man running around the tree.

'...it can store water in its....'

Three times now he had run around that tree. What the hell was he doing? I was just about to say, 'let's go see what that man is doing,' but then he stopped.

'...and one other species is in Australia.'

Henri was a university student doing a master's degree in biology and conservation. He offered to show me around the city which I accepted. I was not under any pretence that he was doing it for free, but sensed in him a genuine interest in chatting with me and showing me Mahajanga. We walked over to the sidewalk that ran along the coast. The road looked new and extended in both directions in excellent condition. I felt I was witness to the best tax dollars spent in the entire country.

A waist-high ledge ran along the sidewalk and on the other side rocks sloped down to the water's edge. Land across the water gave it the appearance of a bay, but it was better described as an estuary. A series of rivers dumped into the ocean at this spot where it formed an octopus-looking body of water. Near the tip of the land across the water, I could see a lighthouse standing alone.

'This is a great spot,' I said to Henri.

'Yes, every night local people come down here to sit on this ledge and talk. Guys bring their girlfriends and parents bring their children. It is very popular. In the rainy season this water turns red.'

I remembered reading before coming that during the rainy season, the top soil in the central highlands washed into the rivers and out to sea, which in effect, turned this whole estuary red.

We walked to the end of the road and turned back towards the city down a gravel road, all the while still next to the water. A lone power line stretched the length of the road across four poles. The road was a couple hundred meters in length and at its end stood a series of small marina shacks with grass roofs. One was open as we passed and had a table and chairs set outside under an awning.

'Fisherman take their lunch in these shacks,' Henri explained.

Behind the shacks was a marina full of boats. There were perhaps twenty dhows that looked like large canoes and each had a naked mast that looked like goal posts at a football stadium. They were yellow, white, blue, green, and red, but filth and the dull erect masts diminished the overall look of them. They were boats for work not luxury.

'These dhows are used to ship things to Morandava. They take alcohol, food, and other things.'

'How long does it take to get there?'

'Usually one week to get to Morandava. Ten men will go on each boat.'

Mahajanga rose to commercial prominence in the eighteenth century as a popular port for Arab sailors. The spread of Islam in the Indian Ocean between the seventh and eleventh centuries eventually touched the shores of Madagascar. Stephen Ellis found in his history of Madagascar that Muslims introduced new concepts of value and exchange which 'revalued existing forms of exchange between people, since various social obligations could now be regulated by money and thus capitalised or imagined as debt.' Increasingly, traders and sailors built mosques in the ports of Madagascar cities.

In the 1700s, Mahajanga eclipsed surrounding port settlements in size and commercial opportunities. It had mosques, schools, and a population of six-thousand Arabs and Indians. Around the same time that Mahajanga was growing into the centre of commerce for the Sakalava kingdom, foreign traders became more interested in the east coast for trade. Meanwhile, the central highlands Merina people had grown in size and power with an aim to control the entire island.

Near the marina where Henri and I were walking, we came to the old part of the city. I looked down a well-designed street lined with two-story buildings built in the eighteenth century. The second stories stood on pillars, similar to the French architectural designs. They looked well-kept for being over two-hundred years old. One hundred meters in the distance, just before the street curved, two people walked in the opposite direction. Other than these two, there was no one around.

'There is no one here on Sunday,' Henri said as a way of explaining the absence of people.

Not far from that spot, we approached a building that faced out to the water. I went up and examined the door. It was thick, wooden, chestnut in colour, had bevels that formed a square, and down the centre were arabesque carvings. The frame of the door was teal green.

'These designs are a symbol of wealth,' Henri told me, meaning the more ornate they were, the wealthier the owner. I reached out and touched a small chain that hung on the door, and Henri said 'no don't touch it, there is probably someone in there.' I dropped it with slight embarrassment for not considering that before. The age of the building made me feel as though I were looking at a relic and not someone's home.

We walked towards the centre of town for about ten minutes. We passed a street of old shops, an old cinema that was unused, and came to the main intersection of the city, which we crossed and continued in the same direction another hundred meters. This part of town was busy with traffic and pedestrians. Henri showed me in the market the ingredients needed to make 'Ravitoto,' a common meat and broth dish.

'Do you like this dish,' I asked him. He put a fist to his mouth like a trumpet and said 'whoooo yes I like it. I took this meal for lunch today.'

Outside the market there was a woman, in her thirties, sitting on the ground behind three baskets of fruit.

'What are these?' I asked unsure what the fruit was. 'It's avocado.' They were so big I did not recognise them. Their skin was the colour of a lime and their size much larger than my fist. The woman had black hair tied in a bun, a brown plaid dress that had blue sleeves down to the wrist where a silver bracelet was worn. I had noticed over the past week many Malagasy wearing silver bracelets. What was most prominent about this woman sitting side saddle and lady-like in her dress was the orange mud smeared on her face like a beauty mask. Many of the Malagasy women wore this type of mud for both beauty and sun protection. It was smeared in a thin consistency that resembled pastel paint.

Across the street from the market was a green mosque where several men sat outside in the shade of a couple trees. 'This is a Sunni mosque. Shi'ite are not allowed to pray here.'

'Where do they pray?'

'They have a different mosque in the city.'

'My father was a Muslim. He is dead now. My mother is catholic. I can show you her church and my primary school.'

The church had a colourless concrete tower that stood in three segments, each smaller than the one below. In the middle segment there was a picture of a heart emitting rays of light, a barbed wreath wrapped around the heart and a cross sat on top of it. Behind the church was a courtyard for the primary school where a group of young girls stood in a circle, holding hands and singing.

I felt a diverse presence in Mahajanga. The city looked every bit as liveable as Diego did. It was nearing the winter season and the sun was a pleasant thirty degrees. The streets were paved. Transportation cost pennies. The waterfront promenade could have been part of any modern city. If I were a youth in Madagascar, I would abandon the farmstead and take up residence in this city like the waitress Koulina did.

Henri liked his city but told me he was interested in studying in Quebec. He asked me if I knew a way for him to study there. 'Did you find a university you want to study at?' The question revealed he had not taken much action or thought beyond the desire to go there. He wanted to see if I would help him. Had I been from England or America he probably would have said he wanted to study there. He said he had access to the internet, so I told him to check the admissions standards of a university and to make an application letter. He was clearly a smart guy and capable of doing this, and there was little I could do to help, even if I wanted to. We walked along for a moment, and then Henri said 'do you want to see my house?'

'I would love to.'

Not far ahead we turned left down a smaller road and entered a residential area. The houses were small, but many were made of concrete, with the properties fenced. Power lines ran the length of the road. A man ahead of us turned around so often to stare at me that he tripped on the shoulder of the road and nearly fell. On our left we passed a small shack built around a well pump.

'This is where we get our water. It is my family duty to get water every morning,' Henri explained.

The road was long and after a hundred meters began to climb up a slight hill. We turned left again down a dirt path worn in the grass. An abandoned car sat at the side of the path and blocked half its narrow width. We walked through a gated fence equal to my height and up a few steps. The front door was open, and as we walked up the steps, Henri's mother emerged from the thin transparent curtain at the entrance. She had short hair, medium build, and smiled at us, welcoming me as though she expected our visit.

Their home was a concrete structure that had three rooms. I entered into the living room which had three small red sofas and light pink walls. The combination of these colours made a clashing but warm hue in the sunlit room. On the opposite wall a curtain blew in the window. The furniture was pointed at a T.V. which was on and showing a Mexican drama dubbed in Malagasy. Henri's brother, Toky, and sister, Salma, came from the next room, from which I only saw a dining table behind them as they entered.

We were all introduced and I shook their hands. They clasped their left hand at the right elbow when shaking mine, so I reciprocated the action. We each took a seat. The mother, Delphine, knew only a few words in English but the siblings spoke English well and asked me questions. Toky asked first 'What do you think of Madagascar?' Tough one first. I said that 'I think the people here are poor and have a tough life. The Malagasy are strong people.' There are few ways to politely euphemise poverty but I wanted to say the truth and not be offensive. This seemed acceptable to all of them and Toky next asked 'What is your job?'

I said I was a teacher and this made Delphine's eyes widen and she stood up and shook my hand again. She was a teacher too and had one year to go before she retired. 'What do you do?' I asked Toky. He studied microbiology, and his sister, who sat shyly on my right next to Henri, studied zoology. 'A family of scientists,' I said smiling. We made pleasant small talk for another five minutes and then Henri and I left. I thanked them for the visit and before leaving Toky said 'Please come back again.'

We continued walking around the city, passing a new hospital and the school where Delphine taught. At the hospital Henri said 'Our new president built a hospital like this in many cities, but it is expensive to visit these hospitals.' We reached the northern part of the city's coastline at a place called Zoma Beach. Like the promenade where we started the day, this area was also well built and had a clean beach. I was impressed with what I saw here.

The sun was beginning to set over the Mozambique Channel and many young people had made their way down to the beach. Small fishing boats with triangular white masts were coming back from a day at sea. Kids played soccer on the beach and many more sat on towels under umbrellas. The atmosphere was great and everyone looked to be enjoying the end of the day.

'In the winter, many people from Tana come here for a vacation at the beach. It is cold in Tana now.'

We followed the coast back around to where we started the day, and then back to my hotel. I gave Henri twenty dollars and thanked him for showing me his city. I had dinner and then went to bed because my bus to Tana left early in the morning.

I left the hotel before sunrise and walked down to the baobab tree and turned right, where just up the road at an office, my vehicle was readying to depart. I booked passage with a company called Malagasycar, which ran a service between Tana and Mahajanga. Their service was a taxi-brousse, but it didn't stop to pick up new people and was more reliable for time, which was supposed to be ten hours.

I arrived early at the office and entered through a gate and up some stairs. It was still dark and everything was quiet. The same ships I saw coming home last night were now setting off for another day at sea. Some of the staff were still sleeping on the balcony and others just beginning to stir as I arrived. I watched them go to a shower room, which was visible from where I sat on a bench. There they performed some morning ablutions: a young man and woman washed their faces while another girl brushed her teeth. Another man approached me and sent me next door where I could have coffee, fruit, and bread before departing.

The drive was quiet and made good progress. I sat with my notebook and recorded the names of villages and the times we passed through them. After three hours, we stopped before a bridge because there was construction on the far side. We had a few minutes to walk around outside where a few huts stood.

The sky was full of thin clouds with little streaks of blue between. Three teenagers sat next to a small pile of stones and hammered at them until they were reduced to gravel-sized pieces. Their pile was small but many sacks sat full behind them. The homes were built with wood sticks and weather-proofed with some type of dried leaves. A support beam in the shape of a cross ran from the ground to the top of the gable which was perhaps seven feet in height. On the roof of one of the huts there were pink and orange clothes placed to dry in the sun.

A passenger from the van, Aarav, said hello to me. He was middle-aged, Indian man who lived in Tana. 'I own hotels in Mahajanga and Tana. I go to Mahajanga once a month.' He held a cigarette up to his mouth and kept it there, the bent arm propped with the other arm slung across his body, the posture looked both frail and philosophical. He wore jeans and a blue striped business shirt. He looked at my shorts and t-shirt and said 'It is cold in Tana. Maybe ten degrees. Where are you from?'

'Canada, O, there is a big fire in Canada now.'

'Al-Ber-Ta' he said remembering each syllable from the news.

The construction crew took a break and we were allowed to pass. In the van, Aarav reached into his bag and found a business card and coupon booklet. He gave me the card and opened the booklet to an advertisement of his hotel.

'How's business?' I asked him.

'It is quite good. We don't have many guests like you, usually business people.' He turned back and listened to a podcast on his tablet. I returned to taking names of villages and times.

After four hours, the land rose in elevation and we ascended into the central highlands, a landscape that filled much of the centre of Madagascar. The road coiled sharply up and down hills making our van feel like a segment of serpent that moved side to side as much as it did forward. I noticed the houses changed to red mud structures and at times two story houses built from wood, but we had not yet reached the arbitrary boundary of the Imerina lands. Perhaps it was the land and available resources that changed the style of living even though we were still among the Sakalava people.

We had left the fertile outer ring of the country. The interior land was a wrinkly, garbage green expanse of tumulus hills that were so barren it looked nameless. The passengers in the vehicle grew tired and slept, their heads sliding left and right as we navigated the winding road. I dozed for two or three hours and remembered seeing little until we stopped outside of a village.

There was a commotion of people standing near the street and a motorcycle lay in pieces on the road. The person next to me shot up in attention. Following this unusual reaction, I shifted my gaze around the head in front of me and could then see what had startled the man beside me. There was a man lying motionless on the road. He had a black t-shirt and his head faced away from us resting on his right arm as though he were sleeping. The pose looked natural, and for a moment I thought maybe he was badly hurt, but this brief wish did little to hold off what I knew to be true. He was dead. Police and army personnel directed traffic and kept the crowd off the road. As we drove by the man I saw his brains and blood draining off the shoulder of the road, and I gave up any illusion he was still breathing.

I didn't feel horror at the sight of the dead man, but had little else to think about as we entered the outskirts of the capital about one hour before sunset. A downhearted mood consumed my thoughts. I considered this dead man's life, a life no older than my own, and projected his loss and my gloomy thoughts on the people walking the busy streets at the end of rush hour. What home were these people going to? What chance did they have for a dignified life in this filth and poverty? What was worse about these ominous thoughts was how a dark lens seemed to reveal more reality than I had previously seen.

I was not going to euphemise or romanticise about the state of their lives. We were driving through typical neighbourhoods in Antananarivo, and I could see hundreds of people out my window who lacked the basic necessities of life, and I was powerless to make any difference. I saw neighbourhoods inundated in black shiny pools of sewage. The poverty was such a depressing mess that I had to put my head down and close my eyes. It took another hour to get through the traffic and people before we reached our destination. I was told in Mahajanga there would be hotels on the street where the vehicle dropped us off, and indeed easily found Independence Avenue around the corner. I had a pizza in the restaurant and went up to bed, tired after a long drive.

Chapter Five
Camp Indri

At three-thirty in the morning, Independence Avenue in Tana was quiet. Other than a barrel fire one hundred meters down the road, the conditions were cold and dark. As I put my bag in the backseat of Ando's taxi, I could make out four men standing near the barrel, but at that distance they were blurry in the lambent glow from the flames. Tana itself was not much brighter. When the sun set in Madagascar, much of a city seemed to vanish. On that morning, widely dispersed points of dim light shone from around the city, but this was little more than glowing embers in a dark pit.

Ando was wearing a jacket and looked cold and sleepy. The passenger seat of the car was cold. I sat with my legs together and my arms held against my body. What was more shocking than the cold was the amount of joggers I saw on my way to the airport, still dark and earlier than four o'clock in the morning. I thanked Ando for driving me so early in the morning and paid him well for his reliability.

In the twenty-first-century, to be an expert in the life of some species of flora or fauna was also to be an expert in how human beings have impacted that species. Millions of years of evolution equipped human beings with the ability to exploit the defences of other life forms. The venom, toxins, speed, aggression, or flight of other life forms were no match for two or three humans who could communicate with grammatical language, make personal sacrifices for non-kin, and use tools, all in pre-planned coordinated cooperation. The various ecosystems on the island of Madagascar had millions of years to develop without the presence of humans, and then one day they arrived, and introduced a bunch of domesticated species to the island along with themselves. And as for the human impact on the natural ecosystems, Dr Steven Goodman told me during our conversation that:

'there are no forest dwelling cultures in Madagascar. For example, if you go into the deep forest of the Congo Basin, you see the dominant tree in the forest is something the people consume. You realise, it's actually a planted forest or a managed forest, that's been managed by people for 10,000 years. It's completely different than the shifts and changes that have taken place in Madagascar over the past few thousand years.'

When human beings arrived to Madagascar from Borneo, they brought chickens, rice, and the agricultural practice of clearing land of its vegetation with machetes and burning it clean; a practice known as swidden, or more colloquially as slash and burn. This technique of clearing new agricultural land left ash in the soil which made it excellent for growing food. The nutrient-rich soil produced healthy yields for a few years, but slash and burn agricultural practitioners had few techniques for maintaining a nutrient-rich soil. When a few growing seasons depleted the soil, a farmer moved on to a new section of land. I learned from Dr Goodman that this new land could have been either fresh water swamp land, rainforest, or wooded savannah. There was not much actual closed-canopy rainforest left in Madagascar, however, up and down the eastern coast of the island there was a thin spine of mountainous rainforest remaining. I flew to Sambava, in north-eastern Madagascar, with Dr Erik Patel, an American biologist and conservationist who has been working in the region for several years.

Before coming to Madagascar, I watched David Attenborough's program on the island's flora and fauna. The video had the familiar shots of chameleons striking prey with their tongues or lemurs sunning themselves on cliffs in the morning. One of the most fascinating creatures of Madagascar endemism was the Indri.

The Indri, at one-meter-tall, was Madagascar's largest surviving lemur. It had black and white fur and could leap ten meters through the forest canopy. The rainforest of Madagascar was the only place in the world it existed; if the Indri disappeared from Madagascar, it would be a global extinction. The stunning and unforgettable feature of this animal was its call, which was a song that carried two miles through the forest, and was then responded to by a chorus of wails. The sound was eerie and poignant and left the human listener in awe at its unique beauty. Dr Erik Patel worked in the northern-most place the indri lived, in the rainforests of Anjanaharibe-Sud in north-eastern Madagascar.

The SAVA region in the north-east derived its name from the four cities of Sambava, Andapa, Vohemar, and Antilaha. Three of the cities, Vohemar, Sambava, and Antilaha, were situated north to south along the coast, while Andapa lay in the rainforest basin one-hundred kilometres west of Sambava, near the base of Marojejy and Anjanaharibe-Sud mountains. The region was home to Madagascar's best agricultural conditions for rice, vanilla, coffee and every other useful subsistence and cash crops grown in the country. The struggle to preserve the remaining rainforests while at the same time having conditions where the occupants of the land can provide for themselves remained in difficult balance. Even with the federal protection of forests, the presence of rosewood trees or crystals and their lucrative market potential made this an on-going struggle.

Dr Erik Patel is originally from Chicago and now a primatologist working for the Lemur Conservation Foundation in Florida. In addition to rainforest conservation, he is a specialist in the vocalisation patterns of the Silky Sifaka, a large white lemur that lived in Marojejy, and Anjanaharibe-Sud National Parks. Dr Patel has been working in the rainforests of the SAVA region for fifteen years, conducting research and developing conservation efforts that incorporate local village economies. The eventual goal was to have Anjanaharibe-Sud become a functioning eco-tourist park, which would provide alternative income to local communities and an incentive to preserve the forest. We planned to visit Camp Indri, a nascent tourist camp that he and his team of locals were in the process of developing.

After we arrived in Sambava, I went to my hotel with plans to meet Erik for dinner later in the evening. This was the one week in my travels that was completely planned, so a relaxed feeling accompanied my excitement about camping in the rainforest with a team of scientists. A man picked me up at the airport, a hotel across town was ready for my arrival, and the hotel owner had arranged everything I needed to tag along with the expedition for a few days. Scientific expeditions into the forest required thorough planning and organisation, so I too needed to be planned and organised.

To have begun this day in the dark cold streets of Tana, the warm sunny climate in the small city of Sambava now felt like a tonic. On the taxi transport to the hotel along the main road through the city, I saw a primitive morning market with chickens in cages and other tables with oranges and bananas. There were some shoppers, but the majority of people looked to be working.

Though right on the coast, I only briefly saw the ocean from a spot where the main road ended its south to north run along the coast and pivoted ninety degrees to the west. At this location, four small river systems converged at one delta point and emptied into the Indian Ocean. Sambava was a flat city with no tall structures. My initial impression was that is looked no busier than a village. It took five minutes to reach the Mimi Hotel where a Chinese man, Bran, was expecting my arrival.

My room had hot running water and a toilet seat so I was satisfied with these luxuries. From my balcony, I could see the large courtyard of the hotel where, at the moment, I saw a couple foreign guests talking to each other. I still had much of the day free and felt exhausted from being up much of the night, so sleep was the first priority. After closing my eyes, I could hear those two chatting in English and I was thankful for its somniferous effects. In travel, the monotonous conversation of locals was valuable; the monotonous conversation of tourists put one to sleep.

I awoke after lunch, showered, and then went out to the street to get a taxi. I needed to go to a bank and get money. A few minutes back towards the airport I found the right bank, but it was closed during the most convenient hours of the day, so I would have to return later. I walked for ten minutes up the street and found a small outdoor diner where I had rice and avocado, and killed a little time gawking.

The sunny weather left an unwashed odour in the air that had begun to bake in the afternoon heat. The 5A highway served as the city's main road and went through town in a staircase of four turns which resulted in its movement in a western direction out of the city. From my seat at the restaurant, I watched two men across the street carry crates of beer from a large red truck into a small wooden bar, its view unobstructed by the truck. It had a low ceiling and thin wooden walls with posters and neighbourly holes. I felt certain that if I entered the bar, I would have to duck under the low door frame, but the men hauling beer into the room were short enough to walk through without any dip. I used this free time to write in my notebook for a while and then later walked back to the bank.

The bank's ATM had a withdrawal limit of four-hundred-thousand, and I needed close to three million, so I put my card into the machine seven times, and each time folded a stack of Ariary notes into my pocket. With my only chore for the day completed, I ambled back in the direction of the hotel, stopping to browse a little in the markets. I had noticed earlier at the bank that my finger nails had grown too long, so I went in search fingernail clippers. I couldn't see any among the various trinkets and curios for sale, so I mimed the action of clipping my nails to a proprietor, and one moment later had what I needed.

The main street was steady with commercial traffic and people, but was not hectic. The city itself was unremarkable, but I liked it for this quality. The sun was warm, the ocean air salubrious, and pace of life simple. It took about forty minutes to reach my hotel where I went up to my room and relaxed until dinner time.

I found Jo waiting in the restaurant at the entrance and together the two of us found a table. A portion of Dr Patel's team were going to meet here for dinner this evening. Jo was a student from Tana who had completed a Master's Degree in biology, and was gaining some field experience before he began a PhD. He had light brown skin like other Merina people I had met in Tana, crooked teeth, and his hair curled into a short afro. I asked him about his family and studies while we waited for the others to arrive. Jo told me he was the oldest of three children.

'My brothers and I all went a different way. I have always loved animals so I chose biology'

He spoke English well but with an accent and cadence that sounded like a mixture of Swahili and French.

'How long will you work with Erik?'

'We will work at Anjanaharibe-Sud until August sometime and then I will return to Tana. I was recently working in a forest near Mahajanga and went back to Tana to come here. What did you think of Tana?'

'I don't really like big cities,' I told him trying to be tactful and omitting that I disliked the city.

'Do you like living in Tana? What do you do for fun there?'

'Make sure you try the nightlife on Friday. Friday is party day all around Tana. The people call it *What's on Friday*, or *Magnificent Friday*.'

I told him my plan to return to the city after traveling down the east coast and that I was interested to learn a little more about the east coast train.

'I read that there is a train that runs from Tamatave to Tana. Have you taken it?' I asked him.

'I have never been on it but I know it doesn't go to Tana anymore. Only to Moramanga. And the train from Tana to Antsirabe also doesn't work.'

This was news to me. I had read there were three trains in Madagascar and planned to ride on all three of them.

'I guess I'll try which ever ones are still working,' I said resigned.

Erik arrived at the restaurant and soon after him two more local men who have worked with Erik in the past but were not coming with us tomorrow. We sat down and ordered from the menu and then the guys discussed some of the plans for the next two months.

They talked about making new transects in the forest for monitoring the lemurs, and Erik pulled out a GPS device and let the guys play with it. After so many years in the country, Erik had developed a habit of sprinkling Malagasy phrases into English sentences in a way similar to how Hawaiians use touches of Native Hawaiian when speaking English. He was a patient man and listened to everyone with sincerity. They discussed finding the northern most point for the Indri and Sifaka, and later in the conversation, I heard it mentioned the Silky Sifaka population numbers were around two-thousand. I naively inquired as to whether or not this was a sustainable population and was told: 'no, that is critically endangered.'

When the waiter brought Erik a cup of coffee, he grabbed a can of powdered cream from his backpack and stirred it in the coffee.

'Won't it keep you awake if you drink it now?' I asked him about the coffee.

'I still have jet lag and a lot of things to organise this evening so probably won't sleep a lot.'

I was still feeling the effects of my lack of sleep last night and did not think that I would have that problem.

The meeting was brief and we disbanded for the night with plans to meet at seven the next morning. Erik's work had many different aspects, and because there was so much to organise, we had a slow and methodical itinerary of moving the team up to Camp Indri. Tomorrow, the plan was to drive one-hundred kilometres west to Andapa, rendezvous with two local conservation workers, and spend the night in the city. The following day our plan was to hike five hours up the mountain to Camp Indri.

The next morning, I bought a bag of croissants and other pastries from the hotel bakery, ordered a coffee, and waited for my ride to arrive. If the French had tried colonising the world through pastry chefs instead of pompous bureaucrats, they may have experienced some actual progress. I sat on the terrace of the hotel to have my breakfast and watched the Sambava morning begin.

Locals walked along the sidewalk and some looked at me as they passed. I felt the presence of an invisible barrier between me and the sidewalk, the way they looked at me as though they were peering into a world just ten feet away but were not allowed to enter. In hotels around the world, this barrier, sometimes actual concrete, was meant to provide patrons piece of mind, but I felt troubled by the looks I received from the sidewalks.

I had come to this island with naïve hopes of understanding the lives of the people here. But I was re-evaluating the likelihood of this possibility. At this point I was waxing idiotically in my notebook about how poverty was the great corrupter of human relations and human dignity when I heard:

'Can I sit with you?'

Jo arrived early from his hotel and I offered him a pastry to eat while we waited. He pulled out a package of cigarettes that had the name *Good Look,* and after offering me one, lit a smoke. 'Today we will go to Andapa by car.' We had just begun rehashing the plan when a woman interrupted us.

'Are you with Guy? He was my guide on Marojejy the past two days and we said we would meet here this morning for breakfast, but I don't have his phone number to call him.'

'He was with us last night but we don't plan to see him today,' I said.

'I have his number in my phone,' Jo offered.

With a slight limp, she approached our table and sat. We introduced ourselves. Her name was Amber, from Toronto, and she was in her late twenties. She had a hearty muscular build and medium length hair.

'Did you hurt your leg?' I asked her pointing to the limp.

'I have blisters on my feet. I got back yesterday from a two-day hike on Marojejy.'

'How long are you traveling in Madagascar for?' I asked.

'I am not traveling,' she said matter-of-fact. Her tone indicated that I had asked the wrong question.

'I lived three and a half years in a village in South Western Madagascar. I worked with the NGO Blue Ventures.'

'Was it with the Vezo people?'

'Yes,' she said, and her eyebrows relented slightly.

'I haven't been to the north yet so decided to come before leaving. Next week I am going back to Canada.'

'After three years in Madagascar it will be a big adjustment to go back to Canada.'

'I think I'll be fine. Are you guys going to Marojejy?'

I told her of the team's plan to spend four days on Anjanaharibe-Sud. She seemed satisfied with this as a worthy trip.

Amber repeatedly made sure I understood she was not the average backpacker.

'Ya, I was on Marojejy. I took a taxi-brousse there and arranged the whole trip myself. They told me they only have guides that speak French. I don't speak French. I told them I'd rather you did the tour in Malagasy. On the mountain, I met a dentist and doctor from Buffalo. They were both young guys but had paid porters to carry their bags around for them,' she explained with the facial features that suggested this was absurd.

'The staff asked me if I needed a porter. I don't need a porter; I can carry my own bag.

But later when we came off the mountain, they offered me a lift in their SUV, so I said sure and jumped in. I even slept on the floor of their room last night.'

I smiled at this and thought '*so you and Buffalo are the bores that helped talk me to sleep yesterday.*'

I wanted to change the subject back to the Vezo people. I told her of the book that I had read last week, *People of the Sea,* and asked her a question about the Vezo way of eating fish mentioned in the book.

'Ya it's true, when they eat fish they put chunks in their mouths and then spittle the bones into the palm of their hand.' She said this with a demonstration placing her supine palm up to her mouth.

I asked about Blue Ventures.

'I came here to travel and offered to volunteer with them for a while which turned into three years. I was part of a dive team that did conservation work on the reefs.'

'I read the reefs are in bad condition.'

'Yes they're nearly destroyed. Lonely Planet listed us as a dive centre so sometimes people would just show up and say *we want to dive*. We had to tell them, ahh, we don't do that.'

Amber was a nice woman and I was interested in her time spent in Madagascar, but she made this difficult because she was also a sanctimonious bore about her ability and the authenticity of her travels. Most sentences were a chance for her to interject 'but I can speak Malagasy,' or 'I don't need that, I lived in Madagascar for three years I can do it like the locals.'

While listening to Amber, I watched Jo's eyes sleepily close for a moment, but then perked open again and he cupped his smoke away from our side of the table. I saw that he sometimes had a look of objection on his face at a comment Amber made about Malagasy people, but just sat there in silence unwilling to even attempt edging in a word.

'…it was a little difficult to get past the—I'm white, you're Vezo—and just become friends. It was hard to form a relationship. When I was saying goodbye they would say things to me like:

I want a present to remember you by; can I have your phone; or can I have your laptop; a souvenir to remember you? I was like, no you cannot have my laptop.' She said re-enacting the affront in a sarcastic voice. 'But, when I was sick in the hospital the entire village came to visit me,' she said in a higher pitch uniting the pro with the con.

I asked her about visiting the Blue Ventures team to see their work and she gave me the contact of a man named Jason.

'He's the guy that replaced me. If you include my name in the email it should be no problem to go see the team.'

I wrote the emails in my notebook as two SUVs arrived in the parking lot. Erik was in the passenger seat of one.

'You guys will both go in that one. I think you'll probably stop at Marojejy, so we'll see you at the hotel in Andapa. This afternoon, we'll likely have time to visit a small nature reserve outside of the city'

The road west to Andapa was paved in the 1960s, but the long mountain curves and transport trucks ambling up and down the steep mountainside made the drive slow. The sky was cloudy but the air was comfortable and got a little cooler as we entered higher elevation. I didn't mind the slow pace because there was plenty to enjoy about the landscape. The land was green with palms, mango trees, jackfruit, coconuts, and the distant hills were covered in vegetation; only some areas had patches of cleared forest. When we slowed to pass through villages, I saw chickens, geese, turkeys, and zebu. The villagers lived in typical small wooden houses lifted on stilts, but I also saw many solid houses of a better quality, which were a sign of the prosperous agriculture in this region.

It was easy to track our progress because every kilometre had a small red and white tombstone in the ditch that marked the distance to the next city. After eighty kilometres of driving, we coiled around a mountain and stopped at a rest point that offered a panoramic view of the landscape. Jo pointed to a mountain ahead saying 'that is Marojejy.' A sign stood on the other side of the road that said *Point de Vue Parc Marojejy*.

Immediately below us the vegetation was dead but the panorama had many green mountains with peaks that reached up into the clouds. I could see hillsides as steep as pitched roofs that were somehow planted with indiscernible crops. I imagined it would have been backbreaking to plant those crops, and that it was either done by hand and hoe or the farmers had yoked mountain goats to the plough. Other mountains had patches of missing trees in their forests which was unmistakably the work of humans.

'That is slash and burn' Jo said seeing where I was looking.

The slash and burn parts of the mountain laid bare. The exposed tawny soil looked aberrant in the surrounding green.

'Some of the areas are not planted. Why do they cut down the trees there?' I asked Jo.

'They use the trees for building houses and making charcoal for cooking.'

It seemed an obvious answer in hindsight. These were some of the problems Dr Goodman described to me in Tana earlier. The people who lived in these mountains used the forest resources to survive because no other option was present here.

Marojejy was centre focus. It stood tall and looked green and healthy. Its peak was covered in cloud which created a trapezoidal symmetry to the base of the mountain. Its summit was nearly seven-thousand feet high and this supported four different types of forest depending on elevation. The cloud that hung over it made it look like it had its own weather system compared to the surrounding mountains. Jo snapped some pictures of the area, I scribbled some notes, and then we continued the final nineteen kilometres to Andapa.

In Andapa we unloaded our gear in the hotel for the night. There were many people in the parking lot, and I was still getting used to all the faces, so was not sure who was going up the mountain and who was not. At this point it was of little difference to me and I felt the best thing I could do was not be an added burden to Erik's list of responsibilities.

Every hotel I stayed at had me fill out an invasive personal information form and I was getting annoyed with the tedious chore. It required your passport number, place you came from, how long you are staying, where you are going next, father's name, mother's name, etc. It was this day, I thought, enough is enough, and began writing amusing answers in the form. I pulled out my notebook and came up with an anagram for my name—*Tryle Leenssok*.

Occupation—Cowboy; Father—Ted; Mother—Teresa.

Mr Leenssok went on to stay in numerous hotels all the way down the eastern coast of Madagascar.

I was introduced to two men, Rabary and Jackson. Rabary was a round man, short, about fifty-five, a local farmer and conservation worker. He wore a Chicago Cubs hat and windbreaker, and had a contagious cackle that he used after giving an observation.

'Do you like baseball?' I asked, pointing at the hat.

'No, I don't know baseball.'

'Your hat is an American baseball team. They're called the Chicago Cubs,' I explained.

'I thought the 'C' was for conservation,' he said thinking about it, and then burst into laughter.

Jackson was a thin man in his forties with a pencil moustache, and he wore a winter jacket and Lemur Conservation hat. Like Rabary, he was a farmer in the Andapa basin, worked in conservation in his spare time, and guided tourists in Marojejy.

We had the afternoon free, so Rabary and Jackson offered to show Jo and me part of the basin where Rabary lived, and a private nature reserve that had bamboo lemurs. The four of us, and a driver Luc, jumped into an SUV and drove out of the city. Erik said he wanted to stay at the hotel and finalise his preparations. As we drove towards the outskirts of Andapa, we passed a large church under construction. I asked Jackson where the money came from to build such a large church.

'The local people all helped pay for this church. I'm a Christian. I also helped. Each person gives a little money. My fady, as a Christian is bad relations with people. I always try to explain a good way. I also don't drink alcohol,' and then he added 'anymore.'

The driver Luc told me he also grew vanilla. 'I sell vanilla to a company in Vancouver.' I later learned that vanilla was more expensive overseas that year because the crops in this valley did not have a good year in 2015, and I wished I had known that at this time so that I could ask these men about it.

After a brief drive through the city, we reached the end of the pavement and followed a country road that took us through yellow rice fields and the occasional homestead. In every direction I saw mountains surrounding the basin and grey clouds in the sky. The colours of the Andapa basin were dull yellows and greens, but it also looked lush and wet, which made it apparent that this was a fertile region for agriculture.

Jackson said from the back seat 'I read about the nature in Canada. You have an animal called the beaver? Yes, I read about their homes in the water. Beavers cut down trees, not good for conservation,' he said mostly as a joke.

I explained to them what Giardia was and how Canadians nicknamed it *beaver fever* which elicited generous chuckles from everyone.

Our first stop was at a small building just outside Andapa in the countryside. It was a two-roomed, wooden building with two entrances, a tin roof, and small gable. In front of the building was a fan-leafed tree about eight feet in height, and a white and blue sign that said: Public Library. The bottom of the sign had a picture of a Silky Sifaka and the word: *SIMPONA*.

Inside I met Pat who worked at the library. He was young, perhaps twenty, thin, and wore a white t-shirt. He greeted me with a smile of big, white teeth. The walls of the room were lined in bookshelves and full of books. Behind the bookshelves I could see red grid-patterned wallpaper, with red and yellow flowers printed in each square. Near the entrance there were educational posters with labelled anatomy, and in the middle of the room, a long table with several chairs, which made the walking area narrow.

I browsed through the English section and found Dr Goodman's *The Natural History of Madagascar,* and another one that interested me, a book called *Lost People* by David Graeber, about the legacy of slavery in Madagascar. There were all kinds of books on trees and nature; I saw the novels of George Eliot, both *Silas Mariner* and *Adam Bede*; and I found *King Leopold's Ghost* by Adam Hochschild, a book I considered required reading in supplement to Conrad's *Heart of Darkness.*

I went around the back of the room past a French section and turned towards the door and asked Pat: 'are there books in Malagasy language?' Nearer the door, Pat pulled some thin books off the shelf and showed me. They looked to be manuals on gardening and agricultural techniques.

'How long has the library been here?'

With his left hand, he played with his chin and mouth while answering my questions and I had trouble hearing him.

'2012?...Yes, 2012,' he repeated.

'Where did the books come from?'

'From Erik,' he replied. 'Maybe Duke had a program to do this library. Because they support the Antanetiambo Nature Reserve.' That was the first time I heard its name, but on the way to the reserve, we passed a sign that marked its location and I copied the name down.

The Antanetiambo Nature Reserve, I later learned, was the result of Rabary's work in collaboration with the Duke Lemur Centre. In a rare example of sacrifice, Rabary used his own funds to buy land and then planted endemic species of trees and bamboo, an effort that won him the 2010 Seacology Prize and a trip to America.

We drove down a country road in the basin of rice fields and stopped next to a field in a place that looked like nowhere in particular. To reach the Nature Reserve we had to walk along the mud wall that separated two rice fields, and once across, we entered a forest of bamboo.

'Welcome to the Reserve Antanetiambo. Be careful,' Rabary warned us. 'The bamboo has sharp stems that can hit your eye.'

We formed a train and hiked on a narrow trail through dense bamboo. Rabary and Jackson led the way and they chatted to each other briefly in Malagasy. Their dialect sounded more expressive and had different noises and inflections to emphasise a point. After five minutes of light marching we stopped. Rabary looked back at us, and without saying a word, pointed upwards ahead of us. Through the thick shoots of bamboo, I saw two dark figures the size of cats, but between the low light dappling through the canopy and the dense bamboo stems, the animals were blurry spectres. We sat and watched them for a few moments, until, with two effortless jumps they were gone. In a flash, they had moved ten feet, and we had to find the best path through the bamboo to reposition ourselves. The best possible positions offered a fuzzy glimpse of them, with no distinct features visible other than a brown blob moving in patterns recognisable as life.

'They like young shoots on the bamboo,' Rabary whispered.

Jo knelt to the ground and changed his camera lens. He raised it up and snapped a few pictures, but after looking at the resolution, he whispered 'it's too dark, I can't get a good shot with all the bamboo.'

We stayed with the pair for thirty minutes and then continued to see the rest of the reserve.

On the hillside trail, Rabary began telling me the story of the park and as a result, we fell behind the others. We came to a bench among trees and flowers. Rabary was an idealist and an optimist when it came to conservation. We stopped at a tree and, pressing his lips in consideration, he told me: 'we planted this tree…native to Madagascar; the bamboo lemur likes it a lot; they appreciate it.'

I asked Rabary to tell me about his trip to America.

'The people here can see the power of conservation. I went to San Francisco, Yellowstone Park, Chicago, and New York. The people here see, wow, conservation takes you to America.'

'What was your favourite place in America?'

'Just as a snake, prefers mouse to cake, I preferred Yellowstone the best.'

He touched every leaf and tree trunk in reverence. We reached a sign that said—*It is forbidden to cut down trees or hunt here.*

'People even see the quality of this sign and think—conservation made this sign. It is important. Thanks to the work of Dr Erik, you see these plants present here; the forestation. Among all of the conservationists, Dr Erik has done the most brilliant, very important things in this region. About conservation, development, protection of nature, and environmental education. Highly positive. Thanks to his presence in this region, this region has more advantages.'

He used both his supine hands, extended his arms, and pointed 'people are working down there, in the flatlands of this region, while this park is conserved forever on behalf of humanity, all over the world. Thanks to the support and help and initiative of Dr Erik. He is really a conservationist, but also he cares about education because without education, there can be no conservation. There are few people that do what he does.'

Rabary impressed me with his tone and sermonic way of speaking about the forest. So much of what I had read and heard about the future of the forests in Madagascar was negative, so to witness this level of optimism and commitment reset my perspective. He sounded like a preacher speaking about the glory of god, and hearing his pride and respect for this patch of forest made this tone feel appropriate to me. Why shouldn't he marvel at the forest that he planted?

We caught up to the others who had stopped to look at a boa constrictor. It was coiled, but I guessed its length to be nine feet. I had read in a book that most Malagasy people feared snakes, but none of these guys seemed afraid. To the contrary, Jo was gently handling it and trying to prevent it from leaving, long enough for him to get a picture.

That evening at dinner, Jo told us about a problem with invasive toads in the Tamatave region. The toads came to scientists' attention in 2014 when a man curious about the species he saw, emailed the biologist Jonathan Kolby to ask what this big bumpy brown amphibian was. It didn't take long for Kolby to confirm what he suspected—that this toxic toad was an invasive species and a serious threat. Scientists believed that the first toads made it to the island from industrial shipping containers. After the history of the cane toad in Australia, scientists were eager to try and contain and eradicate the toad while it was still in just one region of the island.

A few minutes later, while I was scooping some rice onto my spoon to eat with some chicken, I heard Erik say:

'Show Ty the video of Rabary.'

We watched a YouTube video entitled *2010 Seacology Prize Ceremony—Rabary Desire and His Accomplishments*. The video showed Rabary and Erik, and also had multiple views of the Andapa Basin where we had visited earlier that day. This video made me sit back for a moment in reflection, as though at that moment I finally had the right depth of appreciation for the special nature of this opportunity I had to be with these men. I looked forward to the next few days in the rainforest alongside Rabary, Erik, Jo, and Jackson.

We began our hike early the next morning as planned, and we had a lot of stuff to take to base camp with us. In addition to the five of us, a cook and two village locals were going to be at camp for the next four days. We had bags with tents, clothes, equipment, and lots of food. We drove to a small village outside of Andapa, where we procured a team of porters to carry the extra bags halfway, and there they would hand the bags off to another group of porters who would bring them to camp. The system was designed to involve as many people as possible in some paid work. Once we were organised and everyone had their bag to carry, we started off in a train of people up the mountain.

I hiked abreast of Erik and we chatted the whole way up the mountain about each other's lives, education, and his work in Madagascar for the past fifteen years, which started as PhD research for his Cornell University Doctorate. Erik was a genial guy, and I thought, also humble, intelligent, and accomplished. I asked him if he would tell me a little more about Camp Indri.

'The LCF had a small conservation near Tamatave but they wanted a new project. Anjanaharibe-Sud was a park with no infrastructure, but it was a place that had good potential. It's the only place where the silky and indri live side by side. And I did my PhD research in this park, so it was a good park for us to take on. We have tried to develop the park by involving the local villages as much as we can. We built schools, libraries, hold language classes, develop tree nurseries; some villagers get employment.'

When I first met Erik at the airport in Tana two days earlier, at four in the morning, my first impression of meeting him was that he resembled Ronald Regan's son Ron Regan. While hiking, I finally mentioned this to him, and he confirmed my observation with a laugh.

'Ha ok, I'll have to tell my fiancée you said that. We were out eating dinner one evening and some of his fans came to our table and began asking me questions.'

The first two hours of the hike were steep and the trail was rutted and challenging. The sun was warm and made me sweat through much of my shirt. Through more conversation I learned that Erik was born to a German mother and Indian father. Both his parents were well educated, so this played a part in his chosen profession, though he told me it took time to find the right fit. He completed his PhD in his early thirties, which encouraged me in my thoughts about doing the same.

'Both my parents were professors, so they understood the time it takes to finish a PhD and they supported me in finishing it.'

On a well-trodden trail adorned by dull green grass and palmy trees scattered nearby, we reached a small village that had a couple dozen wooden stick shacks along the trail. One of the shacks had a red blanket hanging from the roof over the gable and wall, and nearly reached down to touch the almond-coloured soil. Upon turning around and looking in the direction we had been climbing from, I saw a range of green hills that, from my vantage on the trail, had higher elevation to my left, with the ridgeline sloping downwards to the right. Behind, on the horizon, I could see the dark line of another series of hills that were mostly obscured by thick white and grey clouds.

In the village, we stopped at a tree nursery enclosed in a perimeter of yellow woven fence. Each row of infant trees was growing under a table fashioned to act as a roof to protect the trees while they were still vulnerable saplings. There were three men there who looked after the trees. Outside the perimeter was a yellow tent where a night guard slept each night. Erik chatted with the men for a few minutes and then took a picture of them. After we continued our hike, he explained the project to me.

'We set up this tree nursery with the local school there. The kids learn about the native trees here, and once the trees are big enough, each of them will get a tree to plant.'

This reminded me of a similar project I had done in the fifth grade with a pine tree.

'If they grow up appreciating the time it takes for a tree to grow, and how unique these forests are, hopefully it can develop a new relationship between the people and forest here.'

The difficult part of the climb was done in the first three hours. It was a steady ascent into the mountains and then the trail levelled and gently rolled up and down. The scenery was green, the air warm, and the exertion and pleasant conversation with Dr Patel energised me. This all chimed with one of the most vivid feelings of being in the right place with the right experience—and I thought—this feeling was why one travelled. This was not luxury nor leisure. It was the raw exertion of hiking alongside primordial forest on a mountain that formed two hundred million years ago, and I had to journey to the other side of the world to be here.

On occasion we met people walking and at other times stood aside as motorcycles flew by without consideration. Portions of the road were so rutted, washed out, and multi-tiered, that parts of the trail were two to three meters higher than the section of trail right beside it. We paused in a village where the first round of porters received their pay and the next group took over the duties of carrying bags up the mountain.

Erik said to me 'See that man over there. He used to be in charge of policing the forest but he lost his job. They think he was taking money to let people dig for crystals inside the park. This is the first time I have seen him since he lost the job so I'm wondering how he'll react.'

I watched but nothing seemed to develop from the encounter.

We rested for ten minutes, bought some bananas from the local growers, and sat down to eat them. Jo, in the same manner that I had seen him approach other animals, had found a flea next to where he was sitting, and employed his hands-on style of observing something with benign curiosity. Soon we were back on the trail, with a new train of porters, for the last remaining two hours of our hike.

At the top of a hill, we met two men on either side of a bicycle, which they were using to transport a one-hundred-and-ten-pound bag of rice. Their t-shirts, shorts, sandals, legs, and arms were covered in mud, and they looked tired. Erik spoke to them in Malagasy.

'Wow, they said they came from a Tsmimihety village west of the mountain. They will walk fifty kilometres pushing that bag of rice to the market in Andapa.'

'Why bring it all the way here?' I asked trying to make sense of such an effort. It was hard enough to hump this trail with one pack on my back, and these men were carrying an awkward, heavy package for a much longer distance.

'The market in Andapa is so much better, the price is worth carrying it there.'

Erik had his new GPS device out and was keeping track of different elevation readings as we ascended the hill.

'We're above nine-hundred meters, so the turn into the forest should be somewhere around here. Let's wait for Rabary, because I'm not sure if I'll be able to find it.'

He came along and we were indeed not far from the spot. We climbed up a small bank and disappeared out of the sun into the cooler shade of the forest where the air was moist and mouldering. We descended down a slippery hill covered in leaves and shallow roots.

'Do you know about the leeches?' Erik asked me.

'No,' I replied, ready to listen.

'They're not big but you have to watch out for them. They are everywhere in here and in narrow trails they have no trouble hitching a ride. They're actually interesting. They stick their body up into the air and sniff around. They can sense when you're near.' He said this wiggling his finger as a demonstration.

In a couple minutes we arrived at camp. There was storage shed, and beside it, a large concrete slab under a picnic shelter roof. Forty feet from this dining area were three slabs of concrete where we would pitch the tents. While looking at the progress of the camp since he had visited last, Rabary was beaming:

'All of this is made possible by the help of Dr Erik.'

Erik said 'we just had running water put in last year. Pipes were run from up the mountain at a stream. There is a tap by the fire pit and one in that shed over there where we shower. And if you have to do a number two, we have a toilet over there as well.'

Some of the porters were awaiting their pay and the rest trickled in soon after our arrival. They all received their five bucks and departed back home. Though it doesn't seem like much money, in this remote village five bucks in one day went a long way and all of them looked happy for the work. Erik said to Rabary, while pointing at one of the men, 'ask him if he wants to cut this grass over there for another ten-thousand?' The man agreed and went to work cutting the knee-high growth with his machete.

We made it to camp in the early afternoon and had three hours to set up the tents before nightfall. Everyone in camp appeared to be in high spirits. The man hired to do the cooking went to work organising his different plastic containers of plates and food. It was discovered that no-one brought charcoal and he looked hurt when the others told him it had been his responsibility. He and another found some branches and wood from the forest floor and he made do cooking dinner on a fire.

A gentle-flowing river passed by, just through the tree perimeter opposite from where we entered camp. Before coming, I imagined the forest to be sweltering in humidity, but after sunset the air was chilled enough to see my breath in the candlelight as we ate our dinner. Our meal that evening was rice, with veggies and meat. The cook made two giant bowls full of rice, enough to feed at least a dozen people. When asked why he made so much he said something and Erik laughed and said to me 'he thought you would eat a whole bowl yourself.'

'I have a friend who can eat that much rice,' Jo said, 'and drink eight big bottles of beer.'

I asked Jo, 'do Malagasy people like alcohol?' But this question animated Jackson, who told a story of how Africa was measured to be the biggest consumer of rum drinkers in the world and Madagascar was a big reason why that was true.

'Madagascar makes Africa first place,' he said smiling.

The Malagasy men all finished their meal with a large cup of brown water, a traditional way to end the meal in Madagascar. Water was added to the caked rice pot, and boiled, producing a drink similar to tea in appearance. They were not asked if they would take a glass, it was just assumed; I was offered and said I would try it.

'How is the taste?' Jo asked me

Its warmth was soothing and it had a taste similar to a roasted buckwheat tea I had tried in Japan.

'It's not bad,' I responded, feeling as though I wanted to say more but couldn't find anything more on which to comment. The nineteenth century European traveller Ida Pfeiffer encountered this drink in her travels in Madagascar and was not a fan:

"The usual drink is ranugung, or rice water, which is prepared in the following way. Rice is boiled in a vessel, and purposely burned, so that a crust forms at the bottom of the vessel. Water is then poured on, and allowed to boil. This water assumes the colour of very pale coffee, and, like everything else that is burnt, tastes abominably to a European palate."

In a world that has changed a lot since her day, I found her account of travel in Madagascar valuable for the comparisons it offered with what I was observing in the present. One clear difference was the population had exploded over the past eighty years, a phenomenon the historian Stephen Ellis classified as more altering in the Malagasy way of life than the start or end of the colonial period.

DAY TWO: CAMP INDRI

I remained dry and warm in my tent but all night heard the steady sound of water outside, either from rain showers, or the river passing by camp. This was dense rainforest so the weather choices were rain or heavy rain. I exited my tent before daybreak and found the cook working near the fire where he was when I went to bed last night. It was five in the morning and he already had hot coffee prepared. I had a chance to write a few notes and visit the outhouse before the rest roused from their tents. I could hear stirring in the tents but no one joined me at the table until after day break. When the sun did rise, it revealed a morning that was cloudy but had let up on the rain. A little later, Rabary, dressed in a red windbreaker and, this time undisputedly a conservation hat that said *Duke Lemur Conservation*, had his binoculars and was scanning the distant forest canopy.

Erik looked well rested after getting his first full night's sleep since being in the country. He pointed to the top of the trees behind our tents and said to me 'sometimes we wake up and the silky are in the trees over there.'

Rabary said without removing his binoculars, 'I think I can see them.' The other guys jumped up and stood behind him. They confirmed what he saw—the silky sifaka were about two-hundred meters from camp.

'I was looking for the fruit they like to eat, and found them,' he said. Now there was some energy in the group. Erik said 'Jackson, you and Jo eat quickly and go and find them, and see if you can stay with them for the day.'

The idea of following them around was to get them used to the presence of people so they did not jump away the second you track them down. This was a technique scientists used to get close enough to monitor their behaviour and it involved no contact of any kind. The rice was not cooked but they and one of the two spotters from the village quickly ate and were gone in under five minutes.

We left twenty minutes later in a group of four: Rabary, Erik, a local spotter, and me. Our goal for the day, besides seeing the animals, was to take elevation readings along the transect. Just as I had learned from Dr Goodman in Tana, on mountains like this and Marojejy, the elevation determined the type of flora and fauna that lived there. The taking of these readings also helped determine where new transects will best be placed.

We walked along a narrow trail that had sharp changes in gradient. The density of the trees and the closed canopy made the light shadowy, which created the feeling of being engulfed in forest. The ground was slippery and required caution as we navigated the narrow openings between trees and over logs. When the terrain descended, we had to be careful not to grab the trunk of a dead tree, which fell from the slightest pressure. Shallow buttressed surface roots were often useful as steps, but they could be a hazard when covered in dead leaves and stepped on without awareness of their sharp angles. Other trees were thorn-studded and an accidental touch taught me not to repeat the mistake.

At one point, we heard a chirping in the nearby trees that Rabary pointed out as a blue cuoa bird, but most of the time, the sodden air in the forest was calm enough that I could only hear water dripping.

'I'm surprised we haven't heard the indri call yet,' Erik said. 'They didn't call yesterday or this morning. There is some research that suggests they call fewer times when the weather is colder, but usually at least once.'

Decayed tree trunks lied across the forest floor and replenished the soil with nutrients. Closed canopy rainforests support all kinds of life that prefer growing in the shade of the towering trees. The leaf litter on the ground covered the forest floor and sustained insects, fungus, and bacteria. About six weeks after falling to the forest floor, what was left of a leaf had broken down to nutrient form and was ready to be absorbed back into other plants. The rainforest's ecosystem thrived and sustained itself on this equilibrium.

We spent several hours hiking in the elevation range designated humid forest, and Rabary used his encyclopaedic knowledge of the flora and fauna to rattle off more names that I could remember or write down in the wet atmosphere:

'This is the…native to Madagascar.'

'This bush is the…endemic to this region.'

'The leaves of this tree are eaten by lemurs.'

'This bush is appreciated by local villagers.'

He knew absolutely everything that lived here. The tree canopy dripped with water and occasionally hit the top of my ears. The branches scratched my arms, even on the paths that had begun to take form from previous visits. Every five minutes one of us swiped a leech from our exposed skin, and though they posed a threat to our eyes, most times they were easily removed. We continued in this way for four hours before we froze at the sound of a monkey-like bark that we heard call seven or eight times.

'That's the alarm call of the Indri,' Erik said.

We abandoned the trail and increased our pace through the denser trees. The thorns and branches scratched my forearms and shoulders. At the moment of the call, the local spotter with us disappeared into the forest, and the three of us moved quickly, nearly tumbling down a crater and crawling up the opposite side. Rabary let out a high-pitched holler and the spotter responded from fifty meters away. Erik explained 'we found that if you use radios to communicate, the noises scare the lemurs, but you can holler like what Rabary just did and they won't even look in your direction.'

Our pace and energy was heightened for the next hour, and we heard six more small barks from the indri but we had no luck in finding them. After six hours, we arrived back in camp tired, scratched and filthy from the exhausting hike, but there were no negative feelings about the day. The search was thrilling and left me eager to try again.

Jo and Jackson were back and greeted us with the good news that they had found the silky and followed them for a few hours. Jo showed me some pictures he had taken. Their bodies were completely white and their faces had a black snout with spotty pigmentation that was pink in places. This pigmentation was one of the features of this lemur that distinguish it as a separate species. We had a late lunch, it was now 2:45, and after Erik and I chatted about various things.

'There is a lot of crystal mining in the forest. They have trouble policing the national park. They will hire someone to patrol the area, but we have had trouble in the past. Crystal miners will pay the man off and he allows them to dig in the park.'

And then he told me about a different initiative.

'One of the programs we are doing with the local villages is with family planning. The birth rate in Madagascar is going to double in the next twenty or thirty years. But we have to be careful how we do the program. It is easy to be charged with unethical aims when offering the communities birth control, so we train nurses who speak the local dialect to visit the villages and talk about it with the women. They then have the choice and they have to pay for it as well. That way there is no problem on our end. It's been a successful program. A lot of the women have paid for it and have birth control for five years.'

Erik then went on to tell me about a birth control program that was part of the Catholic Relief Services that had enjoyed some success until the Vatican learned of it, and squashed the funding for the education. Sex education, for teens in a country that had been experiencing worrisome population growth, seemed an understandable approach to reduce the number of teen pregnancies. On this topic, Erik said:

'In the villages in Madagascar, it is common for women in their teens to have their first baby.'

I asked Erik some questions about Rosewood trees and their illegal global market.

'There was a group that put trackers in some of the rosewood trees and confirmed that they ended up in China. A guy named Armand Amarzafy was publicly outspoken against rosewood activity and was put in jail. The American embassy has found evidence that the president's wife is the head of the rosewood mafia. It's dangerous.'

It was interesting to keep an eye on the reaction of Jo at times. He was an educated man, and facts guided his life, but a natural defensive emotion hit his face at times, before he surrendered to reason. When hearing that manioc tubers, if not boiled properly to remove a toxin, could impair the cognitive development of children, or that the president's wife was the head of the rosewood mafia, his initial reaction looked naysaying, but I watched his face change, as he considered—it seemed to go through a reasoning process that said: if there is evidence than I guess it is true.

Since the coup d'état collapsed the economy in 2009, illegal logging became much worse because there were many more people looking for ways to make some money. More desperate people were willing to risk going into the national parks to take the rosewood trees and sell them on the market, where the logs will end up as high-end furniture and guitars. Erik told me he took part in a documentary called *Treasure Island* that was done by Dan Rather, in which he reported the issue as an ecological nightmare plundering the island. The trees sold on the market for thousands of dollars, yet brought just a few dollars a day to the locals who cut them down and transported them to the port.

From this topic, Erik began telling me about some more positive initiatives he and his group have implemented in recent years.

'We started a fish pond and bred a native fish. Tilapias are taking over the rivers. The city of Andapa has dried fish but not fresh fish, so once a year a harvest from the pond gives the city thirty kilos of fresh fish. The fish are fenced in and guarded, and their diet is twenty-five percent protein in dried shrimp and husks of rice. That's the beauty of it because they are fed a waste product.'

He also mentioned some of his future plans for this trip.

'In a couple weeks we will take a break from up here, while Jackson and some guys do some work at the camp. Rabary, Jo and I will visit Diego, Ankarana and the Tsingy Rouges.'

I told him about my time there and said I had enjoyed it.

He asked me, 'Are you taking malaria suppressant? Have you had nightmares?'

'Almost every night,' I said. They were not terrifying, just more vivid than usual.

That evening, after the sun had gone down, Rabary, Jo and I went for a brief walk through the forest with flashlights to see if we could find any nocturnal species. Our search turned up nothing. After the first day, most of the group retired to their tents soon after sundown to get a good night's sleep. I dreamed that hundreds of giant ants had infiltrated my apartment, and when I woke from this dream, I could hear a fire crackling outside. The cook was the first one up again.

DAY THREE CAMP INDRI

I was back in the forest with Rabary and a spotter and we were trying to find the Indri. It was raining that morning, but once we got under the forest canopy it was reduced to constant dripping. Jo was on a different assignment plotting coordinates and finding new areas that would be ideal for new transects. Jackson and Erik planned to hike to a different part of the mountain to do other tasks.

My group was off to an auspicious start. In the first ten minutes we found a family of brown lemurs in a group of tall trees thirty or forty yards in the distance. One moment they appeared, moved across our line of sight, then a moment later they bounded through the trees and vanished. It occurred to me after spending over ten hours hiking in Madagascar's forests how much work it takes to find the animals. When you watch nature documentaries like the David Attenborough one I mentioned earlier, they rarely explain how much work it took to find the species. The program just moves from one species to the next, and the viewer sitting on the sofa at home has no way to appreciate the effort put into the film. It takes days and weeks to go from forest to forest, and perhaps days to find the animals.

'You have a leech on your forehead.'

Rabary had turned to say something to me and said that instead. Not wanting to knock the thing into my eyes, I asked him to take it off for me, and thankfully, he was able to do so with swift resolution.

Again today the indri were not calling, but like yesterday we heard their barking alarm after about four hours of trekking. Rather than scramble after the noise, we moved methodically in what we believed to be the right direction and came to an opening where the river runs down the mountain. We stayed in the opening and scanned the canopy for around twenty minutes.

The spotter crouched down so low his bottom nearly hit the ground and his hand shot out pointing at the tree tops. He signalled with his other hand to come over to him. He had found them. I looked up and indeed saw two, and then a third, black figures moving in the trees at roughly fifty meters' distance. We started celebrating and grabbed each other's shoulders as we stood and watched them with big relieved smiles on our faces. Later when writing this, I further realised how much I appreciated their joy; they were not happy at seeing an animal they had seen hundreds of times. They were happy that I got to see it.

For a minute, the indri stayed in place, perhaps eating, but at this distance it was hard to see what they were doing in specific detail. Then, one at a time, they dashed through a tree top and then leapt twenty feet between two branches that reached across the river opening. They accomplished this feat with minimal effort and expert dexterity, and at the moment they passed by closest to us, I could see that their hips moved in a seemingly unnatural motion, almost as though they were stuffed animals swinging from tree to tree. Yet how could this strange observation be true, because when they had a mind to move, they bolted out of sight with legendary agility.

The three of us congratulated each other on our accomplishment. In that moment, I thought about many days ago in Ramena, when the lemur had jumped on my chair, and I now thought to myself: it can be easy to see lemurs in Madagascar, but it is not easy to see them in their natural environment. Like all the other species of lemurs I had seen during my time in Madagascar, the indri came and went in a flash, just long enough to confirm their elusive inimitable renown. I had spent hours, no, days, to get this glimpse of the indri and the moment was glorious. The lemur leapt through the treetops with as much ease as humans sitting and chatting around a fire—it was what we were born to do.

In the evening after dinner I moved over to the fire and sat next to Jo. The rest of the men were telling stories and laughing.

Jo said 'did you notice at dinner they didn't speak much. Malagasy men don't speak much at dinner, they wait until after to sit and talk by the fire. In Malagasy we call it Tarariva Amorom Paharana. It means stories told around the fire as the sun goes down. Typically, in Malagasy villages in the evening, the elder or grandfather will gather the children around and tell stories and fables of the Malagasy people. Many villages don't have schools, so children learn from their grandfathers in this way. It is Malagasy culture.'

I asked Rabary to tell a story. He first told me the legend of the crocodile lake near the village I had visited near Ankarana. The story told of a thirsty man who entered a village and went from person to person asking for a drink of water. All across town he was denied a drink of water. The village denied him water, so he flooded the village and turned it into a lake and all the people became crocodiles.

Jackson told a humorous story about how a pack of dogs had a meeting with God and one of the dogs farted, but nobody knew who did it. God said, *find me the dog that farted.* Dogs are still looking for the one that farted. Every time a dog meets a new dog, they sniff each other's butts to see if that was the dog that broke wind in God's presence. The searching and the sniffing continues.

I had read in a book that there are many legends of the Indri. In one version of the story, a child who was lost in the forest was taken in by an Indri. Later when the boy was found, the people saw that the Indri was like a father to the boy. The Indri's name in Malagasy is Babakoto, which is derived from the combination of father and child.

That evening, by the fire, once more I had the feeling that I was in the right place. The indri were dozing in the tree tops and men were sitting and telling stories round the fire.

Chapter Six
Sambava to Maroantsetra

I was the only person on the bus who had the feeling of being free, as though I were making an escape down the coastline.

There was something life-affirming about coming to this SAVA region and spending valuable time with a serious group of people who were doing challenging and important work, but then jumping in a taxi-brousse and blasting down the coast to a new destination. The decision and the departure gave me a feeling of freedom like a caffeine-high as I began my journey down the coast of eastern Madagascar.

There was a train from Tamatave (or Taomasina) to the capital Tana, and I intended to ride that train. Though Tamatave was just a few hundred kilometres south of my current location on the eastern coast, the way to get there overland was full of washed out rutted country roads, many of which were impassable in a vehicle. I was not certain how I would get there, but I had time and was determined to find a way.

The eastern Cape of Madagascar was part of a small parrot-billed land formation called the Masoala Peninsula, which enclosed a small body of water called Antogil Bay. The first stretch of my journey meant making it to a city called Antalaha, and then finding a way through the countryside to a bay city called Maroantsetra. Before leaving the Mimi Hotel in Sambava, I asked the hotel owner Bran how to go from Antalaha to Maroantsetra and he suggested that I speak with a man in Antalaha named Fernand.

'If you can go that way, Fernand at the Vitasoa Hotel will know about it.'

The drive from Sambava to Antalaha in a taxi-brousse was along a straight road that ran parallel with the Indian Ocean. About sixteen kilometres outside of Antalaha, we passed the confluence of two rivers. There the Indian Ocean became visible, which until that point, had remained hidden beyond fields of planted coconut trees and other vegetation.

Antalaha was a small decent looking port town that stretched tightly along the coast. Not far into town, the RN5a highway hit a roundabout and then turned into the RN53, which travelled another fifty kilometres down the coast before ending. The downtown square in Antalaha was located at the point where the RN53 began, and on the south-eastern corner of this main square was where I found a room at Hotel Vitasoa.

I asked a staff member of the hotel where I might find Fernand and she told me that he will be back later in the afternoon. With that I went back to my room where I decided to get a little rest to see if I could get over a slight onset of fever that I had felt weakening me for the past hour. The condition worsened for a while to where I had cold sweats and was quite uncomfortable with stiff aching muscles, but later in the afternoon, I managed to throw on some clothes and go look for Fernand.

I found him working at the front desk. He had short thick black hair, thin eyes, with round cheeks. He was not a tall man, but looked young, lean, and athletic. I asked him about going to Maroantsetra and he replied to my question in a deep and confident voice.

'You can walk there but it is a difficult hike. Maybe I can go with you. You will need a guide because it is easy to get lost and security may be a problem if you are alone.'

'How long does it take to walk?' I asked.

He pulled out a map and showed me the peninsular region.

'We can walk for one week around the Masoala Peninsula, or we can do four days straight to Maroantsetra.'

The forest in Masoala interested me but there was still a lot of country I needed to see and I had just spent a week in the forest.

'Let's walk straight there,' I said.

'Yes, it is better I think,' he replied.

We agreed to leave the day after tomorrow which I was hoping would give me enough time to get over whatever condition was causing my fever.

'What is GIDA?' I asked Fernand, who was wearing a shirt that had the acronym printed on it.

'It's a club I started. We do community projects; did you see the garbage cans by the beach? Our group put all those along the beach to help keep it clean.

We have dancing, massage classes, English classes. We have an English club tomorrow night. If you want, you can come with me. The group will enjoy talking to you.'

After I agreed, he said 'okay, I will come here tomorrow night at seven and we can walk there.'

I spent the next twenty-four hours resting and convalescing, and towards the evening I felt well enough to eat dinner at the hotel restaurant. Fernand met me at the hotel, on time, and we walked through the dark streets of Antalaha for about five minutes before reaching a large city building which looked to be French colonial.

We went inside to a large town hall room that had a stage and many folded chairs and tables. I helped him set up four tables in an 'L' shape and while we did this, group members filed in, grabbed a chair, and set it down at the table. Before taking their seats for the meeting, many stopped by to shake my hand, not so much as a self-introduction, but rather as a gesture to smile and say—*you are welcome here*.

Fernand and another young man did some talking in the beginning, which I took to be administrative discussion, but after a few minutes of this, they introduced me to the group and invited me to speak to everyone. I spent some time introducing myself, my background, and where in Canada I came from. Then I spoke a little about my time teaching in Japan and Russia, and ended with telling them why I came to this region of the island. Though there were about fifteen people ranging from high school age to young adult, only about six of them asked me questions.

I got asked why I was in Madagascar, what do I think of life here, and how can I learn English faster. I talked to them about studying English and how I thought there were no shortcuts when learning a second or third language. I told them that it required a lot of memorising and a lot of practice speaking aloud. They should find things they love like music or movies and practice using these mediums as well.

Overall, though a shy group, I saw many smiles and genuine interest in improving themselves and their community. Like what I saw in Tana with the ICE English Club, I thought this group showed initiative to voluntarily begin a group together and try to strengthen their community, better educate themselves, and improve their lives. I thanked them for making me feel welcome there and wished them success with their organisation. After the event, Fernand and some of the others returned the chairs and tables back to their organised storage space, and then Fernand and I walked back to my hotel. His last words were 'See you early tomorrow morning.'

The following morning Fernand and I met early and went to the western edge of town to a perpendicular intersection that functioned as a bus centre. For the majority of our journey to Maroantsetra, we would have to walk, however, the first twelve kilometres we could get a ride. At the bus stop we found several drivers heading to Sambava, before finding a man who planned to drive a large old truck the twelve kilometres to the end of the road. The only issue was there was no scheduled departure time and we would have to wait until he filled the truck with passengers.

Fernand said to me 'I think it will be better if we take a moto, we can leave now.'

I told him I would rather not ride on a motorcycle and would prefer to wait for the truck, suggesting that maybe it would only be twenty or thirty minutes before it filled with passengers. We took a seat on a bench on the other side of the road with our backs to some trees. There were many people standing around, some looked to be peddling food or drink and others perhaps waiting for a bus like we were.

'I think I will take some tea-cola. I didn't sleep last night. I watched soccer at the bar.' Fernand stopped a man who had a large thermos and pail with metal cups and had a glass of tea, which looked to be a mixture similar to Indian chai. After about thirty minutes, Fernand pressed again to take a motorcycle.

What I didn't tell Fernand was that I was afraid to get on the back of a motorcycle with another person operating it. To put yourself in such a vulnerable position as to be precariously hanging off the back of a machine that goes incredibly fast, and crashes easily, was the height of bad sense to me. Furthermore, I had just witnessed a man who had been in a motorcycle accident and was subsequently lying dead on the road. The whole scene was a macabre spectacle for gawking villagers, none of whom were bereaved, and the dead man's only observable hold over those still alive was that he was the cause of some traffic congestion. I was not interested in putting myself on one of these contraptions of death.

'The truck maybe will not leave until eleven or twelve o'clock and it could take one hour to drive to the end,' Fernand said.

We procured a motorcycle driver and strapped our bags on the back of the bike and then the three of us, me in the middle, got on and we started off down the road. The road was rutted and rocky enough for the driver to use some caution in his driving, and when added to that a heavy cargo and a large foreign man squeezing his thighs as tightly as possible, he never achieved any reckless speeds that caused any outcry from me. The truth was, he operated the machine quite well. The ride never achieved any sustained cruising speed; it was a succession of accelerations, slowdowns, swerves, and my prayers every time we idle-glided through low spots filled with mud and rain water. For me the ride was tense, uncomfortable, and images of the bike tipping sideways and falling on our legs, burning and breaking them under the mass and momentum, replayed over in my head. Despite all of this nervous ruminating and torturing myself, we made it to the end of the road with little more than some mud splashes on our legs. Now dressed like the locals, I strapped on my pack, and Fernand, brandishing a machete, did so as well. He said: 'we walk from here.'

We began from a small collection of huts and after a few hundred meters of flat trail, quickly found ourselves entering the green mountainside that stretched into the horizon. Some of the distant mountains were quilted with patches of brown deforestation, but the predominant view was of lush fertile green rainforests. The trailside was thick in light and dark hues of green vegetation, and at various points, small tufts of desiccated grass grew on our rusted orange trail. A few puffs of clouds hung in the sky, but for the most part the morning was sunny. 'We are lucky today,' Fernand said. 'There is no rain. It has rained every day for the past week.'

The trail pig-tailed through the mountains in ascents and descents. In many places the angle was steep enough that it seemed to me for every meter we traversed in a western direction, we had climbed and descended one meter as well. The trail was a type of three-dimensional trekking I had never before experienced.

We kept our pace light and at times walked several meters apart from each other. This light quiet pace suited me fine because I was still feeling slightly ill with residual fever, and it had to have suited Fernand, who had been up all night watching soccer. It also suited the type of trail on which we were walking.

The trail was rough, hilly, and required full attention to the placement of each step. It was not the kind of hike where one could escape into lucid imagination and leave the body on auto-pilot. It was as cognitively draining as a long drive in a car. I watched where I put each step, paid attention to my breathing which had increased to a heavier, more laboured rhythm, and took rationed sips of water. At times, I could feel my heart thump; other times, my legs required focused encouragement not to give up—to be told to keep climbing because we were nearly at the top of this corkscrew and there was no turning back. Fernand and I methodically plodded forward over the challenging gradient.

Once in a while we would pass by a lone traveller and at other times we met small groups of people. A new appreciation for Malagasy life emerged in me while I was walking through these hills. As I struggled up and down the challenging terrain, most of the people we passed looked as though they were walking casually through Central Park. And though they were able to walk this trail with far less exertion than me, this didn't hide the austere nature of people's lives in these mountains. My trek through these mountains was an artificial introduction of struggle to affirm life; for the Malagasy these hills were an affirmation that their lives were a struggle.

The people who lived in these mountains were used to making journeys like this on a regular basis. If a villager wanted to go to Antalaha or Maroantsetra, the only option was to walk. The land was everything to the villagers in these hills. The river and streams that kept intersecting our trail provided drinking water and a place to bathe or wash clothes. The fertile soil provided great conditions for vanilla, rice, coffee, oranges, bananas, and various other crops.

After several hours of walking, Fernand and I stopped in a village to get something to eat and to take a rest. Many of the villages along this trail were used to local people passing through, so each community had at least one hut that offered food or a bed to wayward travellers. We sat at the edge on a decaying wooden terrace that was part of someone's simple wooden home.

The woman who brought us a bowl of rice and a scrawny chicken wing in a bowl had three children also sitting on the terrace. Two girls appeared to be of mid-teenage years, and the third was a young boy of no more than two years old. As I looked over my left shoulder, the younger of the two teenage girls was lazily lying in a pile of laundry.

I ate all the rice in my bowl and picked at the sinewy grey chicken wing looking for a piece of meat. I finished it, and as I set the tray behind me, an unusual thing happened at the same moment. I turned over my right shoulder and set the tray on the terrace behind me, and as I did this, the teenage girl sitting there, popped her large breast out of her shirt; its big dark nipple pierced the air and pointed right at me. This flooded my mind with confusion as to what was happening, and before I could figure it out, the answer came from the two-year-old boy.

The boy, who I had taken to be this girl's younger brother, was in fact this girls' son. A moment later he was sitting on his mother's lap, ape-like against her chest and having his lunch. I asked Fernand to ask the girl her age.

'She said she is seventeen.'

'And how about the child?'

'The child is more than one years old,' Fernand translated, after asking her my latest question. So it was certainly possible that this young girl had become pregnant at the age of fourteen and at the latest, fifteen. But wasn't this minor shock and initial confusion just me trekking modern views into the country highlands where life was still pre-modern?

I later read an article that explained that one third of teen girls under the age of eighteen are pregnant or have been pregnant. Teenage sex was common in most countries but in Madagascar pregnant teens usually quit attending school, which had left nearly half the country remaining illiterate. To put this in perspective, England had achieved this level of literacy by the mid-seventeenth century. Teenage pregnancies were also contributing to a growing population and an average of just over four children per mother.

The population of Madagascar had been steadily increasing by around one million people every year. The problem with population growth was the lack of infrastructure and economic growth to match the pace of the rising population. Looking at the small village I was sitting in, I imagined that youths likely walked to the cities looking for work. The village we sat in had two rows of housing along the main road, and perhaps was home to a few hundred people, though it was hard to tell because at this time, in the middle of the day, there were not many people walking around. I assumed they were working somewhere in the fields.

Fernand and I rested and hydrated in the shade for twenty minutes while our shirts dried in the sun. We had trekked for about four hours that morning, and we had enough daylight left to trek another four hours that afternoon. And four more hours we did go. After some food and a quick nap, Fernand seemed energised, because he was far more gregarious with people we passed along the trail while walking. Each person got at minimum a standard greeting and a 'where are your heading today?' After chatting for thirty seconds, we would continue, and Fernand would say to me things such as

'he is going to Sambava'

'he is going to Antalaha'

'those two are going to Maroantsetra,' he said about the two young men who were walking so fast that they passed us. Not understanding the language, I observed other cues. For example, I picked up on a common pattern of behaviour when passing someone new. Each would look at me and then immediately look down to see what kind of shoes I had on my feet. I assumed this was of interest because everybody we passed was walking barefoot. In fact, as I started taking note of this little pattern, I did not remember seeing a pair of shoes the entire day. These men and women walked in sandals or barefoot, and must have had iron soles on their feet. The one advantage to this was that everyone but me walked through the ubiquitous puddles with indifference, while I always had to go around or hop over.

The reaction of villagers to the sight of me was further proof of how remote this area was. Upon entering villages, a child from a group of playing children would notice me, shout something, and point at me. I imagined them to be saying things like 'the Vikings are coming,' or 'the French are back,' but more often than not the reaction I got was 'Vahaza.' On occasion they would run inside their hut and tell their mother that a white foreigner was passing through their village. But to me it seemed that this was done mostly out of interest rather than fear or suspicion. Upon entering one village, a young girl who was playing atop a small hill about three meters higher than my position on the trail, looked down at me, and said in the politest tone 'Bonjour Vahaza.'

Vahaza was a word on everybody's lips when they saw me. Some people did not even say it to another human, they just muttered it out like a reflex. My visit to the village seemed to me to be a rare enough event that it would make some kind of town newsletter if such a thing existed. This kind of contact with the people in these mountains made me glad I chose this route, and made me appreciate how resilient they were to live here, just as their ancestors must have been. We reached one of these small villages every thirty minutes to two hours of walking.

The trail remained demanding and even capricious in its steep ups and downs. Fernand and I continued to walk in a train, only conversing once in a while such as when we took a minute to catch our breath at the top of a steep hill.

The river meandered back and forth over our trail causing us to cross it many times. Each time there was no bridge, so we had to hop along stones to get across. The trail and the countryside remained unchanged in its appearance and difficult for the rest of the day. Near dusk, we made it to a village where we found a place to sleep for the night.

The proprietor, a middle-aged man, had a large hut split into four tight quadrants. The side where we would sleep had a small bed in the back and an old wooden table in the front. The man's sleeping quarters were opposite ours on the other side of a small wall dividing the two rooms.

We dropped our packs, walked through the village and down a hill to the river, where we both stripped down naked and waded out for a bath. As I walked into the chilly river, I heard some laughs and hollers, and following the sounds, I saw a group of women sitting at the riverside forty meters downstream. The water was too cold to be relaxing, but after such a long day of sweaty trekking I would have jumped into the Drake Passage for a wash.

The village was simple and had few indicators of modernity. The men I saw had western raggedy clothes and their principle cash crops were grown for sale on the international market, but other than that, this village may have looked exactly the same in the nineteenth century as it did this day.

Fernand and I had rice and chicken and then, exhausted, we crawled into the bed which was only large enough to fit the two of us on our sides. I closed my eyes but before I fell asleep, I heard two women begin singing in some kind of phrasing that repeated, to which two male singers seemed to respond in a kind of musical dialogue. I did not know what they were singing about but they sang in lovely tune and harmony. A small smile formed on my face as I fell asleep listening to this beautiful music, and the last thought I remember having was— *I'm glad to be here.*

In the countryside, all alarm clocks were fowl. I opened my eyes the next morning to the sound of vociferous honks, croaks, clucks, and crows. I next heard a man clucking to call these birds for breakfast. My boots had not dried overnight, so I pulled the soles out of them and put everything in a plastic bag. Today I would have to wear my shoes. I ate some bananas and drank some water for breakfast. While sitting at the small table Fernand appeared in the entrance.

'If you have to put, you can do it out there,' he said to me while pointing to behind the hut. I went outside to look around but could not find anything resembling a toilet. I stared for a moment at a cement structure that stood knee-high, and had a flat surface with a large hole that tapered to the bottom. Fernand came out and saw me eyeing this thing with intent to squat over it, and said 'no, that is for hitting rice.'

'This,' he said pointing to a small room, 'is the toilet.' It was a small shack erected for privacy with a level dirt surface. I decided not 'to put' that morning.

There was no trail leading out of the village, so that mornings' hike began walking across a mud wall barrier between two rice fields. By the time I was on the other side, I had mud and water in my shoes. Annoyed, I swapped my sodden shoes back for my damp boots and we continued. The first hour of the morning's hike was difficult to navigate because there was not much of a trail. We walked through a series of trees and bushes and the path was so narrow that the branches scraped along our arms as we passed through this area. We picked up the trail on the other side and were back to a steep path moving through the mountains.

By the middle of the second day, we reached the northern part of Masoala Park, a protected expanse of rainforest that covered much of the peninsula. Due to its location on the peninsula, the park received the most rainfall of any place on the entire island. The government designated this a protected area in 1997 and it was one of the biggest national parks on the island. Despite this protected status, this was one of the areas where people trafficked in illegal rosewood trees.

The trail, up until that point, had been in tough mountainous terrain, but now we were in engulfed in a three-dimensional rain forest. Immediately after entering the forest, we saw a family of brown lemurs just a few meters from the trail. Fernand and I were only briefly cutting across a northern section of the park so it was not long before we had left the forest and were back to the familiar grinding trail.

Keeping my feet dry was the most difficult part of the trekking. Fernand was walking in cheap plastic water crocs, while I struggled over numerous river crossings and around large puddles. As we descended one hillside we approached a river with a village on the other side. At the river's edge, Fernand said:

'I think you should take your boots off.'

Many of the rocks that formed the path across this river were slightly submerged, but visible. I judged that the water level was not high enough above the rock for it to be a problem. What I did not consider was the current of the river and the slippery rock surfaces. At the fourth step, my foot slipped off the rock and my boot plunged into the water nearly up to me knee.

'I told you but you didn't listen.'

This mistake had me fuming. I was so angry at myself that I was overflowing to the point that I wanted to yell at Fernand for my own stupidity. But this would have been insane and foolish and I did not.

At the other side of the river, I put my boots in the bag with my shoes, and put on my sandals, the last of my footwear. At least with the sandals, it did not matter if they got wet. But this too was an erroneous assumption I had made. The leather stretched and when the soles got muddy my feet slid right out of them. They fell off at the next river crossing. With wet shoes and boots, sandals on their way to Australia, I continued on in bare feet, which turned out to be a massive improvement over the sandals. My feet grew sore at walking without any protection, but I also realised that I felt a small tinge of pride when the locals who passed by did their usual look at my feet and this time saw the local footwear. I recalled reading a passage in Robert McFarlane's *The Old Way* where he recounted taking off his shoes to walk barefoot and 'began to feel the changes of habitat underfoot: the temperatures of the leaf-litter…it is true that I remember the terrains over which I have walked barefoot differently.' When shed of all my footwear, I felt a lot more concerned and became more vigilant about not stepping on any of the cow turds that were everywhere on the trail.

We trekked for another three hours that afternoon, and just before dusk, we made it to a town called Tanambao. This village was larger than the one in which we spent the previous night. Fernand and I found a small operation with four huts that served as individual rooms for the itinerants of the trail. A lady showed us back to the chambers and said something to Fernand, which he then passed to me.

'They only have this one room, is it ok for us?'

We took the small room and tried our best to find spots to lay our clothes to dry for the evening. I pulled the insoles from my boots and shoes in hopes that they would dry overnight. Fernand suggested that I stay in the room while he went to shower, then he would do the same, when I went to shower. A precaution for security, as he put it. He left, and I finished hanging another shirt to dry for the evening. I soon heard water splashing on the ground behind our room.

When it was my turn, I found a small three-walled enclosure, and inside on the ground, a bucket of water with a scoop. The water was icy but it felt good to wash after another long day on the road. The only issue I had with the shower was each time I tried washing my legs and feet, mud splashed up and dirtied them again. I did the best I could with that, then slipped on my last pair of clean clothes from my pack.

Fernand and I went looking to see if I could buy a pair of sandals. Dusk had just fallen to nightfall which made it impossible to get a decent look at the village. We walked through many rows of housing with an old man following behind us, trying to offer his services as a guide to whatever we wanted to find in the village. When we found a shop that sold sandals, I bought a pair. The shop had a few other dry food goods and bottled drinks for sale. The old man pestered us for a little cash for showing us the way to the shop. After a quick meal of rice and chicken, we both crawled into our bed. The bed was uncomfortable, but I didn't mind, and instead understood the sentiment in Nicholas Nickleby, that a long journey was 'one of the best softeners of a hard bed that ingenuity can devise.'

The next morning, Fernand suggested to me that for the first part of the day's hike, I should wear the sandals to make the river crossings, and he would let me know when we had made our last cross of the trip. Unlike the previous day, I intended to listen to his council today. We began our trek at six in the morning which opened with a climb up and around a mountain pass. As we came down the other side, there were a few river crossings to make, but it didn't take long before he said to me 'you can put your shoes back on, that was the last one.'

With my shoes back on our pace picked up substantially. For the first time on the hike, I took the lead up and down the hills and through the valleys. There was no rush, because we were a-day-and-a-half ahead of schedule, with over three-quarters of our trip already completed, but I felt like a man with new feet, no longer handicapped by the ignorance that had led to so many prior difficulties.

After an hour of this pace we came to a small country city called Mahalevona. This town had larger buildings and sturdier homes than the village where we slept the night before. The town was still a country village with at least a thousand people but I could not tell if it was much bigger than this our not. One new experience here was the first sighting of motorcycles since leaving two days before, and like all motorcycles, they were a noisy nuisance that terrorised the road. I saw a school, a football pitch, a store, and even a bank. But what differentiated this large town from other large places around the country was that this place had no French influence in its architecture.

Its buildings were all in the style of huts, with a few structures made of wood. I judged that everything here was built with resources from the surrounding area. We stopped in a small restaurant where Fernand wanted to say hello to a waitress he was friends with. As we entered the restaurant, in the distance, down the long village road, I could see a large group of people walking with a purpose in our direction.

The two of us went inside and Fernand chatted a bit with his friend. I watched out the door as over one hundred people passed by in rows and columns. Women had lambas wrapped around their waists and many of the men carried flimsy sandals in their hands. Everyone that I could see was wearing a hat, though none of them were similar.

I asked Fernand what was happening and after conferring with the waitress, he told me 'a boy in the next village died. This is a funeral for him. They started walking from the last village and will walk to the end of this one.' There was light singing that was graver and more sombre than the mellifluous storied-singing I had heard two nights ago.

The next village we reached was similar in size and appearance. Along the main road, there were town buildings built with lumber, and some were even two-stories. This village had a nineteenth century American West feeling to it: the dirt road, two-story saloon, restaurant, and locally-built bank. At the far end of town, we approached a group of men holding a town meeting. Fernand listened in for a moment then told me 'they are talking about vanilla farming. Maybe the prices and protecting their plants. In this country, it is forbidden to walk along this trail at night. It is security for vanilla plants.'

'Do people steal vanilla?' I asked.

'If vanilla is not close to home, the security is dangerous. Someone might take it.'

We exited the town across a series of bridges and walked by the last scattering of homes where just beyond were fields of rice. On the way out of town an older woman stood in front of us and gently grabbed my wrist with her left hand. She uttered something as I gently pulled back. I was slightly startled by her wretched appearance but more so because she held a machete in her left hand.

'She asked you to buy her alcohol at that store.'

I said, 'tell her to buy her own alcohol' a comment which Fernand found hilarious.

At the edge of town, there were a series of houses that had trees, fences, and gates, which I thought were more for privacy than security. There we heard a woman shout at us.

'She invited you to stay at her home.'

'I'm busy, but thank you,' I shouted to her.

Fernand said, 'This town is different. In Antalaha, people would never talk like this.'

'I heard things like that in Tana,' I said.

We were now on a trail that could pass for a road, and this stretch of road led several kilometres ahead of us towards a large mountain covered in clouds. Seeing where I was looking, Fernand said 'that is the last mountain we have to pass.' I asked him how long it would take and he said 'maybe two hours.'

The path ascending up the mountain was steep and unrelenting. It took close to two hours to reach the top of the trail, which I judged to be five- to six-hundred meters high. We passed some men carrying bundles of firewood down the hill that we had just climbed. A light rain began which reminded me of the fact that in the last two days we had had almost completely rain-free days of trekking, something that was rare in an area designated the wettest region of the island.

The trail down the other side was slightly worn and etched into the edge of the mountain where I could see lava rock exposed. As we were walking down hill we approached two men and one of them stopped to ask me if I was an English speaker. He told me he was from Somalia and that he worked in Madagascar as an English teacher.

'We are walking to Sambava. I teach English classes there.'

On a normal day, I would have been more interested in chatting with him, but my feet were aching, it was raining, and we still had at least another two hours to our destination. Fernand talked with the man for a minute and they exchanged contact information. I heard him mention an idea of bringing his group from Antalaha to Sambava to meet each other.

Towards the bottom of the mountain we came to a sign saying *Entrée Parc Tropical Farankaraina*. The words were printed in green capital letters and the background picture was of a rocky hill next to the ocean.

The forest thinned to our left and we now could hear gentle waves hitting the coast. We exited the mountain forest and rain, and walked the remaining portion of distance along a flat sand trail that ran parallel to the water. At the end of this trail, we would have to take a ferry boat through some reedy water to get to Maroantsetra, but we still had several kilometres to trek before we arrived there. However, the knowledge of nearing our destination revealed just how beat up my feet were. The onset of more pain made me wince a little as I walked, slightly more laboured down the final stretch of trail. We reached the water's edge where I saw two men had brought a small fishing boat up to shore where they were met by their ladies. Motorcycles and scooters were frequent, and each time they roared by we had to stand off the trail in the grass. We passed a cemetery in which I saw large square tombs adorned with crosses.

We were nearing a short bridge at the edge of the town of Andranofosty. I saw three zebu foraging near the bridge on our side, and a young man rode his bicycle in a wobbly reckless manner all over the trail in front of us. As we approached the zebu, Fernand was about to shoo them out of our way, but before he could do this, the wild hollering man had u-turned on his bicycle, threw it to the ground, and walked over to the zebu and began smacking them and yelling at them. Then, with his head titled up and in a mocking rage, he yelled something to nobody in particular. This made Fernand buckle over in laughter as he said something to the man.

'He asked me if it is ok to fuck this zebu. I told him to go ahead.'

We entered town and the bicycle man sped past us again. A moment later, he lost control of his steering causing the front wheel to jack-knife, sending him over the handlebars landing on his shoulder and face. He gasped as though the wind had been knocked out of him and then he curled into the foetal position and moaned in pain. This too caused Fernand to continue howling with laughter, who then shouted 'Hooa, nice job man.'

No one felt sorry for this ridiculous and aggressive drunk. He seemed determined to hurt someone, and the indifference of everyone who saw this accident suggested they all agreed, that it was just deserts that he ended up hurting himself. We walked through town, turning left once and went for the water's edge where a long transport boat was full of passengers and readying to depart. We did not have to wait for more than five minutes.

The final hour was spent on this water taxi, which coasted through a marshy waterway bound for the city of Maroantsetra. Fernand and I were in great spirits, having completed our hike. I felt like treating myself to a nice meal and thought that I will look for the nicest hotel when we arrive to the city. As it happened, a large peachy-orange coloured hotel stood right at the marina where we docked, and it looked like the gates of heaven after the three days of arduous trekking.

After walking nearly one-hundred kilometres over steep rolling mountainous trails, it was a great feeling to be here. I said to Fernand, 'let's go eat the best meal in that hotel's restaurant. My treat.'

'It is still morning. I think I will take the next boat. Maybe I can reach Mahalevona tonight.' And when he said this I felt slightly deflated.

'Can I change my shirt in your room? I don't want them to see me with the same shirt on.'

I did not know what Fernand meant with this request, but I did not press the issue. I paid at the front desk for a couple nights and then we both walked up to the room. I suspected that this was what he wanted to do; he just wanted to see the room.

Fernand changed his shirt, took one last look out from the balcony, and at the soft white luxurious queen-sized bed, then we went back down to the boat. He asked me to take a picture of him in front of the hotel.

I shook his hand, thanked him, and gave him a hug, and then told him that I really appreciated spending the past four days together. As I watched him go back to the boat, a part of me felt lousy. The end point of my trek, which for a moment felt triumphant, was the halfway point for him. As Fernand sailed away, I went into the hotel restaurant and drank a few bottles of beer and ate steak with mashed potatoes. Then I went upstairs and washed my bleeding, blistered, swollen feet in a hot shower, and fell soundly asleep in a large feathery white bed. Meanwhile, Fernand had turned around and did the same walk over again. This long trek through the mountains was, for me, meant to be a struggle to affirm life. For the Malagasy of this region, hiking through these mountains was nothing more than an affirmation that their lives were a struggle.

Chapter Seven
The Train to Tana:
Maroantsetra to Antananarivo

Throughout my time trekking in the mountains, the goal of reaching Maroantsetra remained a fixture in my mind, and that helped keep my feet moving through challenging moments of fatigue or discomfort while on the trail. Overall, I felt happy at having gone this way and having seen such a remote region of the island. I would never look at a container of vanilla ice cream again without thinking of those remote vanilla growers in the north-eastern rainforest mountains of Madagascar. Now with that complete and having had great rest, hearty meals, and enjoyable writing at my desk with a view of Antogil Bay and Mangabe Island, I wanted to find a way to leave the city.

Maroantsetra was at the inner-most point of Antogil Bay and had one road going south. I wanted to avoid this route because I had heard that this road was notorious for being one of the worst roads in Madagascar, and that was not an easy distinction to earn. At times during the rainy season it became impassable from flood and washout. Option two—I could take an airplane. A flight left the city once a week but I felt that I had done enough flying already and there was a third option that I preferred to them all—I could go by water.

A ferry service ran from Maroantsetra to Soanierana-Ivongo, a port town with access to Sainte Marie Island. This option was not without its perils. The constant rain and wind from the Indian Ocean had sunk many ferries and boats in the past. But I reasoned the odds of this could be no higher than the odds of an accident on the road. The morning after my second night, I asked at my hotel about buying a ticket and was able to get one there in the lobby. I asked when the ferry will leave and was told 'when the weather is good.'

This could become an issue, I thought. The previous day when I had hobbled to the main street of the city, I went to the bank and found they did not accept my credit card. Not only that, neither did the hotel. I had a MasterCard and this city only had machines that accepted Visa credit cards. So without access to additional cash, I was held up in Maroantsetra for an indeterminate amount of time with a depleting fold of cash in my wallet.

Maroantsetra was notable to the region for its seaport and its role as a transition hub between the capital city and Masoala National Park, but from the two days I had spent there so far, I could see no remarkable features. It had dirt streets and a conglomeration of buildings, the best of which were peeling and decaying. And now that I was stuck here for an unspecified length of time, I began looking at my additional time in the city as an internment. I definitely had to find a new hotel. I was paid up for the last two nights and one more tonight, so I decided that after breakfast, I would go out for a walk and find a cheaper place to stay while I waited for the ferry service to depart.

After breakfast, I met a man and his daughter outside in the parking lot of my hotel. He was tall, wore glasses, and I judged him to be a few years older than me, perhaps in his late thirties. In his hands he held a hard yellow plastic box, which looked like the kind used to protect an electronic device. We greeted each other and he told me his name was John. On the yellow box, I saw the name *Pettersson* and asked him if he was Scandinavian.

'No, we're American, but I'll take it as a compliment. Why did you guess that?'

I told him and then asked him some more questions. John told me he lived in the Masoala National Park with his wife and their two daughters.

'My wife is a scientist in the park and I am an artist. I do watercolour illustrations of wildlife. We've been here for a year.'

He gave me his website address so that I could see his work.

I asked him 'is it difficult to live with your family out there in the forest?'

'It's no more difficult than living in American right now with the economy. Both my wife and I have good work here, so for now, it's a good fit.'

John told me that his wife was a researcher in conservation biology and human ecology.

'She studies the effect of people on the forest and the forest on the people.'

We chatted about the American presidential race, religion, and conservation work in Madagascar which prompted John to say.

'The people here need some nationalist cause to rally behind. There is not enough collective focus. They had it when the French were here.' I told Joel that

I thought a lack of economic opportunity was the biggest concern here, and then I mentioned what I had learned in Ambanja, about how the government sold lucrative land to the Chinese government and the effect was a net benefit to the Chinese people and the Malagasy governors who brokered the deals. The regular Malagasy people get bilked because the land gets used, politicians get paid, but the economy does not grow nor do the local people have access to jobs. As for the mention of the French, I said.

'The French were interested in implementing French rule, rather than a rule of law. They had three-quarters of a century to implement modern political institutions in Madagascar and failed to instantiate a capable state, a rule of law, nor any shred of accountability.'

'It's nice to talk about these things with someone,' John said. 'I haven't had a conversation with anyone other than my family for months. We come here for supplies every so often and then return to the park. How long are you here for?'

I told him that I had a ticket to leave on the ferry but was not sure if it would leave tomorrow or next week. The mention of the ferry had him bent over in sarcastic laughter.

'That thing has sunk like two times in the past year,' he said still clucking in laughter. 'Make sure you wear a lifejacket.'

John finished his laugh over this and then called to his daughter, who had patiently gone over to a bench where she had been sitting with an iPad tablet.

'We have to go meet mommy; get ready to go.'

He looked back at me.

'I'm supposed to meet my wife. Nice talking to you.'

The marina front in Maroantsetra was part of an estuary for the Antainambalana River that formed half a rectangle surrounding the city, and also had a series of smaller streams that ran through the city. Mirroring the river, the RN5 went through the city in a rectangular shape before following the coastline all the way down to Tamatave. The main activity of the city operated around this river and marina. I crossed a bridge over one section of the river and while crossing, I could see a lone man in a thin small motorised watercraft, and some red-roofed buildings among some palm trees across on the other side. I went across the river and turned right and found a series of bungalow rooms called the Coco Hotel on the south side of town. I took up residence there the next day and waited.

The first two mornings at the new hotel, after breakfast I walked back across the river and down the main market street to go and check if the ferry planned to leave. Both mornings I was told no, then I returned back to my hotel. I tried not to let the situation frustrate me.

One day while sitting on my terrace writing notes, a middle-aged woman from the adjacent room approached me.

'Excuse me. When do you plan to leave the city?'

Her voice was kind and she approached with the intention to discuss the ferry delay. I had heard her and her husband speaking earlier that day. At first, I took them to be Russian, but after hearing them speak some more, I changed my guess to Slavic Eastern European, which turned out to be correct. She told me her name was Jana and her husband's name was Lukas. The door to their bungalow was open and I could hear her husband fumbling with something in their room.

'We don't know if we leave tomorrow or next day?' she said this with her arms and shoulders raised. Her English was decent, but perhaps under-practiced, causing her to pause during sentences to find the right word. Lukas said something from inside the room and Jana leaned her head in the direction of the door and said, 'Nie, Kanadsky.'

She looked back at me and said, 'He is Spanish and I am English.'

'Where are you two from?' I asked.

When she said they were from Slovakia, I tried to chat to her about her homeland. I told her about the time I went to the Tatra Mountains and my beautiful train ride from Kosice to Bratislava. I said I was really impressed with how green and scenic the Slovakian countryside was when I was there. But she did not want to participate in this conversation because the current predicament was more pressing.

'We have to leave the country in five days. I wanted to see the whales at Sainte Marie but now we can't. It is a big regret. We can't see them now. I think we will fly to Tananarive on Tuesday to get our flight. We can't wait here longer.'

I could relate somewhat to how she felt. It was not exactly the easiest place to visit, and traveling in Madagascar, one was not filled with a sense that—*I'll just see it the next time I come here.* These delays were frustrating but I said to her that they were a normal part of travel on the island of *Mora Mora*. Floris's lesson for me about the 'slowly slowly' philosophy came in handy several times throughout my time in Madagascar, but nobody found it amusing or useful as I did.

As it happened, this delay also altered my plans. I had planned to visit the islands in search of pirate history, but I decided to cancel this and go straight to Tamatave. Two more days passed with much the same routine; got up, went to check at the ferry office, walked a little around town, and returned to my hotel room. On one morning, I awoke before dawn and the electricity was not working. I went to the sink to brush my teeth. I had my toothbrush in a plastic case that had one end open. As I pulled out the toothbrush I also pulled out a large cockroach, and seeing the creature caused me to drop the whole lot into the sink.

After gaining my composure, I trapped the cockroach and threw it outside, and then went back inside to throw the toothbrush in the garbage. Later that day, I remembered Somerset Maugham's short story *A Marriage of Convenience,* in which the narrator stated: 'however placid your temperament, it is difficult not to be startled when you go to the washbasin to wash your hands and a huge cockroach stalks leisurely out.' The grotesque is bearable when you can relate it to a book.

After a week in Maroantsetra, the lady who worked at the ferry office finally had good news for me. I was instructed to return to this office at 11:00pm in the evening. There was a light rain during the day, but to me the wind conditions seemed calm, and I remained optimistic that they would not cancel the departure. At 10:45pm, I left for the office. The bridge and town were dark and visibility was poor. As I walked down the dark street, I had a strong sense of insecurity and vulnerability in this situation. I moved quickly and anxiously towards a dim light and vehicle over one-hundred meters in the distance. I could only make out the shadows of the sides of the street and the occasional outline of buildings. In the immediate darkness, beyond my limited visibility, I heard a roar that made me jump. A large dog charged me and barked in a state of alarm and a show of aggressive dominance. My instinctive reaction to this attack was to throw off my bag and hold it at knee level between me and the dog. The dog however was not interested in taking the matter further; it just wanted to stake its territory and tell me to move along. With my heart now pounding in my chest, I obliged.

I scampered across the remaining distance and then sank down among the dozen people also waiting for the ferry. Even though I now felt more secure, I could still feel my heart thumping in my chest. The distance from the bridge to this spot was perhaps three hundred meters but I felt relieved that I had made it.

I sat there for about twenty minutes, occasionally looking at some of the new arrivals to our group, until a bus came and took us to the port on the east side of the city. There we were left in darkness; the only sound I heard was from the light raindrops hitting my jacket. I could barely see a thing and would have been alarmed in this situation had I not been with about fifty other people. Nobody said anything. We all just stood quietly in the rain for over an hour, before the staff arrived and punched our ticket, and permitted us to board the ferry. I didn't get a good look at the ferry because it was too dark, but it was obvious from its size that it was a passenger boat and not the kind of ferry that carried vehicles. Inside, there were seats in two columns, each having three seats to a row. We all put on an orange life jacket, and then I put my head against the window and fell asleep with the happy thought that I would not be waking up in Maroantsetra.

I awoke with the sun on my face and the taste of salt on my lips. I soon identified that the salt had come from a small mist that was spraying through the edge of the window frame. The view from my window was empty miles of beach with palms and green bushes growing beyond it. Bunches of thick white clouds floated above the horizon, but above us was nothing but blue skies. I rested in a comfortable position with my eyes lazily watching the coastline and did not move until I felt the boat turn and begin idling into the coast.

We were approaching the remote coastal city of Mananara, where small taxi boats awaited us one-hundred meters from the coast. Some of the passengers were awake and others lay in a variety of contorted sleeping positions. A small number of our group disembarked to the taxi boats, which rowed them to shore to the dozen or so onlookers awaiting someone or perhaps just watching for something to do.

It was a brief stop, and then we continued our course south towards Soanierana-Ivongo, at which we docked and disembarked six hours later. From here, onward passengers had the option of catching a ferry across to the island of Saint Marie, or boarding a bus to Tamatave. I waited to do the latter.

I stood and watched some workers transfer the baggage from the boat to a truck, which I learned was going to follow our bus to Tamatave. This was the first time I saw the ferry in daylight, and looking at it just then, I felt glad it had not sunk. It was mostly white, had a blue fin, and letters which said *Melissa Express*. The craft had an aerodynamic design that looked like a missile with a front end like an under-bite.

Two awaiting vehicles were backed in near the dock, and beyond them, I saw a road leading about eighty meters up a hill. I noticed some of the passengers walking up the hill and a moment later a man came to me.

'Please walk up the hill and wait for the bus.'

I did as he instructed and waited with the group and a few locals who looked like they were waiting for a different bus to come along. An older man, not from our group, approached me and said something in Malagasy. A younger man said 'he wants to know if you have medicine?' I did not and said so.

The bus drove down a beautiful road and coastline, where I could see the ocean for much of the day. After several more hours we arrived at the outskirts of Tamatave just as the sun was going down. The parking lot was muddy, noisy, and chaotic, with people waiting for their bags, and taxi and tuk-tuk drivers waiting to get a fare. Drivers harassed me, perhaps because I was the only discernible foreigner among the crowd, and if they had me as a patron they would be able to charge me the foreigner rate.

It had been another long journey that took most of the night, and all the next day, and I was tired and hungry. I hadn't eaten anything all day. In the bus station, I asked a man about a nice hotel in the immediate area and he recommended I go to Hotel Joffre.

'Don't take a rickshaw, take a tuk-tuk,' he warned me. 'At night the security in Tamatave is not good.'

Listening to everything the man said, I hopped into a tuk-tuk and said, 'Hotel Joffre please.'

We embarked down a busy road, but after a few minutes and a couple of turns, we were driving down a dark quiet street. Here the driver began pestering me about how much was I going to pay for this ride. Wise to this, I just said in a calm and polite tone 'Hotel Joffre please.' And this seemed to work. We arrived at the hotel and I paid him what I considered to be triple the standard fee. He came after me and aggressively implored me for more money. He did it with such a convincing demeanour that he made it seem like I was the one cheating him, and for a moment I thought he might follow me right into the hotel.

Up until this point, I had been as polite as I possibly could with this man and even overpaid him for a job well done. Hungry and impatient, I turned around, looked at him with widened and angered eyes, and said, '*STOP IT!*' I stood my ground and stared at him until he turned around and walked back to his tuk-tuk, no doubt cursing me for being a cheap so and so. Over the past several weeks, I had dealt with this situation far better than I did here. I had no issue overpaying because overpaying often meant perhaps a dollar or two. What made me lose my cool was that this man was not friendly, did not smile, was not interested whatsoever in me other than in how much money he may be able to get out of me, and had been pestering me during the ride here because, in my opinion, he would have stopped and refused to go further until I agreed to pay him an extortionate rate.

The Joffre Hotel was an upscale, French-owned hotel that had three stories, and with its white balconies, looked like a square cruise ship. When the lady at the desk saw my dishevelled state, in her French upper-class manners she made sure that I knew the price of the room, just to inquire whether or not I was in the right place. I smiled and said, 'One night please.'

After the best shower I had had in weeks, I went down to the restaurant where I drank beer, ate baked crab crepes, *emince de poulet* with mashed potatoes, and fruit salad for dessert. There were two other couples in the restaurant but I paid little attention to them. I ordered another beer and wrote in my journal for a while.

At the front desk, I asked about the train and was told that it left in the morning at 8am. This unexpected pattern had emerged in my travel across the island. Long, challenging journeys ended with a great meal and a soft bed, followed by another long gruelling jaunt across the island on the other side of the world. I lied in my soft comfortable bed that evening and told myself to enjoy it, because I had no idea where I would sleep the next evening.

Independence Avenue in Tamatave was a wide two-road thoroughfare lined with ten-meter palms running the length of the street. The towering trees had a uniform white substance painted around the base about five feet in height. I did not know what this substance was, but believed it was there to repel insects from wanting to crawl up the trunk.

I took a tuk-tuk to the train station early the next morning to buy a ticket. The Tamatave Station was a large train warehouse built on a huge slab of concrete that stood about four feet high. It was effortless to place my hands on the edge and jump up to the platform and I saw many other people performing this same movement. The train was not there yet but I found around twenty-five people sitting or standing around the platform. I walked to the end where I found a small booth and purchased a ticket.

Brief showers came and went but I remained dry from an overhang on the roof. A steady flow of bicycle rickshaws and tuk-tuk drivers arrived and dropped off more passengers for the train, soon transforming twenty-five people into one-hundred. There were three different mobile vendors carrying large plastic tubs with some kind of bread cake, samosas, and individually wrapped bags of nuts and snacks. The men balanced these tubs on their shoulders, and the woman vendor balanced it on a cushion placed on her hat. As she turned her back to me to serve a customer, I saw that she had a folded umbrella hooked into her shirt collar. I bought some snacks for the ride and two drinks from a gas station across the street.

I had little idea how long the train would take to Moramanga other than what Dr Patel had told me in Sambava: that it was a long journey. It was a well-travelled stretch of land. The journey from Tamatave to Tana was a common journey for visitors in the nineteenth century after ships docked at the Harbour of Tamatave. Ida Pfeiffer arrived at the Harbour of Tamatave in 1857, where she stayed briefly, before traveling inland. She described Tamatave as a large but poor village of 'four to five thousand souls.' Besides a few residences belonging to wealthy people, Pfeiffer described the village as:

'nothing but little huts, some scattered about without order or arrangement, others forming narrow streets. These huts rest on poles from six to ten feet in height, are built of wood or bamboo, thatched with long grass or palm-leaves, and contain a single room, of which the fireplace occupies a large part, so that the family can scarcely find sleeping room.'

The Hotel Joffre was an improvement on Pfeiffer's stay in Tamatave. The city had remained significant to the island's international trade, and one-hundred-and-fifty years later the city had many paved streets, decent buildings, foreign shops, cars, industry, and a quarter of a million people. Despite the changes, there were still useful comparisons to make between her visit and my own.

Pfeiffer's description of the homes showed a continuity between the past and today. The huts that I saw in the countryside did not all resemble each other out of rare chance. There was an informal institutional wisdom handed down over generations that instructed people how to make these dwellings. What Ida Pfeiffer saw in the nineteenth century can still be found in Madagascar today, just not in downtown Tamatave, which was too important a colonial city to remain small and primitive.

Three decades after Pfeiffer, Colonel Francis Cornwallis Maude of the British army spent five years in Madagascar. He made the journey from Tamatave to Antananarivo in 1888, at the age of sixty, but gave few details of the journey other than to say, after completing it, that he 'would welcome the conquest of Madagascar by any country which will provide decent locomotion.' Less than ten years after Maude had these thoughts, the French took control of the island, and in ten years more, they were busy constructing the rail line that I was about to take.

The train arrived at about ten o'clock, and when it did, the warehouse doors slid open and the passengers filed inside to the platform on the other side. The platform was hectic with people hauling their large bags and baskets into the train. I entered a car parallel to a woman entering the adjoining car. She carried two flat bags on her head, had a baby secured to her back with a thick-striped lamba, and held the hand of a second child who hurried along beside her.

The train cars had filled by the time I stepped into the seating area. From what I could see with a cursory glance was that each set of benches facing each other had room for four and already contained six people. Feeling slightly timid and not seeing any possibilities, I just hung around the door and stood. A seated woman in a black shirt signalled to me with her hand to come and sit across from her next to a plump middle-aged woman. As I approached the bench, I saw that the woman in black had been indicating that the two remaining inches of seat across from her was an open spot where I was welcomed to sit. I thanked her in Malagasy, then turned forty-five degrees and placed my tail bone up next to the hip of the plump woman on the seat, pushed with my feet, and tried to rotate my way into the small spot. I wedged myself in as best I could and felt satisfied that should the train suddenly stop, the plump woman beside me was secure in her seat.

My legs were spilled out into the aisle near the seats across from me, where a young woman was busy with different containers, bowls, bottles of water, and in the corner had a basket of baguettes sticking in the air. She was busy scooping cold spaghetti into bowls and putting four to a tray, then stacking a new tray on top. Her co-worker was a young man with a nice smile who chatted like a host with several of the passengers. When the food was ready, he went up and down the wagon aisle serving the baguettes and cold spaghetti to paying customers.

The train shifted into motion and made a light clicking noise as it crawled through the city. I saw a few stacks of shipping containers and also made note of what I thought were unusually narrow railway tracks. Only a few minutes passed before we made our first stop at a different station in Tamatave. I presumed we were picking up more supplies or new passengers, but it turned out to be the hitching of a new engine car to the train. After a while it became apparent we had an issue, because we continued to sit in this spot and no one seemed to know what was happening.

One hour turned to two, then three. A few passengers grew impatient and disembarked, presumably thinking *ahh nuts to this, I'll take the bus.* As I watched them go, I had a strong desire for the train to leave at the moment they were just far enough away where they couldn't get back, but our train had no sense of the ironic. Never mind them, I was pleased because this opened a new spot, which the woman in black gestured that I move to. I gently peeled myself off the cosy plump woman I was attached to, and moved to sit beside a woman in a much more comfortable pair on the seat.

After hours of stillness, my mind began creating small hallucinations where I imagined the train juddered into action. These re-occurring phantom jolts created a flash of relief at what I thought to be movement, but then the realisation of continued stillness compounded the needling ache to be in motion. This was a lesson on maintaining the right state of mind in travel. A wish to be moving when delayed, or a wish to stay put when forced to move on, can detract from the experience of travel. After all, wasn't something happening to me? I was in Madagascar on a train with local people, some of whom were laughing with one another. Nobody bothered me, the sun was shining, and, there was cold spaghetti. I had my notebook in hand, in which I wrote, and I resigned that the delay *was* the experience on the island of mora mora.

Sometime after four hours the whistle blew and we departed. We first passed an industrial factory that looked like a petroleum plant or storage area. We winded this way and that as we left the city, and when we reached the countryside, passing by trees and crossing rivers, I was thrilled to be slowly chugging down the southbound tracks. For the next three hours of remaining daylight, I stared out the window at this landscape. Out the window to my left, in the offing some dark rain clouds had formed over the Indian Ocean, and their colours blurred into each other in a way that obscured the horizon line in a mercury haze. Out the right was a clearer view of marshy rivers, coconut fields, rice fields, fruit trees and the eventual sunset over the Panaglanes Canal.

As we entered the first stop of our journey at the village of Voheza, the trees alongside the tracks were so close that the train brushed against the branches, which ruffled in and out of the windows that were open. Voheza was a small country village among many trees. When the train made its stop, the inhabitants of the village rushed to the wagon cars. The passengers hung their arms and torsos out the windows to buy oranges from some of the women from the village. Activity swarmed around the train for a few brief minutes and then we continued. The interior of the train now smelled of fresh citrus from all of the passengers, including me, who were munching on orange pieces and spitting seeds out the window. We were like Napoleon or General Sherman's army, living off the land as we moved southward, stopping in each village for a short amount of time, buying snacks from locals reaching up to the windows, then continuing again. I bought some spaghetti and a baguette from the gregarious worker. He gave me a warm reaction and said 'tsara be vahaza,' which literally meant 'very good white man,' but I took to mean, *thank you for sharing our food stranger*. The noodles were salty but when combined with the dry crumbly baguette, the two reduced each other into a palatable substance that washed down with sips of water.

As dusk fell and the sun disappeared, the cabin grew dark and the chatter in the wagon quieted. Some passengers lit candle sticks and put them on the window sill giving some spots a warm glow. In some villages we picked up several passengers whose addition made our cabin fuller than what we started the journey with that morning. Every bit of floor space, every inch of seat space, was crammed full. I drifted in and out of sleep, sometimes rousing from the train's movement, and at other times awoke to find many new faces in the train and that other faces had departed. I heard birds rustling in the overhead storage. I smiled at this motley bunch and felt happy to be among what I took to be good people.

The next time I awoke the first indications of dawn were visible. I was glad that our arrival would not be in the middle of the night. Just before five in the morning, we made a stop at the station of Andasibe. I recognised this name but had to think for a moment. It hit me. A few months before coming to Madagascar, I had read David Quanman's brilliant *Song of the Dodo*, a book about island biogeography as evolutionary history, but also its development as an academic discipline. For his research, he visited Andasibe where he saw the indri. On a traveller's whim, I jumped up and grabbed my bag and leaped off the train just before it took off again. I wanted one more crack at hearing the song of the indri.

I met a young local woman named Nirina at the park office. She was short, thin, and had coarse unwashed hair which came down to her shoulder. From Tamatave to here, I had travelled less than two-hundred kilometres but the elevation in that distance rose to over two-thousand feet. The air was cool and the sky was overcast with light rain clouds. Nirina wore a warm jacket and a pair of sneakers.

Andasibe was a small village that lied in a basin of rainforest hills about one-hundred and forty-five kilometres from the capital Tana. Its location and presence of wildlife made it a well-visited spot on the tourist circuit, but at that moment in low season, there was not a soul around. The region had one-hundred-and-sixty square kilometres of protected rainforest called Andasibe-Mantadia National Park, with several conservation efforts in the park to plant native species of trees. Nirina also told me that they recently reintroduced two species of lemur back into the park. The lemurs used to live in this region but they died out back in the 1970s. Nirina was self-taught in the flora and fauna of the region.

'I didn't have a chance to go to college. At high school, my mother was dead, and my father didn't have money for college. I read books about plants and animals, and took a test to become a guide.'

The park office was a couple hundred meters from the train station, along the road that connected the village to the main RN2 highway that ran from Tamatave to Tana. The edge of the forest was behind the office building, so Nirina and I entered the forest trail and began the search for the indri.

The trails were well-trodden and it was easy to walk through their wide transects and over the minor elevation changes in the land. I had had only two or three hours of sleep, but the fresh air and easy trail felt stimulating and kept me energised. The forest canopy was similar to a pine or popular in height, and on the leaf-littered forest floor there were shade-thriving bushy plants. With the forest canopy and the overcast sky, the air in the forest was dull and moist. I saw a small brown tree frog sitting on a pandanus plant leaf. The pandanus had flat narrow sturdy leaves that stemmed from its centre, with tiny sharp thorns along the edges. The leaves fanned out in a palm-like-fashion in low, round volume.

With little effort, we came upon a small family of brown lemurs jumping around branches at about four meters above us. They hopped casually from tree to tree with no concern for their on-lookers. Their size was perhaps only five or six pounds, and other than their long tails, seemed to me to be similar in size to a cat or the crowned lemurs I had seen in the northern part of the island.

A little further along the trail we found a large chameleon clinging to a network of sticks and branches. When I was with Floris at Amber Mountain, I was lucky enough to see the chameleon's masterful ability to camouflage against a tree branch. But today, it was as though this chameleon wanted our attention, because amongst the brown sticks and dark green leaves, this creature was ten inches in length and the brightest colour of orange I had ever seen.

I knelt down close to the animal. Its body was spear-like, with four stick legs designed for the type of small branch to which its tiny mitten-like claws were attached. Its tail was a little longer than its body. Its head had a flat top casque and cone-shaped pinpoint eyes that had a full range of motion. I sat crouched down and marvelled at this creature, appreciating the unusualness of my encounter with it. It kept an eye on me and decided to try and put a little distance between us by moving in peg-legged steps along the tree branch. While I remained still and let the chameleon move away, an eerie siren wailed through the forest canopy. Wide-eyed, I stood. It was the song of the indri.

A high-pitched call resonated throughout the forest. Several indris called in response, their voices filling the forest canopy with orchestral noise. An individual call lasted around three or four seconds. My mind was flooded with comparisons of how to describe this unusual sound. An eerie call; a whale's sonar and wailing siren; even a wheezing pitch of air released from a balloon while the hole is stretched by both thumbs and index fingers pinching and pulling. I had barely slept and perhaps I was hallucinating a *Through the Looking Glass* scenario replete with orange lizards, eerie indris, and next a Bandersnatch perhaps?

Nirina and I followed the direction of the sound and had no trouble finding the family five meters up in the branches of some trees. The small group I had seen in Anjanaharibe-Sud were active and leaped through the tree canopy so quickly that we did not have a hope to keep up to them. This group in Andasibe were lazily sitting around in the trees, perhaps a little slow to get moving on this chilly early morning.

Nirina tried to get the attention of the animals. She placed the palm of her hand to her lips and made a kiss sound, then dropped her hand while making a sound as though she just had a refreshing beverage.

'Kiss haaaa, kiss haaaaa.'

Faeces and urine fell from the tree tops. I sat and watched the indri for several minutes, hoping they might make another call, but they didn't. Nonetheless, I had heard them call and I was now thrilled with my decision to get off the train.

I asked Nirina to show me around the village. We walked back to the train station, across the tracks and up a small path. The main part of the village stood on a flat area a little higher in elevation from the train station. The houses and shops along the cobbled market road were different from the village homes I had seen in the north. Many were two-story wooden buildings with balconies large enough for one person to stand.

One of these buildings was currently under construction. Its walls still had a bunch of exposed timber but enough had been finished to conclude it would look like the other houses in the village. Here was the cradle of a new home, directly opposite it was an older decaying home that had withered from a lack of weather proofing into what was now a grey corpse. Despite lacking any aesthetic beauty, these homes were better than anything I had seen over the past weeks of traveling down the east coast.

Nirina showed me her primary school where I saw an American woman playing a game with several elementary kids. I asked about a high school.

'I had to go to Moramanga for high school.'

'Did you travel there every day?' I asked.

'I lived in a school dormitory and came back to Andasibe on free days.'

We next went to the maternity ward which was a well-constructed concrete building that had plaque- and mercury-coloured walls, small gables and a tin roof. Inside was nearly empty except for a maternity bed. A little farther down the road was a compound for a Catholic Church, Catholic school, and private medical centre. Nirina told me that she was a member of this church and she attended services here. It was built with dark grey stone and it had windows in the shape of obelisks, with blue in the frame and window sills. A Madagascar national flag and Vatican flag flew on two separate poles along the side of the church. For the most part, it was a building that would not have been out of place in a European village.

The pews inside were from rosewood and the wall behind the alter was the same colour of blue that I had seen outside. When the Malagasy used colour, they had great taste in rich powerful hues.

'I'm always first at church,' Nirina said meaning that she sat in the first row. We walked to the front where she sat. I do not remember exactly how our conversation fell to local taboos, but she told me:

'We cannot wash red clothes in the river or it will bring death.'

After thinking a moment, she told me another.

If you eat pig before going to the forest you can get lost, but I like ravitoto with pork,' she said with a sly smile. After a couple more minutes we continued. Our walk through the village arced around north of the train station and ended near the road back to where I had found a hotel earlier that morning. I made plans to meet Nirina again that evening, then went back to the hotel to sleep for the afternoon, eat dinner, and do some writing.

That evening at a street corner, I found Nirina, who was wearing a hood over her head to protect it from the light rain. We both had flashlights turned on because there were no lights anywhere where we planned to walk. Not long after setting out, Nirina found a large chameleon in the trees. When I got close to it and targeted my light on its large body, I could see its skin was shades of brown and grey and it stood motionless, perhaps alarmed by the bright light shining in its eyes.

We walked around for twenty minutes scanning the tree branches. Occasionally our lights illuminated the eyes of a lemur but they were deeper in the trees and difficult to approach. We turned around and retraced our steps to go back, moving a few steps and then pausing and scanning the branches and bushes. I scoured the trees determined to find something but had no luck.

'I found a mouse lemur,' I heard Nirina whisper from five meters away.

The mouse lemur was a nocturnal tree dweller and the world's smallest primate. The creature sat at chest level on a branch angled at twenty degrees. My flashlight reflected two little dots of white light from its dark eyes. It was grey in colour and its body was plump. Its size was a little bigger and longer than an actual mouse. It had big round eyes, tall ears, and a thick tail; features which resembled the paedomorphic bush baby. After a few minutes of being perched still, it reared around and scuttled away with an unannounced quickness. This sighting gave the day a sense of completion. That morning I saw the island's largest primate and that evening I saw its smallest. Nirina and I walked back to the perpendicular intersection at the train station and I thanked her for showing me the lemurs and her village.

In the morning, I returned to the station to wait for a taxi-brousse to take me to Moramanga, where my train journey would have brought me had I stayed on for its full length. But I was delighted with my felicitous leap from the train the previous morning in this very spot where I now stood.

The Andasibe train station was a beautiful pre-war building, but unfortunately its operational use had ceased and was now empty, with broken windows, discarded garbage, condoms, and human shit dumped in its small porticos. On the wall there was a sign advertising an upcoming concert of a woman named Black Nadia. Her portrait was on the poster with two red hearts near her head, and two blue hearts near her waist. I could hear the sound of a small gander of geese hissing and honking. I walked a short distance away from the building towards a series of bungalows not too far away. From this view, I could take in a better profile of the train station.

The building contained two long wings with pitched roofs running east-west, which disappeared into the sides of the tall-gabled centre building aligned north-south. The entire structure was made of orange brick perhaps fired from the local earth. The east wing of the station had square windows at ground level, and small uniform triangle windows jutted out from its shingled roof. At both ends, the word *ANDASIBE* hung on the wall.

At a distance, from where I could not see its dispiriting neglect, the building still looked attractive, and I hoped that one day when I returned here, I might find this building restored and operational. Perhaps I may even be able to use a train schedule and hop on a train passing through and take it the rest of the way to Antananarivo. At this time, I took the bus. Just before I hopped onto the bus, I heard the indri call good morning, and I took it as well-wishes for an onward journey.

Moramanga owed its little prominence to a favourable location between the capital city and the large port city of Tamatave. The train passed through the northern part, but I found most of Moramanga concentrated in the south around the RN2 highway. A steady stream of transport trucks rumbled by on the narrow road, kicking up dust, spewing out exhaust, and sending every rickshaw puller to the side of the road.

The city was remembered in Malagasy history as one of two places where a March, 1947 nationalist uprising led groups with spears to attack the French military base in a move for independence. The French countered in May with reinforced troops from African colonies and violently crushed the uprising.

There is no exact figure on the number who died, but some estimates were around the one-hundred-thousand casualty mark.

I took a room at a hotel right off RN2 and then had lunch at an Indian restaurant. I noticed many Chinese stores varying from common foodstuffs to pawnshops full of merchandise. I browsed through some tall glass cases inside this store and found a blue plastic stencil in the shape of the island of Madagascar and bought it for a few pennies. Along the side of the main road, most of the buildings were two or three stories high, some had handmade signs advertising rooms, restaurants, or other commercial services. There was a network of power lines running in all directions. Though the city centre was bustling, I walked around for a couple hours and found nothing much to do at all.

The following morning, I went back to the taxi-brousse station and bought a ticket to Tana, then waited until we had enough passengers to fill our vehicle. The station was south of the main road in the middle of a market. The large parking lot, made of dirt, had bricks lying around everywhere to aid the many vehicles with traction, which they needed because that morning the ground was sodden.

At this hour, the market was still setting up and school children were off to morning classes. While I waited, I watched the local merchants prepare their booths for the day. The street was busy with people walking to their workplaces, rickshaws hauled workers, schoolkids, and some transported cargo. A large bus drove by and splashed water across the road when its tire sunk into a pothole. The passengers on the bus were all construction workers, destined for a site just down the road, where they were building a series of commercial buildings.

Immediately in front of me, at the edge of the wet, dirty street, I watched a plump woman in her forties prepare a table for the market. She arrived by bicycle rickshaw with two large baskets of oranges. While the driver heaved these to the ground, she sent another to go into the lot behind us, from where he re-emerged carrying a wooden table on his head. I had to move my own head back a few inches to avoid getting smacked with the table as he passed. He placed the table at the side of the street, and to compensate for the uneven ground, used two bricks from the lot to prop up one leg, levelling it with the others. A second rickshaw arrived and delivered a small bag of charcoal to the woman.

Behind the table, directly in front of me, the charcoal man prepared a small round metal stove that resembled a bongo drum. I wondered who these men were helping this woman. One had arrived as her chauffeur and then unloaded her oranges and another fetched her table. The charcoal delivery apparently included the service of starting a fire for the client. Was this woman paying for these services, or was she some kind of matriarch that could command extra services not usually included? When the wood kindling lit the charcoal and slowly heated, the man placed a greasy wok on top and dumped oil in the pan. The woman was picking through her basket of oranges, selecting nice ones, which she set on the table.

Three more passengers had bought a ticket and our drivers decided our bus was full enough to begin the journey. We passed a few villages and I pencilled some into my notebook:

Manjakandriana

Sambaina

Nandihizana

In the Merina villages, and somewhat greenish countryside, I saw two-story high-gabled houses, Eucalyptus trees growing on hills, and at times I saw the now defunct railway tracks that no longer brought the train service all the way to the capital. My reason for riding the bus for the remainder of the journey to Tana.

Chapter Eight
The Land of the Invincible Multitude: Antsirabe, Fianarantsoa and Manakara

There was a time in the past when there was a train from Tamatave to Antananarivo and another from Antananarivo to Antsirabe. The former had its line shortened at Moramanga for reasons I did not discover and the latter train to Antsirabe was out of commission. I went to the southern part of Tana to a muddy chaotic meeting area where taxi-brousses departed for various southern locations.

I found a booth where I could buy a ticket and then took it over to the large van that was departing for Antsirabe, in what turned out to be ninety minutes. There I showed the driver my ticket and then I moved to hand my bag to the roof of the van where another man was securing the passengers' luggage with rope, but before I could get there, the driver stopped me and indicated that I needed to pay him more money. I laughed at him and said 'don't be silly,' and then walked by him as though he had told me a joke. Another man standing witness to all of this roared in laughter, perhaps at my plight as a targeted walking dollar sign or the driver's feeble failure to shake me down for extra money.

As we left the outskirts of Tana for Antsirabe, the city thinned into rice paddy slums. I noted many brick-making sites that had smoke billowing from their kilns and thousands of bricks stacked like shipping containers in a large port. The journey from Tana to Antsirabe was an easy journey of just a few hours, and after arriving, I walked around the streets for about twenty minutes and found an inexpensive tourist hotel. I had nothing planned in this city other than a stop along the way to Betsileo country in the south-east where the only other working train ran between two cities called Fianarantsoa and Manakara.

Antsirabe was on the tourist circuit due to its role as a colonial town, spa waters, and decent climate. It was still in the highlands and part of the central territory of the Imerina. My first thought in the town was that it was a relief I was not in the capital Antananarivo. Some streets lined with colonial buildings had many rickshaw pullers, but on the street where I had found my hotel, things were relaxed. I took an early dinner that evening and was in my room by sundown, reading a book and then falling asleep early.

The following morning after breakfast, I was at a table in the hotel lobby writing some notes when I was asked a question. It was a man who introduced himself as Jan, a German, who looked to be in his early thirties. He asked me if I was busy:

'My wife and I want to see the turning bones festival. That man over there said he can take us,' he said pointing to the connecting passageway between our room and the front desk where I could see the arm and leg of a man standing mostly obscured on the other side. A woman approached us.

'This is my wife Paula,' Jan said, introducing the two of us.

'Nice to meet you,' she said curtly and then spoke in German to Jan.

Jan was tall and had two or three weeks of beard growth added to his thin flaxen complexion. Compared to Jan, Paula was more buxom and very attractive with medium-length golden hair. She seemed vivacious, and at the moment, was focused on what I soon realised was a negotiation with the man in the other room who had stepped off and was no longer visible to me. I also learned the main reason that Jan had targeted me for conversation.

'If we split the cost of the trip, it will be much cheaper,' Jan said to me.

'Are you sure that this turning the bones ritual is actually happening?' I asked.

'That man says he knows a village that will have it today but wants one-hundred-and-fifty Euros for the trip.'

'That's way too much,' I said.

'Yes, we refused this cost.'

I told them that it sounded a bit convenient and that I was reluctant to believe that we would actually see this ritual performed. I had read about this cultural practice before visiting the island and understood that it was an important ritual for the Imerina people, but I wrote it down as something I could do without seeing. It seemed to me the perfect way to spread disease and I had already had one bout with the "Malagasy fever" as the Rev. T.T. Matthews called it in the nineteenth century. However, since the opportunity had implausibly fell into my lap, I told Jan and Paula that I would very much like to join them for the trip.

Jan and Paula told me that they had been traveling in Madagascar for the past two weeks. They had just arrived in Antsirabe from Tulear after spending all night on a bus. It took another hour for Paula and Jan to negotiate the price of one-hundred-and-twenty Euros, which must have been the right price because everyone involved felt ripped-off by this amount. I pitched in my equivalent of forty Euros and then we waited for our transportation to arrive.

Jan and Paula had been travelling in Mozambique for a couple weeks before coming to Madagascar.

'There are rebels in Mozambique in the centre of the country. They shoot at the buses passing from south to north. It is not a nice place. It is corrupt.'

The man who had agreed to show us the village was short and had sore-looking red eyes. I was certain that he was full of it when he said 'only I can show you,' but I was open to see where this adventure was headed. Instead of going to the bus station that morning, I spontaneously agreed to go with these two who seemed agreeable enough travellers.

Jan and Paula protested the minute an old clunking van arrived.

'What? This is not a private car?' they both were saying in demand of an explanation. It was a taxi-brousse that was falling apart and had five other men in it.

The man who had made the deal with us pointed at two men who got out of the van and said 'these two men will be your interpreters and these two need a ride.'

I suggested to Jan and Paula that we make the best of this and that we get in the vehicle, but they wanted to moan and grumble a little more. I was busy trying to write all of this in my notebook.

'What do you write down?' Jan asked me.

'I like to write down what happens when I travel so that I can remember the details in the future,' I told him.

'Are you writing something? If you are writing a book please use my name, put me in your book, I would love that,' Jan said with a large smile on his face.

'Come on, let's go,' I said. With Jan snooping around my notebook, I decided to put it away and piece things together later.

Jan and Paula acquiesced enough to get into the crumby old van and once we were on our way they settled and we were able to have a nice conversation about travel for a while. If they were not complaining, Jan and Paula were nice to chat with, and for some of the time on this trip we managed a nice conversation.

We were driven about twenty-five kilometres into the countryside where we stopped in a small village to eat lunch. The guide took us to a dark and aged wooden building that had two rooms. There were only a few other dilapidated buildings in the surrounding area. The structure we entered was makeshift; tall distorted wooden posts that were perhaps three inches in diameter supported variable planks of wood that reached down to the loose dirt in some spots, and in other spots left large gaping holes. There were stacks of grey bricks and stacks of wooden baskets in a small shed next to the room we entered. The whole scene was void of colour except for a rooster, who had a thick orange neck thrusted upright in the air atop tiger-patterned breasts and legs.

Jan and I had to lower our heads to clear the ceiling until we sat down at the table. The meal, the room, and the toilet afterwards were all filthy but none of this seemed to bother my husband and wife companions who were prone to griping. I too did not mind because nothing about this experience thus far was any different than what I had experienced in every other location I had visited in Madagascar. I had had this chicken and rice amongst a swarm of flies in Ambanja, in the middle of the night on the way to Mahajanga, at Camp Indri at Anjanaharibe-Sud, in mountain villages near Maroantsetra and in a small Merina village north of Tana. At this point it was familiar. After lunch the driver and two guides took us to sample some locally-made rum which we each tried in a small capful. It burned my throat, and even in its small quantity my stomach did not welcome it. Like Jan and Paula, I declined a second taste.

Unbeknownst to us until that moment, this small village was where we began walking along a trodden trail into the hilly surrounding country. From atop the first ascent I could see that the hilly landscape looked barren and eroded in every direction. Scarce trees offered some green to the eye in the immediate area, but when I took in the landscape in its full panorama, the trees only highlighted the desolate hills in a manner I lamented. But perhaps this was a fitting scene for the morbid intentions we had of intruding on the Malagasy tribal custom of interacting with the dead.

The climbs up and down the hills were steep but did not compare to the difficulty I experienced between Antalaha and Maroantsetra. Jan and Paula began grumbling about the climb.

'They didn't tell us we would have to do this hiking,' Jan said and Paula exhaled with frustration in response.

I decided to tell them a little about my trip hiking through the mountains. I mentioned the adorable little girl who said 'Bonjour Vahaza' but this seemed to be something Jan had heard before.

'I usually respond to them *bonjour niggerkind*,' Jan said with a poor attempt at humour.

I was about to respond to this comment with disapproval, when I remembered what Jan had said to me earlier.

Are you writing something? If you are writing a book please use my name, put me in your book, I would love that.

As I thought this over in my head it made me smile and Jan, seeing this, understood that he had hit the mark with his joke.

Down the other side of the hill were a few square two-story houses that looked like rectangles stood vertically. Each had a small window in the gable and the steeply pitched roofs looked to be constructed with some kind of thatch. The land was highly contoured at the bottom of the hill just before the area where these homes stood, and beyond them were quilted plots of land worn from seasons of agricultural use.

The whole scene of dull greens and tawny, ochre, and russet browns gave the houses a sense of belonging to the land at least in terms of colour. As we walked by them, it seemed to me that the second story could only be reached by the external ladders leaning against the houses. If that was not the case, then I had no explanation for the ladders positioned as they were. Some of the homes had windows with exterior wooden shutters, none had glass panes, and other houses lacked windows altogether.

We trekked for an hour through the hills and crossed a bridge that looked ready to collapse at any moment. We followed a trail through a valley whereupon we met a local woman. The main guide talked with this woman for a moment and then she continued on her way. The guide did not continue and he said something in Malagasy. The other guide said 'that woman told him there is no festival today.'

'Do you smoke?' Jan asked me. 'No? Well now's a good time to start.'

Paula began saying in the direction of Jan and me, but in actuality it was for the guides and host: 'this man brought us out here. We paid him a lot of money because he said he is the only one who knows where the ceremony is. He doesn't know anything!'

'He didn't plan this,' Jan said now building on the anger of his wife.

This went on a little longer before I quietly suggested to Jan and Paula that we still needed a ride back to Antsirabe. We were an hour's hike from the vehicle and perhaps thirty kilometres away from the city. So we turned around and went back the way we had come, and the hike was enough to postpone the ire of my two companions for a time.

One of the guides apologised for the problem and seemed to have been hired as an English speaker but had no involvement in the actual planning of the excursion. To take our mind off the current frustrations, Jan and I fell to chatting about the war in Afghanistan and the Second World War. I told him a story that I had read in a book called *The Red Circle* written by the Navy SEAL sniper Brandon Webb. According to Webb, the German soldiers who served alongside him in Afghanistan sung old World War Two era songs, which they explained as honouring the brave sacrifice of people such as their grandfathers and great-grandfathers who were just common folk who stepped up to serve their country. Even though the cause was not just, their bravery was admirable, according to the soldiers. Jan asked me if I had read any novels by Ken Follet to which I replied that I hadn't.

'I like the novel *Storm Island*,' he told me and then explained its plot about a German spy trying to collect intelligence about the movements of British troops. He chatted a little more about this and another novel, which was perhaps *Fatherland* by Robert Harris. It was a novel that presented the counterfactual story that Nazi Germany had won the Second World War.

'Don't misunderstand me,' he then added. 'I am glad that the Nazis did not win.'

I told him the books sounded interesting and that I would look them up to read.

I was later surprised to learn that one of the early Nazi "solutions" to the "Jewish Problem" was to ship the Jewish people of Central Europe to the island of Madagascar. According to the foremost historian of the Third Reich, Michael Burleigh, the plan was set to go ahead as long as the Germans were able to defeat the British. What happened instead was that the British fought for and took control of Madagascar. Furthermore, when the Germans opened up the Eastern front against the Soviet Union, the expansion into new territory unfortunately led to new ideas for how to solve the "Jewish Problem." Interestingly, in the theme of Jan's fictional reading interests, Guy Saville has imagined a counterfactual scenario where a victorious Nazi Germany did exile five million Jews to live in ghettos in Madagascar. Saville's book *The Madagaskar Plan* was an enjoyable addition to my reading on all of these interconnected historical topics.

We made it to a spot near a road where we were told to stop and wait. Soon the battered van appeared. Before we got in the van, Jan and Paula resumed their yelling at the others.

'Do you have our money?' Jan said. The look on his face had hardly transformed from five minutes previously when talking about a novel he liked. He flashed his teeth and his eyebrows crinkled but instead of light chuckles he was indignant.

'We came all the way from Isalo to see this festival and tomorrow we have to leave,' Paula said. 'I want my money back.'

'Money,' she repeated, looking at them with obstinate emphasis.

I too was not pleased that this man contrived this whole excursion for quite a lot of money, assuring us that only he knew where the ceremony would take place, and did all of this knowing that it was going to end with the discovery of his duplicity. Either I was entirely passive or well-used to this behaviour because I was not shocked to learn he was trying to cheat us out of money. Nonetheless, I felt a pang of shame and embarrassment at the level of anger that my companions where spewing towards the others in our party. I thought—when it was revealed that there would be no ceremony, was it really such a surprise? I felt that everyone was behaving poorly and I could think of no way to include myself.

'Money,' Jan said echoing his wife.

The man who arranged our trip reached into his pocket and revealed about thirty dollars' worth of Madagascar Ariary and handed it to Paula.

Our ride back to Antsirabe was quiet and tense. As we entered the city Paula repeated several of the things I had heard her say earlier and then added 'if you don't give us back our money we will go to the police.' And to Paula's credit, she remained true to her word. When the van stopped, she spotted a foot patrol on the sidewalk across the street and went straight over to him. I could see some chatting and pointing and the police officer approached the van.

'He said we must all go to the station,' Paula said translating the French for Jan and me. What further surprised me was the men all willingly complied and began marching to the police station.

'Walk at the back,' Jan said to me, indicating that we should be the last in the train walking to the station.

'They may try to run away.'

But they didn't.

We walked to a large building, through a compound and up some stairs to the second floor. Paula went into a room with another officer and gave him a statement. Jan and I, with the two guides, sat in the next room from where we could hear the muffled conversation between Paula and the officer.

'Where is the other man?' I asked the guide.

'He is down stairs in jail,' the guide explained.

After about fifteen minutes of waiting, mostly in silence, the rest of us were invited into the room where a large desk took perhaps one-quarter of the otherwise empty space. As much as I did not like losing the forty Euros to this scamming man, I was hesitant to be at the police station where we could just as easily wind up behind bars if the officers felt capricious and in need of a sizable bribe. This turned out to be a mistaken anxiety, because the police officer in charge handled the situation with poise and as well as anyone could have hoped for.

'Where is the rest of our money?' Jan asked the guides. 'Do you have it?' He looked at both of them not just with anger, but also with aggression. The police officer asked the guides to explain what happened and they began doing so until Paula interrupted.

'Speak in French or English so we can understand what you're saying.'

They continued in Malagasy and then we were asked to wait for a time while presumably the officer made some deliberations. We waited in the corridor—the European couple stewed and fumed and the two guides looked apologetic, bothered, and annoyed. We waited out there for about thirty minutes with little happening and little being said. I could see from the entrance to the hallway twenty meters away that the sun had gone down.

We returned back into the room. Pointing, anger, aggression, questions, money, money, money, this went around in circles for a few more minutes until another officer escorted the man from downstairs into the room with us.

This is who the couple wanted. Jan and Paula went after him with bellicose accusations asking him where the rest of our money was. This behaviour was so strong that I could hardly bare to watch it. But then, as if to exceed my timid expectations, Jan grabbed the backpack right off this man and started digging through it. I had to avert my gaze as though he had started flaying him alive. I walked out of the room back into the corridor for a minute, but returned when I had heard Jan's expression change.

I re-entered the room and saw Jan holding a whole stack of clean Madagascar money notes. I recognised them because they were the notes that I had withdrawn from the ATM earlier that morning. My mouth fell open at the audacity of Jan's actions but also that he actually found most of the cash in the man's pack. This made the man furious and he started to protest in a threatening enough manner that the officer seated at the desk bellowed and the other officer grabbed him and was ready to throw him out of the room.

What I hadn't paid much attention to earlier I now noticed in full scope. Earlier today when we had sampled the village rum, this man had bought a small bottle of it and had been sipping rum for the past four hours. When he spoke in English, his words were slurred. He said to Jan:

'Do you believe in god? I believe in god. What do you call god?'

But this talk was not meant for Jan to reply because he continued.

'That money is for my children. My wife gave me that money. Now I have to call her and tell her to bring me dinner in jail.'

This was a skilled attempt at manipulation because if it was true, it made us seem like horrible people for stealing a week's salary from him and his family. If he was lying, which was the highest probability, then he was indeed demonstrating himself to be a first-rate scumbag. This confirmation then came with a more ominous comment.

'But you know, something might happen outside.'

This was an unambiguous threat that we would not be safe if we chose to keep this money and not return it to him. Eventually, because he was obnoxious and drunk, he was returned to the prison cell down below where the officer explained to Paula he was going to spend the evening.

In the end, it took about two hours and the whole process was emotionally draining. But, about eighty percent of my money was returned to me, something I had never expected to happen. I left the police station that evening wondering if all of this trouble was worth the return of a few Euros. The man who had arranged our trip gambled that it would not be worth it, and if it had been just me, he probably would have been correct. What he had not counted on was the fact that Jan and Paula were the kind of travellers who would negotiate for hours to receive what they deemed to be a fair price. In this respect I was not like them. What was depressing about the whole experience was the feeling as though everyone involved behaved indecently.

The next morning, I changed to a new hotel and spent the day in a dark room and a dark mood. The yelling, fighting, and levels of deception from the previous day, added to the amount of shady dealings I had had until that point and left me in need of a day to recharge mentally. And so I did.

For my southern departure, there was no station in Antsirabe, just a taxi-brousse parked on the side of the road. I threw my pack to a man on top of the vehicle, paid another man my fare plus extortion, then took a seat in the front of the vehicle. It took about ninety minutes or so for the vehicle to fill with passengers and then we left for the city of Fianarantsoa. Fianarantsoa was the capital and main city of the Betsileo region, and lied two-hundred-and-forty kilometres southeast of Antsirabe. The day was a typical long day of travel on the island of mora mora.

Throughout the journey, the countryside was mainly treeless highlands, where the one remarkable feature I noticed was the prevalence of potato farmers in the region. At several points again, I saw earthen brickworks operations with crude kilns and hundreds of bricks stacked on the ground in large steaming piles. The exposed ground surrounding it was russet in colour which seemed much duller than the various orange and red soils I had seen elsewhere. At times along the winding road, the landscape appeared to me that we were driving to a lower elevation.

While taking one of the ubiquitous sharp curves, our van surprised a dog who was trotting along the side of the road. In a casual and careless manner, it seemed the dog wanted to cross the road and in doing so, stepped onto the road directly in front of the vehicle.

The vehicle did not collide with the dog so much as we ran it over. There was a plastic heavy thud at initial impact with a brief tumbling and scraping under the vehicle as the dog emitted its final breaths in a high-pitched wail. This noise caused me to wince and feel an acute stab of guilt and sorrow for the poor creature who we left fatally mangled behind us on the road. That feeling of guilt and sorrow compounded into loneliness when I next discovered that not another of the twenty souls in the vehicle even blinked their eyes in concern over what had just occurred.

Why was my reaction one of concern and pity when everyone else in the van seemed indifferent? Was that stinging feeling of concern an imagined ordeal that I made too much of, or should the rest of these people have their moral compasses checked for deficiency? But just then, the driver stopped. I exhaled in relief that he was shook by what had happened. After all, he saw the dog and didn't slow down or swerve the vehicle. He got out of the vehicle with a heavy look of concern, but this look was alleviated when he examined the front of his van and saw that there was no damage. His features softened with relief, and my loneliness returned and accompanied me for the remainder of the nine-hour drive.

So often experienced in travel in Madagascar, the afternoon hours dwindled, and I began wondering whether we may reach our destination before sundown. These thoughts always began optimistic, that we may just get there in time, but the result was always an arrival in a dark strange city alone and without a plan. I arrived in Fianarantsoa after sundown and had to fend for myself among the swarming drivers who had been waiting for our arrival at the bus stop. As we had been driving through the city streets, I spotted a decent looking hotel which turned out to be not far from the bus stop where we made our final stop.

I stepped out of the vehicle and had to wait for my bag to be tossed down from the roof. The other passengers and I stood near the van with our backs to the mob of taxi and rickshaw drivers. The driver of our vehicle was atop the van with another man, untying ropes and loosening bags to throw down. In an instant, however, the driver stopped what he was doing, looked down at one of the taxi drivers and yelled something at him. A moment later he was on the ground and these two men were pushing and swinging and wrestling in the parking lot. This drew the crowd around the two combatants. Nobody dreamed of separating the two; the violence was entertainment to the mob who maintained the exact same pitch and volume of chattering as had before been directed at the passengers of the vehicle.

I received my bag and a smart young man, who was smiling at me because he knew the rest lost their chance at my fare by chasing the cheap entertainment, said something to me and directed me to his tuk-tuk. I made it to the hotel just in time to eat a great meal of French cuisine before the kitchen closed for the evening. The good news about my location was that it was just a few minutes' walk to the train station, and the next morning the train was planning to leave. So the next morning I had some breakfast and went there.

The train station in Fianarantsoa was a high-pitched building with two stories and a clock above the entrance. I bought a ticket in a busy waiting room full of people whom I presumed to be taking the train as well. The Fianarantsoa East-Coast Railroad ran one-hundred-and-sixty kilometres southeast to the coastal city of Manakara. The French colonials built the FEC railroad between 1926 and 1936 to speed up the export of coffee and other cash crops to the east coast. The French brought the tracks from the Alsace region after it was re-acquired from Germany following the First World War.

The train had green wagons for passengers, several black cars for cargo, and a red engine car at the front. Unlike the train I took from Tamatave to Andasibe, the FEC passenger cars had small stepped-platforms at the ends of each wagon rather than entrances on their sides like the majority of modern trains. I found a spot in the storage rack to put my bag, then returned to the platform outside at the end of the car where I hung on to the balustrade and waited for departure. I could smell freshly butchered meat in the black cargo car connected to the passenger car.

The train jolted into animation and slowly crept through the city and into the countryside. There was a raw sense of freedom that accompanied the fresh breeze and the small risk of standing out on this observation platform with its open sides. A man exited the train car and joined me in the open air. He was a Malagasy man who wore a dark blue hooded sweater with a black baseball cap. He put his hand up to the beak of the cap and shielded the breeze long enough to light a cigarette. When he inquired in French where I came from, he switched and spoke in English.

'The bus is faster, but I like to take the train.'

He introduced himself as Faniry and that he came from a southern city called Ambalavao.

'I do construction; anything in construction. Build houses, bungalows, shops. You are going to Manakara? Yes, me too. I am going to see my friend. I left my family in Ambalavao.'

Faniry spoke in a soft gentle voice that made him seem more white collar rather than a cigarette smoking construction worker. He returned back in the carriage when he finished his cigarette.

The initial countryside outside Fianarantsoa was mostly low hills where the locals had planted every usable acre with rice or vegetables. In a treeless landscape under a grey-clouded sky, I could see a small village on a hill. The square houses were two stories giving them a rectangular appearance. They looked like the houses I had seen in the countryside outside of Antsirabe just a couple days previously when I was with German Jan and Spanish Paula. Each house here had the same charcoal coloured roof and one window at the gable. These were the homes of the Betsileo people, a name that meant the *Invincible Multitude*.

The Betsileo had a reputation for their terraced rice farming skills, and in spots they had rendered the landscape in much the same way the Chinese or Vietnamese tiered their rice fields from the side of a mountain down into the valley. In some flatland fields I saw families standing shin-deep in the mud and water, harvesting yellow stalks. Some fields were finished and all that remained was yellow stubble. In other fields, I saw men cutting and women thrashing the rice stalks on a mat. The word 'paddy,' meaning rice plant, originated from the Malay family of languages. The travellers who had brought their knowledge of rice planting to Madagascar a long time ago, left generations of descendants who enjoyed the staple crop. I was later to learn, after making these first impressions, that in addition to rice, the Betsileo region was also notable for its tea and wine production.

Though at the moment, we were still traveling along the outer edge of the central highlands, soon we would reach the mountainous spine of rainforests that ran north to south along the east coast of Madagascar. All that remained of the rainforest here was a strip twenty-five kilometres in width, and interestingly enough, the train played an important role in conserving the remaining forest.

The train served around one-hundred-thousand rural inhabitants who had little other means of connection to the outside world. For many of the villages, there were no roads that served their communities. The train allowed for the shipment of rice and other goods to these villages, which played an important role in conservation. Because the train gave the villagers a means for shipping cash crops to the markets of Fianarantsoa and Manakara, they chose to grow coffee, oranges, bananas, litchis, and avocadoes. Whereas rice cleared away the land and depleted the soil in a few years, causing the farmer to prepare new land, fruit trees could annually produce for around fifty years making them far more conducive to conserving the forests. For many of the villages in this region, the continuation of producing cash crops rather than rice fields relied completely on the existence of the train. A persuasive argument followed that if these farmers lost the commercial transport for their cash crops, they would give up the enterprise and clear trees to grow rice.

It was for these reasons that every stop we made in a village took between thirty minutes and an hour for supplies to be loaded and unloaded. Our progress towards the coast was glacial. We would make a stop in a village for an hour, then chug along the tracks for ten or fifteen minutes before making our next stop. An hour in Andrambovato, then back to the picturesque cloudy mountainous rainforest on our antique train, then an hour in Madiorano, and on it repeated. As passengers, we were on this train to be whisked through the rainforest to the coast, but it was more accurate to view the train as a commercial part of the economy. However, having passengers on the train gave villagers other means to earn some money.

While young men were put to work carrying goods off the train, others had tables with food to sell to the passengers, who walked around on the platform during the stops. Most of these villages looked like the inhabitants lived an austere life, just as the country inhabitants that I had visited in the north east certainly did. Each village had a decaying French-built train station that no longer served any purpose, or if it did, it was not obvious to me.

The women were attired in traditional lambas, while the men and children all wore dirty clothes that had probably began as cotton in the United States, then shipped to China and assembled in a clothing factory, then shipped back to the United States where it was purchased and worn for several years, and then when its owner no longer wanted it, it was donated to a company that shipped it to Madagascar, where now these young men and children wore them. The travels of a cheaply-made t-shirt were extensive; and for some of them, this train was their final journey in the world.

The mood in each village was in high spirits, as though the stopping of the train was an important event that gave everyone something to do. It was a weekly event that broke up the regular and uneventful country routine. In one village I watched the locals unload their cargo of soda, the hind-quarter of a zebu, and other small market goods. I bought some fruit and fried bread and ate it while nosing around a little.

In many of the villages, children pestered me to give them something. None of them looked wanting for anything, so it gave me a negative impression that they viewed a foreigner as someone from whom they could ask for something. They crowded around the foreigners repeating the word 'vahaza.' I found these children annoying because they were not homeless or hungry, but used to passengers on the train giving them things.

At another stop I heard children screaming. I looked to see a European couple blowing up balloons and spiking them in the air for the children. When the novelty of this passed, the children were relentless in their harassment of the two European balloon blowers. I stood safely up on the observation platform, shelling and munching on peanuts, all the while feeling that the European couple were getting what they deserved. I spent about six hours riding the train on this platform like a hobo, hopping on and off the observation platform in each new village and watching the locals unload sacs and crates of goods, then returning to my post as we moved through the forest to our next stop.

At times there were actual vagrants who jumped onto the platform and hitched a ride from one village to the next. A ticket man who doubled as security popped his head through the door on one occasion and scolded the stowaway, but this young man just ignored him, and there was nothing more that could be done about it on a moving train.

Our train passed through several tunnels which blackened the cabin for about thirty seconds at a time. I grew tired of standing on the platform by the sixth village and went in to take a seat. My carriage was not full and several of the passengers were foreigners. I could overhear an American couple opposite me.

'We should have brought a joint for this.'

'There is a police man right there.'

'Ya, but that would have been good.'

By the eighth stop we had been on the train for close to ten hours and most of the passengers were losing their spirit. What had been novel was now becoming mundane and feeling more like delay.

One man sat scrunched up in the corner of his seat and seemed to be growing impatient with the length of the journey. His Korean girlfriend didn't share his demeanour. She was friendly, moved about the car and chatted with other passengers, and snapped pictures of every detail that caught her interest. The man sat in his seat the whole time and did not speak. A little later in the journey I saw the Korean girl move to the seat behind me, where she now sat with Faniry.

As for me, I sat with French Christophe and German Tomas. Christophe was a muscular, bald, freelance journalist who spent much of his time in Western

Africa. He had a soft voice and manicured appearance that seemed homosexual to me, but I never confirmed this because he rarely spoke. German Tomas was abrupt, opinionated, and self-righteous. I liked hearing his opinions for their sanctimony and at times I encouraged him, but over the course of the journey, our conversations were brief and interspersed.

He was slightly cryptic about what he did for a living. He told me he was an economist of some kind, but it seemed he just spent his time travelling the world. We had both lived and worked as teachers in Japan so he asked me questions about what it was like now. I told him how a teacher typically finds employment in Japan.

'I just went there in the 1990s and was able to find a job while I was there,' he said in contrast to what I had told him.

He told me, 'I have been to America one time. New York, Philadelphia, and Washington D.C.'

'What did you think?' I asked him.

'The biggest problem with the United States is there is no culture,' he said.

In my travels, I had heard people make stupid comments like this on more than one occasion. I suggested to him that the differences in history do not mean the U.S. is absent culture.

'No, there is no culture in the United States.'

I thought to myself, the United States created and refined the modern political institutions that were now slowly lifting the entire world out of poverty. Their traditions of business, industry, innovation, cuisine, cars, cowboys, and music have been the most successful cultural exports in the history of humanity. Not only that, but they have had democracy and free speech for longer than Germany has even been a centralised state and they were kind enough to leave both there in the forties.

I said to Tomas 'I have heard people say that before, but I think it is a comment that comes from jealousy of their success as a powerful and rich country. You do not need a deep history to have an interesting or robust culture. Furthermore, just like the rest of Europe, the United States has a right to claim the three-thousand years of Western history as their own.'

Tomas, a sober man, to his credit did not mind my riposte to his comment, but he chewed on it for a while. Christophe remained laconic and uttered something softly in French once in a while.

Each time we stopped at a village, Tomas seemed in near disbelief at the train schedule and there was a hint of disgust in his voice. 'Uggh, how long will we stop this time?'

I wondered how a man who was so well-travelled was not used to inefficiency or delay?

'These people have nothing. They have nothing,' he'd say. 'What a life.'

This phrase was used to explain everything that we saw.

Sometime after sundown, our train was stopped at a village. After a few moments, a pig began squealing in distress and this attracted some to the opposite window. The squeal had roused a dozing Tomas, who groaned.

Three men outside were laughing as they tried to lift a struggling sow into the cargo wagon. This was repeated with three more pigs, one of which, kicked free from the men's grasp and fell to the ground wailing and squealing. This caused the men to laugh so hard they could barely complete their task, but eventually they calmed themselves long enough to get the noisy struggling beast into the car with the rest of them.

'What a life,' uttered Tomas as he tucked his chin to his breast and closed his eyes again.

At the next stop, I could see no station or village, but two passengers jumped off and disappeared into the forest.

'What a waste of a day,' I heard one passenger moan.

Later, I heard another man utter 'How much longer, it's been fourteen hours.'

Indeed, it had, and the answer to his question was only two more hours. Our journey on the train took sixteen hours in total, and though long, I enjoyed the journey, and it completed my desire to ride all the trains in Madagascar. I had made use of most forms of travel: I had two domestic flights, two trains, a ferry, a motorcycle, over one-hundred kilometres of trekking, and many unforgettable taxi-brousses.

The city of Manakara was pitch black, quiet, and felt abandoned. Had there not been a couple rickshaw bicycle drivers hanging around the station for a fare, I don't know what I would have done. Luckily, having learned from my many night-time arrivals, I prepared in advance the name of a hotel I wished to go to, so I knew what to say to the driver.

The only sound in the city were the squeaks and rattles of the rickshaw as my driver peddled through the empty streets. The darkness was unnerving and it heightened my sense of vulnerability. This reached a peak when I understood that he was peddling into a shipyard. It looked to me like a good spot to be ambushed, robbed, or killed if an attacker was so inclined. I asked the driver about the hotel.

He pointed and said 'it's after bridge.'

As this bridge came into view an instant later, I calmed slightly, and we rattled across it leaving the shipyard behind.

We reached the hotel without a problem and I gave the man lots of money because I appreciated the fact that he had delivered me to a safe place where I could spend the night. I had to rouse a security guard who opened a gate and showed me to an empty room. It had been a long day and I had a handsome bungalow for the evening. I checked the bed for creepy-crawlies and then wrapped myself in the blanket. Before falling asleep, I heard the sound of waves hitting the coast which reminded me that I had travelled all the way back to the east coast of the island.

The next morning, I had coffee and breakfast on a terrace with an ocean view. The temperature was pleasant and the breeze mild. When I was in Fianarantsoa, I read about a hotel that, according to the description, was located several kilometres down the coast. If I understood it correctly, it was completely secluded and alone along the coast. With nothing else planned or desired, I resolved to see if I could find out some more information about this secluded inn, and if possible, go there later in the day.

After breakfast, I walked up and down the beach for about twenty minutes. There were no skylines in Madagascar cities. A look back towards the city revealed the first layer of colonial buildings and nothing behind them was tall enough to be visible. I saw a fisherman setting up a fishing pole in a holder, and then casting a second fishing line which he held. I found a driftwood log where I could sit and enjoy the sound of the waves and sight of the ocean. Two middle-aged women approached me and showed me hand-woven mats, vanilla, curry powder. They spoke no English and could only say the price of their goods in French. A teenager approached as well and sat on the log. At first I didn't pay him much attention but I heard him say 'this vanilla is too expensive.'

I turned my head to him and said hello.

Joseph was eighteen years old and currently finishing his final year of high school in Manakara. He had a small, thin body, orange hat, and green bag; in total a youthful appearance.

'I saw you walking on the beach but I was afraid to come and talk to you.'

As my attention turned to talking with Joseph the women went away. When I glanced to see where they had gone, I noticed four young men taking a few steps into the water.

Joseph said 'I belong to an English club but I don't get much practice.'

I asked him what he was doing today.

'I'm a high school student but today is a holiday so I am walking along the beach and riding my bicycle. Where do your come from? Ahh Canada, it is very far and cold. The south of Madagascar is very hot. Do you know, soon we will have our Independence Celebration?'

Many weeks ago when I was in Diego Suarez and saw the little boy with his mother in a small park, the black obelisk that I saw there was a monument dedicated to this upcoming 26th June national celebration of independence from French colonial rule. In Canada we had a similar Independence Day holiday on 1st July, in which people often celebrated at a lakeside cabin, barbequing and enjoying evening fireworks.

'How will you celebrate the day?' I asked him.

'My parents live in the countryside. I will visit them to celebrate.'

'Where do you live in Manakara?'

'I live with my sister and her husband here until I finish high school.'

I asked him why he thought those four young men were splashing around gaily in the water so early in the morning.

'They are from the countryside. They are happy to see the ocean. Maybe it is their first time. Some people from the country put some sea water in a can and take it back for their children to see.'

I asked him what his parents do in the countryside.

'My parents are farmers; I help them when I can.'

He showed me his calloused palms which were incongruent to the youthful appearance I had first observed.

'This is from working in the rice fields.'

'Will you go to university when you are finished high school?' I asked him.

'Here the corruption is very dangerous. It is difficult for someone from the countryside to get a job or go to university because they don't have any money. If you want a job or to take some exam, you have to pay money.'

A young man in a black sleeveless shirt approached and said something to Joseph and this caused him to reach into his bag and pull out a pen. This prompted a lesson for me.

'You see, here in Madagascar, if you have a problem, it's ok to ask someone. I don't know this boy, but he needed a pen and come to ask me. We are like a family. It is different in Canada?'

I said that borrowing things from others is acceptable, but in Canada we try not to borrow money from others. If we need to borrow money, we go to a bank.

'Banks can't give people money here,' Joseph responded, which was something that I had assumed to be the biggest difference between my chances for social mobility and his: credit. The great historian Niall Ferguson wrote in his 2008 book, *The Ascent of Money,* that:

'Credit and debt…are among the essential building blocks of economic development, as vital to creating wealth of nations as mining, manufacturing or mobile telephony. Poverty, by contrast, is seldom directly attributable to the antics of rapacious financiers. It often has more to do with the lack of financial institutions, with the absence of banks, not their presence.'

We got up and walked back to the road, Joseph pushing his bike beside me.

'The French built this city but I don't know why?'

I suggested to him that it was because of the beach and access to water but he was not sure about that answer.

'Perhaps you can study this question in school for an assignment,' I said to him, which he considered out of politeness.

I took the opportunity to ask him about the hotel down the coast. I described the hotel and he recognised what I was asking him.

'Yes, it is down this road,' he said pointing to the road on which we were standing.

'But it is very far.'

I grabbed my bag from the hotel and began walking down the road through the southern part of the city. The Manakara River nearly made it to the ocean several kilometres south of the city, but just before reaching the ocean the land caused it to veer north. It ran parallel to the coast before reaching a path to empty into the ocean. The French no doubt chose the delta of this small river as the spot to build Manakara into a city. As I walked south down the coast, I had this river not too far to my right, the ocean not far to my left, and I followed a sandy path between the two, which began in the city.

The last part of the city had two and three story colonial buildings that had been converted into a bank or other government offices. Others looked abandoned and in a state of decay which was apt to occur in poorly-run colonies after the imperial power left. It was a familiar site at this point in my travels. After about one kilometre of walking, the city thinned to a village and then turned to sandy trail.

Somewhere down the path, I reached an unusual looking white structure that said *FASAN'IREO MAHERY FO* and under this it said *AMBALAKARARAY MANAKARA*. Below this was a thick white cross and a fence. It was some kind of compound; the walls were tall and had seven arches along its length. There was no roof and it had no enclosure; it was as though it were made from thick white popsicle sticks. When I got close enough I realised it was a structure built around a cemetery.

Soon the city was out of sight behind me and I felt completely alone. In previous days, being alone, while among many, at times produced feelings of melancholy. This solitude, however, was exhilarating. As far as I could see in front of me there was nothing but scenes of paradise. The sand below my feet was thick and loose, causing my feet to slip in the lack of traction. Trees enclosed the trail, but at most times the Indian Ocean was visible through the ringed palm trunks to my left; I was close enough that I could hear the waves amidst the ocean breeze.

I could not see the Manakara River to my right but reckoned it was not far. On occasion I passed a villa or two, and a small village where the locals smiled at me, but I then walked for a long stretch of time seeing no signs of human life. Never in my life have I felt so far on the fringe of the world. What began as a quaint train journey the day before, was completed with trekking down the coast until I vanished. I imagined that if I ever had to run from the law and disappear, that this place would be perfect. It was ideal seclusion.

After two hours of walking I began to have doubts creep into my thoughts that maybe there wasn't a hotel down this coast. I walked from the trail out onto the beach to see if I could see anything in the distance. In both directions, I saw only a view that was a million years old. I had come far enough from the city that I couldn't see it, and there was no structure visible south down the coast. The first humans that visited this coast likely saw the same view that I could now see.

I kept marching along and it wasn't much longer before I could see something in the distance under some trees. As I got closer I was relieved to see that I had indeed found this mysterious hotel at the end of the world. Nestled among a variety of green leafy trees was a small sun-faded thatched roof overtop a sign saying:

BUNGALOWS
RESTAURANT
La Vanille

And to complete the picture of desolation, I was the hotel's only guest.

I had a bungalow with a shower, toilet, and comfortable bed. The bungalows were set a hundred meters from the beach in a quiet grassy enclosure. I walked across the trail to the beachfront restaurant and took a table outside and had some lunch and drank a beer. With the ocean wind and waves this spot was much noisier than my bungalow just beyond the trees. The restaurant was run by a lady and her two daughters. One of them approached my table and asked me a question which I pieced together as 'do you want lobster for dinner tonight?' I smiled at this thought and indicated that I would indeed like this very much.

I went down to the beach and shuffled up and down the water's edge for a while. I heard in recent news that debris from the Malaysia flight MH 370 had been found washed up on Madagascar's eastern coast. I walked up and down the coast to see if I could spot anything but came up empty. That evening I gorged myself on a large lobster and drank beer. After finishing my meal, I wrote in my notes for a while. The evening felt unique, peaceful, restorative, and I was happy I had found this interesting place.

The next morning, after some breakfast, I made the ten-kilometre trek back to Manakara, walked a little further across the bridge into Tanambao. I took a room at Les Flagencourts which was on a street full of rickshaw pullers and across from a two-story white building with gabled windows and an arabesque balcony. I went for a walk around the markets, which were similar to others I had seen around the country. The one remarkable feature of the market here was that the traffic was light and made walking up and down the street more pleasant. The sides of the street were lined with shaky wooden kiosks, and down the centre, vendors had laid a row of blankets with goods displayed in an orderly way. The kiosks had selections of meat, fruits, vegetables, plastic water pistols, balloons, and other various knickknacks and bibelots. Some sold clothes, others tools, and yet another cheap radios.

I met Tajona, who was a man in his late twenties. He wore a cap and had the light copper skin tone of a Merina.

'How's business,' I asked him.

Tajona was selling big woollen blankets. He told me 'It's not bad. In Winter I can sell three a day.'

'Where do these come from?' I asked him.

'They are made in Tana. They are shipped here. I usually sell two or three a day. Malagasy people bargain very hard, but foreigners not so much.'

Perhaps he was playfully baiting me with this comment, but if so, he had the wrong vahaza. Then he said something that I had completely forgotten about.

'Brexit, Brexit. England will leave Europe.'

I asked him about this but he didn't seem to know anything more about it so I asked him something more general about his life.

'What do you do in the summer Tajona?'

'I'm here for a few months a year and then I go back to Antsirabe. I am not married but I have one son in Antsirabe.'

He told me that his son was seven years old, was a student, and lived with his mother in Antsirabe. When Tajona was not busy with his business, he spent as much time there as he could to help take care of his son.

'Good luck with the day,' I told him and finished my walk through the market. The people looked poor and so did the city, but like Diego Suarez and Mahajanga, there were a few bright points in these coastal cities. And here in Manakara they had access to a train and decent roads between here and Fianarantsoa, as I was to discover. It was not a bad place to come and start a new life.

In the morning I had a brief conversation with the owner of the hotel while sitting in the gated terrace of the restaurant. He was a French man of about fifty-five years old. I noticed he had pictures of boxers and Japanese samurai figures so I asked him about them. The boxing pictures reminded me that Muhammad Ali had passed away just three weeks ago.

As a teenager I had no notion of politics and little interest in it, but I was captivated by the life and career of Ali, and this inadvertently clarified some nascent political opinions, though I may not have thought of them in that way at that time. I was drawn to his outspokenness during the civil rights era and the stance he took against the Vietnam War. I thought him inspiring in his quest to become the heavyweight champion, and then principled when he was willing to give that up to maintain his stance on the Vietnam War. I remembered, as a kid, finding my grandfather watching a replay of one of his fights from the early sixties. I asked: 'why is he dancing around the ring like that?'

'That's the way he fought,' was my grandfather's reply.

Ali was a stubborn, charismatic, flawed, but deeply talented man who worked hard, accomplished a lot, and tried to live a principled life. As a teenager I idolised him, and when I had heard of his death, I mourned his loss.

Indoors, the restaurant had wooden chairs, orange tablecloths, and a floor of straight and level white tiles. In addition to the Japanese and boxing influences in the décor, there were a few decorative African figurines. The whole building was old and falling apart, yet there were many details and personal touches that gave it charm. The hotel owner and I moved from boxing to the Japanese décor, and I told him that I lived and worked in Japan as a teacher. He walked into the restaurant for a moment then re-emerged with two books.

'I love these books; do you know them.'

They were both plump novels written by Eiji Yoshikawa: *La Pierre Et Le Sabre* and *La Parfaite Lumiere.*

'I read these two and reread them,' he told me.

I asked him what he knew about the English Brexit Referendum.

'I am disappointed by this outcome,' was all he had time to say on the topic before work duties called him. I took my leave from the hotel and the city, and spent the day in travel back to Fianarantsoa by taxi-brousse.

Fianarantsoa was a medium-sized city spread mainly across two distant hills in a subtropical geography. The residential area stretched into some valleys and in other valleys there were rice fields. A few pretty church spires were visible on the hillside, but for the most part it was a city absent affluence, colour, or beauty. On the morning of 25th June, the city had a bustling sense of anticipation for the Independence Day celebrations that evening and the holiday tomorrow. I saw several people who looked to be going about their daily work routines but many others were preparing for the celebrations.

My hotel was near an important road that entered the city. I walked along this road for ten minutes and turned up another and climbed the remaining street to the top of the hill where I watched some people setting up a stage. There were police officers everywhere and long queues at the ATM. This area had large civil buildings, a market, banks, and a library which I tried to enter but was closed.

Later that evening the streets were noisy with car horns and children who lit firecrackers and poppers. Other children wielded plastic swords and slashed them to and fro with devilry. There was widespread dancing in the streets and countless groups who had set up and sat around primitive street-side barbecues that filled the air with the smell of smoke and grilled meat skewers.

I walked towards the sound of music and the louder it became the denser the crowd of people. The source of the music had drawn and pullulated hundreds to watch a full band play fast-paced dance music. A front man moved around the stage dancing, singing, and energising the crowd. After a full look around, I re-estimated the crowd to number over a thousand people. As far as I could see, I was the only foreigner among them and nobody looked at me, bothered me, asked me for anything, nor did they invite me to join them. But then why should they want help to celebrate their Independence? They were celebrating an independence from people who looked exactly like me.

In the centre of the crowd near the stage, young teens pushed and thrashed around. Girls of all ages were shaking their bottoms with such mesmerising speed that they were nearly vibrating. I wondered around some more, but after another hour or so, the noise became too much for me and I wondered back to my hotel. I asked a man at the front desk about the celebrations tomorrow. I told him that I would like to see a village and he said that he could arrange for me to do this with him and a driver.

The next morning, I awoke just before dawn and emerged from my quarters to a sunrise still concealed by the hills. My room was in a separate building behind the lobby of the hotel, so before going for breakfast, I walked to the lower edge of the property to where I had a panoramic view of the adjacent hills covered in clouds and mist. I could still hear music playing from two different locations down below in the valley. The wisps of mist and fog gave the landscape a sense as though a rainforest was supposed to be here, but was, over time, replaced with this city. At the bottom of the valley, a small basin had rice fields and a few farmers were poking around down there.

At breakfast, I was writing scattered thoughts in my notebook while drinking nice coffee.

'You write down your thoughts,' I heard a man say to me in a mild accent. I looked up and saw a friendly face with a grey beard. This man of retirement age told me he was from Paris.

'Me, I am doing the same. Did you take in the party last night? I took many photographs and watched a children's dance competition. It is in their blood to dance this way. Five, six, seven years old; they dance beautifully. The youngest child can...just move,' he chuckled to make up for the unmerited lack of words in his description.

'It's in their blood. Today, I will go watch the...*défilé*? I can't remember the right word...Parade! Yes. I am going to watch the parade.'

I wished him a good morning and went back to my room to prepare for my little trip into the countryside to watch the 'défilé.'

Tombovelo, or Tom, was a local student who was finishing a master's degree at Fianarantsoa University, and was working part time at the front desk of my hotel. His friend had a car and made himself available for me to hire to take us into the countryside. They were both waiting for me at the front entrance.

'I just have to wait for my co-worker to get here and take over for me,' Tom told me. 'He is on his way.'

The driver was sitting on a sofa in the lobby watching a video on his phone. He was a round man with a gap-toothed smile, but at the moment his features had a look of hard scrutiny.

'How will I be able to fuck my husband?' I heard a ditzy voice say from the speaker of his phone. I asked him what he was watching and he chuckled but was unwilling to show me. He stood up before shutting his phone off, and like an incautious poker player who revealed a peak at his cards, I glimpsed his phone screen and confirmed what I already suspected—that this strange man was watching pornography with audible volume in the public lobby of a hotel.

'He doesn't have the internet at home,' Tom said under his breath, as a way of explaining his friend's behaviour.

We got into an old Peugeot car and left the city. We drove down decent country roads for about an hour and I saw much of the same landscape that I saw from the train a few days earlier.

Tom said to me 'after the 2009 political crisis, life became worse here in Madagascar.'

I asked him for an example.

'Before the political crisis, our independence day celebration had two-hundred fireworks. After, for a while we had one-hundred, and last night, only fifty. Economic things around here collapsed.'

'Did people here support the coup d'état?'

'There were some protests but many people who protested were arrested. Life is not well-balanced here. There are rich people and many poor people. I don't know how we will change this.'

I asked him about the Betsileo people and culture in this region.

'Our culture is expressed in wedding ceremonies, circumcision, and funerals. We also do exhumation like Merina.' I told Tom about my attempt to see this in Antsirabe. He then continued:

'the market is important for our culture. That is where you can hit on a girl. If you want to find a girl to flirt with, you must go to the market.'

At this point out the window, I could see the village we planned to visit. I said to Tom: 'a few days ago in Manakara a boy told me it's difficult for people in the country to go to university. Was it difficult for you to go?'

'Our public universities are not too expensive but you need a computer and most people cannot afford to buy a computer.'

We drove through the small village and out the other side, where our driver parked the car near a small factory in the countryside. I could see dark green crops extending up a hill and across a valley.

'This is a tea plantation,' Tom explained to me. 'The government owns this and hires local people to harvest this tea.'

I saw the letters *SIJEXAM* on the building, but there was no activity that day, presumably because it was a holiday. Tom and I walked up a hill a short way to a spot where we could see the tea fields in all directions. Three young women in lamba dress walked by us gabbing about something.

We returned to the nearby village, found a place to park the car, and then we walked through a gate into the main courtyard where many locals had gathered for a school parade. Tom remembered that he wanted to say more about the market and flirting.

'The market is a place where you can meet a girl and flirt with her. If I give her my lamba or a comb, and she accepts it, it means we can discuss dating. People dress a certain way to advertise if they are single or married. But you also have to be careful. If you try to flirt with someone's wife, the husband might kill you.'

A few hundred people gathered in the dirt courtyard where children started to line up according to gender and age. The formal event was about to begin. Some of the groups held banners that indicated membership to a martial arts club. Others had banners that identified them as school groups. When they were all set in position and the organisers seemed satisfied, they began marching up and down the rectangular courtyard which could have otherwise served as a small soccer pitch.

Some of the crowd were dressed in traditional clothes with a cultural Betsileo hat. Others wore baseball caps and the cheap western hand-me-downs. Most were bundled in warm clothing because the morning was cool. The group as a whole had the sartorial look of a train of migrants. One old man came over to Tom and me and told us that he used to be a teacher of one of the classes. I judged this was a tall tale because he was dressed like a bum and smelled like the village drunk.

'That guy wanted money,' Tom said to me, after the man disappeared in the crowd.

The final part of the celebration was a raising of the green, red, and white Madagascar flag, and the national anthem, to which everyone sang along. When the parade finished, the three of us drove to the next town where we stopped at a small diner to eat some rice and fish. A television was on in the diner and the president was delivering his annual holiday message. There was no Wi-Fi in the diner, so the driver was watching the television. He pointed a finger at the screen and said something in disdain.

'He does not like this man,' Tom said to me.

An old man, who looked to be in his eighties, came in the shop. There was a display of conspicuous medals pinned to his shirt. The driver asked him where he got the medals and the old man said that he had gotten them from his career in the army.

'He was part of the Independence movement in the 1950s,' Tom explained to me after the old man left. I was angry with myself for not getting Tom to invite this man over to eat lunch with us and talk to us. I missed what was likely an interesting story.

As we drove back into the city, Tom invited me to his place for dinner. He lived on the other hill in the city. The driver dropped us off at the side of the main road at the top of the hill and we stepped down a trail of steep earthen steps. Houses were scattered along the hillside in no particular design. Tom lived in a small two-story concrete apartment building that had eight rooms altogether. His place was one open room; it had a dining table and behind it his bed. There was no bathroom or running water. To the left, upon entering, he had a television and

DVD player, and to the right was a counter used for preparing a meal or cleaning dishes.

'It's normal to offer guests honey, but I am sorry, I don't have any,' Tom said. 'I do have this local rum though.'

He poured us each a glass and as we clicked them, he said.

'You are the first foreign guest I have had at my house. I am very happy you came.'

I thanked him for hosting me and wished him a happy Independence Day celebration. With that we drank the rum, which burned my throat and warmed my stomach like a furnace. My head felt like I had inhaled toxic fumes.

'My fiancée is coming later to join us for dinner. She lives in the countryside. Let's drink some more.'

We had some time before we had to prepare dinner so we sat and talked. He put on a video of Betsileo music.

'What do you think of life here?'

I told him I thought that the country was very poor and people had to work hard just to survive. I said the island was the most interesting place I had ever visited. I told him how I had travelled in several places in the north of Madagascar and how it took a long time to travel around the country. Overall, it seemed that times were hard for the Malagasy people and I hoped that in the future things become more prosperous, so that people could work hard but earn enough money to live well. I said: 'people who work hard deserve security and some prosperity in their lives.'

'I will work one more year at this job and then I want to find a better position. I want to live in the suburbs outside the city where it is quiet.'

We went outside the open door and Tom climbed a ladder to the neighbour's place. A moment later he climbed back down holding a duck that was bound at the legs. He set the duck down in the corner next to the entrance of his place where it remained in restrained silence.

'I have to get water, please wait here.'

He took two big yellow jugs and walked out of the gate and disappeared. I took a look around the yard next to the apartment building. There was a clothes line, a wooden shack with two outhouse toilets, and a large black punching bag hung from a wooden beam. Straight down the hillside, immediately below the path in front of the apartment building, was a small house that I guessed belonged to one family. A dog wondered around barking and a separate pen housed two pigs, one of whom had sensed my presence and looked at me. I could hear firecrackers and poppers from further down the valley. Tom returned with the water and set the jugs down.

'I want to show you my hat.' It was a yellow hat that had a thin rim and a beehive dome. I thought its shape to resemble a First World War Doughboy helmet. He put the cap on, turned up the music, then started preparing some things at the counter inside his room. Then outside, he lit a fire with wood and charcoal and set some water to boil. Then came the duck.

'It's time to make the sacrifice,' he said to me with a smile.

Tom held the bird down, and with a couple slices of the knife, severed off the head. He poured some boiling water into a plastic tub and threw in the duck and began plucking its feathers. He had told me that he did not need my assistance, so I was sitting at the table and occasionally chatted with him while he worked. The music was so loud that we had to talk with raised voices.

We drank more rum and Tom began dancing and singing to the music. We were drunk, and kept pouring more drinks, taking turns toasting each other, and then slamming back more rum. He danced and sang and I laughed at his unabashed gaiety. A neighbour popped her head in the door. Her name was Mamy and she was a gaunt, dark-skinned woman who appeared to be in her early sixties. She lived upstairs with her daughter and infirmed father. She hauled her two jugs of water up the ladder and left them upstairs for her family's use. We had offered her rum but she said that first she had to finish the water duties.

Tom and I walked down the road a few minutes and bought some bottles of beer. When the sun set, Tom turned on the lone lightbulb in his room. Perhaps it was the sun setting or the alcohol tormenting him, but a worried look appeared on his face. He grabbed his phone and a moment later pulled it from his ear.

'I am worried; I can't reach my fiancée. She should be here by now and she isn't picking up her phone.'

He called his fiancée's parents who told him that she was on her way and this seemed to placate Tom a little.

Mamy joined us at the table and I poured her a glass of beer. She brought fried skewers of Zebu meat which now rested on the table. Soon Tom's fiancée arrived and this made Tom both relieved and thrilled. She was a short woman with an abundance of youth in her round cheeks and kind smile. I found these features radiant in my drunken observation. She said something and he laughed and said to me 'this is my fiancée Andry; she said we have had a lot to drink. I told her we are celebrating.'

Andry took over the cooking duties and Tom and I drank more with Mamy. Tom danced over and over to something called the Kidodo song, which was some kind of bird dance. His enthusiasm for this song encouraged Andry to join in and soon Mamy stood up and lifted her dress a little and attempted to show these young whippers a thing or two about Betsileo dance steps.

A teenage girl and boy arrived. Mamy proudly introduced the girl as her daughter, who moved straight for her mother's glass of beer and took two breathless gulps from the cup. I gave them some money and we sent them to buy us more beer which they brought back in time to drink while we ate the duck. Tom gave what he considered to be the best pieces to Mamy because she was the eldest. We completed the meal with a large bowl of rice.

'Do you want to sit next to my wife?' Tom asked me.

I laughed at him and hollered 'no she is your wife; you must sit beside her.' He looked pleased like he had schooled me well in Betsileo manners. He spoke Malagasy to the two ladies and they both laughed.

'I told them I taught you about flirting with a man's wife at the market.'

For Mamy, the drink made her reflective and she began discussing her life. She was the oldest of many siblings and this meant many responsibilities. She said life in the past was very hard for the oldest child. They had to work hard to help support the family. Most Malagasy families were large when she was growing up. She believed that young people now didn't work like she had to in the sixties and seventies. I silently hoped this was a meagre sign that maybe the harshness of poverty was less severe today than it was forty-five years ago, but it may have just been the universal nature of an older generation to find moral shortcomings in the generation they had raised.

With dinner finished, we prepared to go into the city and enjoy the street celebrations. Tom, Andry and I took a taxi to the other side of the city, on the adjacent mountaintop, to the same concert stage where I had been the previous night. Like the night before, thousands danced on the street and watched a performer from Tana, who I was told was quite famous. Tom was almost a foot shorter than me, so when he said to me 'come on; let's go to the front,' I felt ambivalent because I was not just a foot taller than Tom; I was a foot taller than everyone. We pushed our way to the front. To not feel like a tower, I bent my knees and lowered my head several inches. A circle in the middle of the crowd jumped around and pushed each other. Those on the perimeter did not seem bothered by this wild behaviour. This went on for a couple more songs and then some contest began.

Seven women on stage each had an individual opportunity to dance for ten seconds and then the host of the contest elicited the crowd's evaluation. Each woman turned from the crowd and danced with her rear-end. Some bounced it up and down and others wiggled their asses so forcefully it brought to mind cardiac arrest. This form of dancing was far more sexual than the laid back and joyous Kidodo bird dance from Tom's house.

After the contest, the performer returned to the stage and the winner of the contest danced on stage with her. I felt drunk and was not up to this raucous dancing in the streets. I gave Tom and Andry a hug and thanked them for a wonderful evening, and then stumbled my way back to my hotel which took only five minutes.

I spent the next day relaxing in my hotel room and catching up on all the notes and writing in my journal from the busy day before. I felt uplifted by the experience I had had the day before with Tom and the people in his life. Before leaving Fianarantsoa, I was fortunate enough to see him one more time at his work post where we exchanged email addresses and he said 'we cannot forget this beautiful moment and I wish to stay in touch forever.'

Chapter Nine
Goat, Circumcision and a Crayon Fence: The Last Road to Toliara

There was one more thing I wanted to do before leaving the Fianarantsoa region. I took a taxi-brousse to the outskirts of Ranomafana National Park, which was perhaps the most famous nature park for tourists on the entire island. Before coming to Madagascar, I had contacted Dr Patricia Wright and asked her if she would be in Madagascar. She kindly welcomed me to come to her research centre called Valbio so that I could see their operations in the Ranomafana and Andringitra regions.

Dr Wright was an American anthropologist who came to Madagascar in the mid-1980s, to search for the greater bamboo lemur, which was then feared to be extinct. Not only did she find that this lemur still lived, she also found a new species of lemur now known as the golden bamboo lemur. Five years later, in 1991, Ranomafana National Park was established to protect several species of lemur, birds, frogs, and other wildlife that lived in the rainforest there. Since the 1980s, Patricia Wright had become one of the leading authorities on conservation, lemurs, and Madagascar in general.

When I called on the centre that day, a staff member told me she was out and was not sure when Dr Wright would return. This was alright with me since we did not have any official appointment. Another reason that I could take this news without issue was the great success I had already had in exploring national parks in search of lemurs and other endemic species to Madagascar. With Floris in the northwest of the island, with Rabary and Dr Patel at Anjanaharibe-Sud's Camp Indri, and once again at Andasibe, where I heard the indri call numerous times. At this point in the journey, I still wanted more personal experiences with the Malagasy people if I could manage it. There was also still a fifth of the island's southern territory that I had yet to explore, but even at this point, I knew it was likely that I would not have enough time to see much of what remained.

Since more than half the day had passed already, I found lodging at a tourist hotel called Cristo Hotel Ranomafana, which was a beautiful place located about six kilometres east of Ranomafana. During peak season, I imagined that this place would be full of tourists, but on that day, I was the only one at this large wonderful rainforest lodge. I enjoyed a tasty meal, drank Three Horses Beer, and wrote in my notebook for about two and a half hours that late afternoon.

The following day, I lingered at the comfortable and quiet hotel for the morning, enjoying the cool misty and rainy weather, then made my return to Fianarantsoa, so that I could plan my onward journey the next day. Overall, this was a representative sample of travel on the island of mora mora; things progressed slowly, and at times things happened but progressed none. But I didn't mind a wink because by this time I had made a habit of the travel philosophy: slowly, slowly.

I decided that I would follow the Route Nationale Seven road south, first to Isalo National Park, and then continue the rest of the way to the south-western coastal city of Tulear (Toliara). I made this decision with the awareness that I was choosing a comfortable option of southward travel along a decent stretch of highway.

As our vehicle drove in and out of the terraced rice valleys of the Betsileo, soon, in the distance ahead to the immediate south, I could see the Andringitra mountain range, and Peak Boby (booby), the highest peak in southern Madagascar. This mountain marked a sharp distinction in the landscape between formations that were as old as the hills and others that were very recently formed. When I was at Vahatra, Dr Goodman had put it thusly:

'Now, the thing that's hard to get your head around is, this is the area that was attached to Africa. Everything from Andringitra to the west coast is Neogenic, that is to say it formed since the breakup of Gondwanaland. There is transitional forest, the Grand Canyon of Madagascar, the spiny bush, all of that has evolved since the breakup.'

Dr Goodman recommended hiking in this area but this came with a warning: 'It'll be cold though. I remember vividly we did some inventories, it was on the twenty-first of August, 1993, it got down to minus eleven degrees Celsius; there was recorded snow!'

As we moved on from this region, the road began to angle in a more west by southwest direction. The first major town was a place called Ihotsy, which was a dusty cow-poke town where men walked around with semi-automatic machine guns strapped over their shoulders. This whole region, home to the Bara people, had been a cow-punching territory for the last century. Completing the Wild West image of the place, it was also home to a lot of zebu thieves, which was why I saw so many people strapped with guns. As we left the city, we wound our way up a hill, and then on the other side, the land flattened, the road straightened, and the vegetation changed.

This was a land of isolated mango trees and towering termite mounds. The Bara people, who had a prominent ancestry of African descent, built dark brick-coloured mud huts and shacks. Their world, kinship groups, and economy revolved around raising, trading, stealing, and bartering cattle. If you were a young man who wanted to get married, the best way to demonstrate your worthiness was to provide zebu for the bride-to-be and her family.

From the historical rise of the Merina monarch in the central highlands, the Bara people of this region were one of several groups who remained obstinate and resisted becoming subordinate to the Merina monarchy. Though this region was important to the island for its production of cattle, none of the villages caught my eye as a place I wanted to stop and explore in further detail. For some villages, the full extent of their sprawl could be observed from the vehicle. After leaving Ihotsy, much of the landscape with its sparse scrubby grassland and solitary rocky escarpments could have fit into a scene somewhere among the various prairie landscapes of central North America from Saskatchewan down to Texas, in the Edward's Plateau, for example.

That evening I made it to the Isalo Rock Lodge, a place that Tom had recommended for me back when I was in Fianarantsoa. The Isalo Rock Lodge was located near the village of Ilakaka on RN7 and was constructed to serve tourism into the Isalo Massif, which was a giant expanse of national park immediately to the north. That evening in the hotel's elegant rooms, I sat on a stool at a bar that was built of roughly thirty planks of long rectangular wood sheets pressed together, which sat under a row of hanging lights. There I wrote in my journal for a while, and before going to bed, made some inquiries about hiking in the massif the next day.

The whole complex and grounds, I discovered the next morning, had an Arizona desert theme that was meant to fit the region's close proximity to the arid spiny bush vegetation further south of this location. It was the most beautiful hotel of my journey into Madagascar and also the most expensive. They could charge a lot of money because they offered a refuge of luxury in a remote place where one's other option was to rough it.

The Isalo Massif was a massive sandstone national park that stretched for many kilometres and took at least seven days to fully explore. I found one day to be enough because much of the preparations were an expensive hassle. I took a taxi into the village so that I could arrange to hire a tour guide which was mandatory in a Madagascar national park. I bought a ticket and then I had to hire another taxi to take me and the guide to a place where we could begin our walk. The expense and inefficiency of this whole morning procedure was not an enjoyable way to begin the day.

My guide was Tio, a tall Betsileo man from Fianarantsoa area who had moved to this region of the island to take tourists into the Isalo National Park. His stature was lean and fit from five years of hiking with visitors through the park. Tio knew enough English to explain some things we saw in the park but if I asked a question, he revealed that he had many limitations in his ability to converse in the language. Basically, he had memorised a few lines but couldn't say much beyond that. So I tried to focus on enjoying the mild exertion from the hike and the rather pretty landscape of the park.

One of the things Tio could tell me about the cave tombs in this area I found interesting. The Bara used the caves as tombs, where they sometimes saved a good spot by putting a boulder in front of the opening. When the time came to put the deceased inside, they were walled-in by a pile of stones. During an exhumation, the corpse was moved to a permanent spot, often difficult and dangerous to reach. Young men climbed up vertiginous cliff sides and placed the remains in an opening.

They were not difficult to spot throughout the trek. Tio pointed to a low-arched niche in the rock face perhaps thirty feet from the ground, and then again to another as we rounded a small corner. I asked Tio a question about his life in the nearby village to which he replied 'I don't like the Bara. They are too aggressive. They are not nice people.'

I wondered if my guide had any personal examples but he had difficulty expressing this to me and I let it go.

We came to a ground-level opening that had an old empty casket lying a few feet from the entrance. The casket looked like an old travel trunk, with green metal sides that were faded and rusted. There was a feeble set of wheels under the trunk. I was not sure how this scene came to look this way and Tio said nothing more about it other than that it was another tomb. Perhaps it used to be, but I had the suspicion that now it was left staged in this way for tourists to see. Overall, the hiking was enjoyable, but I found my guide's company underwhelming and I was not eager to stay here another day.

The next morning, I continued on my journey south-west along RN7 to Tulear. It did not take much driving before we left the state region of Fianarantsoa and entered into Tulear territory where the land looked dry and the sky was an expanse of cloudless blue. In the north-east, where I trekked in the Antalaha to Maroantsetra region, it was usual to have rain every day. In this south-western region the climate was arid and precipitation infrequent. To my eye, every twenty-five to thirty kilometres, a new kind of vegetation was prominent. In some spots, cacti and termite mounds, in other spots there were mango trees.

We stopped in a spot of empty landscape to take a bathroom break. Perhaps one-hundred-and-fifty meters south of the road stood a solitary baobab tree. Its loneliness made its root-like branches all the more remarkable and beautiful. While I was standing, basically alone, the others were stretching their legs or finishing relieving themselves, I could see not far down the road a woman in traditional blue lamba dress making haste towards our location. As she approached, it became clear that she had nothing to sell, and what she and her four children were running towards, was me.

Her children were dressed in filthy clothes and two of them were bare-footed. She pointed to the baobab tree and made some motions with her hands and communicated to me that because I took a picture of the tree, I had to give her some money. This was a worse excuse than having no reason at all. I held my pen and notebook in my hands and smiled, but this did not assuage the scowl on her face. As I began to walk back to the taxi-brousse door, she pinched a hold of my shirt sleeve and tugged on it in a manner that despite the gentle pressure applied, was an act of aggression. With minimum-needed force, I maintained my walk and hoisted myself into the vehicle. She continued to stand at the door and pester me for money until the door slid in her face and we departed.

The towns from Isalo to Tulear were built along a straight road on flat, dry land. These towns earned their living from sapphire mining and it was reflected in the construction of some of the housing and buildings. Most of the buildings along the road through town contained some kind of gem business. I saw locals walking around with pails and shovels, the tools of their foraging for gems in the countryside. I also saw lamba-cloaked women with orange mud smeared and caked on their faces and carrying baskets on their heads.

The arid red landscape gave the villages a dry destitute feeling and they stood out compared with villages from the northern parts of the island. They were dusty, flat, mining towns with a Deadwood feel, and often as our vehicle approached a village, from a kilometre or two away, it was possible to see to the other end of the town and long past it to the horizon. I arrived in Tulear that evening and found a decent room at the Chez Lalah for eight dollars a night.

Route Nationale Seven entered Tulear from the south and ran parallel to the coast. In the middle of the city, it turned ninety degrees towards the coast then north again back up the coast and out of the city. It was at this spot where the road transformed into Route Nationale Nine. The Chez Lalah hotel was on a street called Avenue de France, a block south of the RN7 and RN9 connection point. The cheap cost and relative level of comfort in the hotel, and around the city, made me interested to stay for a few days.

The next morning, after sunrise, I took a walk around and found a place called *Le Blu* that served breakfast. The entrance was open and it had a large blackboard menu displayed at the end of a walkway between a series of posts connected by rope. The place looked designed in a theme of an African-style thatched hut.

In the centre of a large shadowy yellow and brown room stood a thick post that supported a pitched roof that was perhaps thirty feet high. To the right of this was a large dining area, and to the left, a long flipped question-mark-shaped bar with a handsome stained wooden counter-top. I took a seat at a stool near the back of the bar, from where I could see a capacious back terrace full of more seating options under some leaning palm trees. Overall, the room was a cosy inviting cave that I instantly liked.

At my seat, I met the owner of the restaurant who stood behind the bar; an affable German man in his fifties.

'I really like the look of your place,' I told him.

'We have the only beach in Tulear,' he responded. 'There is no beach here, so I ordered trucks of sand and created my own.'

He wore a black T-shirt, had grey hair around his temples, and he sipped from a coffee cup that he held at chest level while he talked with me.

I detected a light Australian influence in his accent and asked him about this.

'I was in the French Legionnaire and after the Falkland Island War, British soldiers wanted to join a group where they could fight. I was put with a troop that had people from Scotland, Australia, England, South Africa. We were supposed to speak French but of course we all spoke English,' he said, chuckling at the memory.

'How long have you been running this place?' I asked him.

'I opened this place two years ago. I feel like every day I am living well. I have this place, a young wife and two children. You saw that woman walk by?'

He was referring to an older Malagasy woman, perhaps sixty years old, who walked by a moment before.

'She takes care of my kids during the day. We are young parents; well my wife is, but we are both new parents so we don't always know what is wrong with our children. But this woman. She always seems to know what they need. Between a new baby and a two-year-old boy, she is kept very busy.'

'Sounds like you have enough to keep you busy, between your family and this place,' I said.

'Do you want to try this local fruit? It's called Yevis fruit.' I asked him to spell this for me, which he did, and then he explained a little more about it.

'We are the only ones around here who make this juice.'

He showed me the small yellow fruit.

'The skin and seed are hard to get apart so no one bothers to make juice with it. You see that man out there?'

He pointed to the terrace where a European man in his early sixties was sitting at a table.

'He comes in here every morning, grabs the paper and has a glass of this juice.'

The owner seemed to take his job as host further than general platitudes and I believed him that he actually enjoyed his life and work here, and when I said this to him, he laughed.

'People come here for mood and tranquillity. I love what I do. It's my passion. This is my living room and all these people are my friends. A bricklayer goes to work every day and doesn't like what he does, but he has to feed his family.'

One of his staff approached him and said something, and he then said, 'Please excuse me a minute.'

I proceeded to enjoy the tastiest breakfast I had in Madagascar—a full plate of beans, eggs, toast, coffee and the Yevis juice.

I poked around the city for the day. Tulear was a seaside city located right at the Tropic of Capricorn. On initial impression, I took note of its ubiquitous rickshaw peddlers and pullers, its expat community, and diverse ethnicities representative of the Indian Ocean. It also had an arresting sky that was a deep and cloudless blue that hung over the city like a dome. The population of the city was barely above one-hundred-and-fifty-thousand people.

I found the city quiet and it seemed to me to be a little smaller than Antsirabe but comparable with its rickshaw pullers and mild traffic. The basic areas of the city were all close enough together that I could ignore haggling with the rickshaw pullers. If they accepted my offer, I jumped on and was peddled around. There were other times when I walked around.

The next morning, I returned to have the same breakfast again. I saw the owner of the restaurant after I had finished my meal and mentioned to him that his place had great bread.

'We make our bread here; everywhere the baguettes are liked baked air. There is nothing to them; they just crumble on the table.'

I laughed at this and said 'that perfectly sums up exactly what I have been eating for the past ten and a half weeks.'

I took the opportunity to ask him a question I had.

'Yesterday, I saw a cart being pulled by two zebu out there in the water. Why do they take that cart out into the water like that?'

'The water is low here. The boats cannot come closer so the cart pulls people out to the boat. There are many hotels down the coast. Do you know Anakao? No, ahh, it's a village not far down the coast. The roads are awful and it takes a long time to get there, but by boat, not long. It's quiet there so if you want that, then check it out.'

It was early enough that I was able to buy a ticket to take the boat down to Anakao. Not far off the coast was one of the world's largest coral reefs which caused the waves to break far out at sea, making the bay shallow and the coast muddy. When it was time to go, I was guided to a creaky wooden cart that was yoked to two zebu. Five others were on the cart with me along with two people who operated the cart and handled the animals.

The beasts had no difficulty pulling the cart but their stubborn temperaments kept the staff busy yelling and whipping the animals. The wood on the cart creaked in a rhythmic manner and was accompanied by sharp snaps of the whip hitting the beast's thick muscular backsides, and the driver yelling 'hekh.' When yelling and whipping were not enough to coax the zebu, the driver of the cart grabbed one of their tails and yanked and twisted it. The car was able to bring us right alongside the speedboat, making the transfer into the vessel easy enough for the older lady who was part of the group. When it was my turn, I felt a hand grab my sleeve and I stopped to look at the driver. He wanted money. I smiled at his impertinence and said 'thank you for the ride sir.'

We began out to sea, which first involved a slow circumnavigation of the Tulear port, which was located far from shore in the deeper water. It consisted of two large platforms where cargo was offloaded and then transferred to a smaller ship, which brought it further in to the port. After we made our pass by this area, we sped off down the coast, and the breeze, sunshine, and salt air made for a brilliant morning.

Anakao was a picturesque stretch of beach where local villages and some foreign investment created modest resorts for tourists to visit. All of the hotels looked to be small businesses by private owners, which was consistent with my experience around the country. I took a room at one of these resorts called *Peter Pan Aubergine Hotel*. It consisted of a series of beach-side bungalows and a two-story restaurant bearing the hotel's name. After I jumped off the boat and headed for the resort, a man came out to greet me. He had a weary-face which was perhaps due to the early hour, and when he shook my hand, I saw he had black polish on his nails. He showed me to a bungalow and then said, 'if you see a man with a gun, don't be alarmed. We have two security guards to protect the property day and night.'

After getting settled into my room, I took my notebook to the restaurant and ordered a beer and pizza. The hotel's décor had a mixture of the personal and whimsical, mixed with a healthy theme of counterculture. I saw the libertalia theme of pirates, Cuban Revolution propaganda, Bob Marley, and Lou Reed. On the wall there was a menu written in chalk and in the bottom left corner it said 'rolling papers free for guests.' There were various games and books; hobbies to pass time. But I also got the sense that the whole resort was a hobby. The two proprietors were gaunt Italian men in their thirties who were unlike the hospitable German man at the restaurant where I had breakfast that morning. These two young men were busy doing something the entire time I was there.

One of them later told me 'we are always doing new things; if you have nothing to do it gets boring here.' A few locals were outside working on a new shed-like building that could be used for any number of things. Others were moving a statue into a new spot.

'We push the locals to work hard,' the owner told me. 'We just finished that statue.'

Along the front of the hotel property stood a multi-coloured fence painted to look like a package of crayons, and on the other side was a pair of swings. I sat at a table for a couple hours writing notes and watching local people walk in small groups along the beach. A few flies buzzed around my head and neck, distracting me while I tried to write.

Later, while walking along the beach, a man approached me and said 'my friend, do you want to go diving? No? sailing? No? Do you want some lobster? We have a small shop just over here.' I politely declined his offers and continued walking along the beach. Two minutes later a new man approached me and said exactly the same words as the first man. Three minutes after him, a third approached me, and before he could say anything, I questioned him:

'Diving?'

'Yes.'

'Sailing?'

'Yes sir.'

'What about lobster in a small restaurant?'

'Yes,' he said, smiling. 'Do you want?'

'Not now thank you, maybe later. Good day sir.'

After satisfying myself that there was little to see along the beach, I returned to my hotel and read a book in a hammock for a couple hours, dozed a little, then ate an Italian dinner. I found this place relaxing and oddly charming, but there was no one here and I did not want to spend my final few days sitting here by myself. I still had enough time to make one more trip before my journey was finished, so the next morning, I got on the boat, returned to Tulear by zebu cart, and returned to the Chez Lalah to make some plans.

Many weeks ago, when I was in Sambava with Dr Patel's team, I met a Canadian woman named Amber, who said she could help me visit the NGO Blue Ventures.

'You will want to contact Jason. He's the guy that replaced me. If you include my name in the email, it should be no problem to go see the team.'

I sent Jason an email and he asked me for more details about why I wanted to come there. He then wrote to me and said, 'I am sorry but unluckily I wouldn't be able to accept your visit.' So much for that I thought.

I was in a bit of a dilemma here because I was running out of time before I had to be back in the capital city to leave at the expiration of my visa. My two on-going travel options were, firstly, to try and circumnavigate the southern coast all the way around to the city of Fort Dauphin, and then fly back to the capital. The second choice was to travel straight north to a city called Morandava, from which I could take a quick flight back to the capital city. Both options lacked roads and infrastructure, and had no reliable amount of time that I could expect the duration of the travel to take. Unexpected delay was not just a possibility, rather that was how these regions were travelled—a series of delays pieced together and progressing at the speed of mora mora.

I had few days left, so I decided to arrange a four-wheel-drive vehicle to visit some Vezo villages and then end the journey in Morandava. I found a company, and they said that it would be no problem to arrange the trip. So I returned back to the hotel to get prepared to leave the next morning at seven-thirty. The next morning, I was ready on time and sat waiting on a sofa. Two-and-a-half hours passed, and my driver and guide had not yet arrived, and I was a little vexed, but decided that the trip was cancelled. At the front desk, I paid for another night, and then went back to my room to try and think of what to do next.

There was a knock on my door around eleven o'clock and it was the woman at the front desk saying someone was in the lobby for me. I went out there and found that a driver had finally come. But there were a couple problems. There was no English speaking guide, the driver only spoke Malagasy, and the reason I did not go ahead with the trip was the man was clearly drunk, and according to the hotel worker who translated for me, the drunk man did not even know where we were supposed to be going. So, in anger, I told him to get lost.

The next day, I walked down the road a short distance to the Hippocampo Hotel as a way to try and revive my spirits in a new environment. An Italian woman who owned the hotel told me that she had no more normal vacant rooms, but offered me the suite for the normal price. The room was beautiful and comfortable but it was her casual act of kindness that lifted my spirits back to full capacity. She arranged for me to visit a place called the Antsokay Arboretum, a living museum of sorts. It was a grounds that maintained and protected various species from the spiny desert of the southern region of the island. For the next day, my kind Italian host arranged a trip for me to go to a fishing village with a guide.

That morning, I met the guide, Alain, in the lobby and we went out to the SUV, where the same driver who had showed up drunk and late two days before was going to be my driver today. He did not look at me nor gave any indication about what had happened two days before, and as far as I could tell, he was not drunk that morning.

In the hills to the east of the road, I could see several tombs along the way. We travelled south of Tulear to a village called St Augustine, and nearby, the delta of the Onilahy River. I wondered if this driver was angry at me for cancelling the trip or if he felt, as I did, that he was in error. This mild tension and consideration made me quiet for much of the short drive.

The village area where we parked had numerous square wooden shacks, dirt roads, and a small but busy daily market where the smell of dried fish was in the air and gave an essence to the village. Many were sitting around socialising and others I saw buying fruit or vegetables. The village had a number of drunks who all hassled me for money. One man, who asked me for rum, looked as though he had been drinking the stuff all night. When I neglected him, he went from slurring his words to yelling at me. I stared right into his glossy eyes and told him to bugger off, which he did. We passed through and walked across a small area of wild grass towards the river, where upon two men approached us and asked if we wanted to go for a ride on the river. We accepted their offer.

Along the edge of the river, several wooden pirogue boats sat on shore. I could see a woman standing between two of them washing herself. She knelt in the water, which had submerged much of her legs, and was busy scrubbing a garment with a bar of soap. She had thick coarse black hair, a dark complexion, and her bare breasts sagged and shook, nearly stirring the water as she laboured. A small girl, her granddaughter perhaps, sat at the water's edge waiting for her to finish washing.

The two young men grabbed a boat and instructed us to walk down the river about thirty meters, where they brought the boat to us, and we climbed aboard. We were not yet in the main body of the river, but one of its narrow rivulets that ribboned around the low ground before the delta emptied into the Mozambique Channel. The men walked alongside the boat until they found a spot deep enough and jumped into the boat. The man who jumped in was thin, but as he began to work his single paddle, the large and small muscles in his back swelled and bulged under the constraint and displayed a strength and mass that resulted from a lifetime of paddling.

We made it to the end of our stream and just before we entered the main flow of the river, we passed another boat with three young fishermen that had come back from sea. The man paddling our boat yelled to them something like 'how's it today?'

Their response was 'not a damned thing this morning,' the essence of this exchange translated by Alain. One of the men walked nude alongside the boat, keeping pace with its slow movement, while using the fresh water to wash his upper legs and genitals.

Not far from where we entered into the river was the place where salt water and fresh water merged and created a torrent of activity as the energy from both water sources crashed headlong into each other. When our boat entered the river, I felt the current pull it towards the sea, and at times it felt as though we were pushed back into the river, but the operator of our vessel seemed perfectly under control as he cut our boat through the mild turbulence. Even if this turbulence did not exist, I could have identified the dividing line between fresh and salt water by where the red silty water met the blue water of the Mozambique Channel.

Across the river, upstream, a collection of flamingos, with light pink plumage, had gathered along the shallow water of the river's edge. We rowed for ten minutes across the river to the other side where a large bed of salt-water mangrove trees grew. Each time the tide went out the water level dropped, which exposed the soil and roots of the trees. Here we floated in a gentle manner for a while between the mangroves and the shore. I asked Alain to tell me more about his life.

'I am from the Betsileo tribe near Fianarantsoa but my parents moved to Tulear when I was younger. I live here with my wife and children now.'

He told me that he takes clients all over the southern territory. He just got back the day before from a ten-day trip from Tulear to Fort Dauphin. I, somewhat rueful, wished that I had a few more days so that I could attempt the same thing. But as it happened, I had only three more days until my scheduled departure.

I told Alain some of this and he asked me if I had been to Anakao? I told him that I had, and when I mentioned the name of the hotel I stayed at, Alain said: 'I have met those two Italian guys.'

I mentioned that when I was there, one of them was dressed like a woman. Alain crinkled his face and laughed: 'ahh it's disgusting.'

I next told Alain my history with the driver who had brought us here, how when I had walked out of the hotel and saw his face, my jaw nearly dropped, and that was one of the reasons why I was quiet on the drive here. Alain howled so loudly I feared the flamingos would scatter and never return.

'I know this man a little,' Alain said after regaining his composure. 'Two nights ago, he was at a circumcision party. After a boy's circumcision, the men often drink late into the night to celebrate the boy becoming a man. In September, my son will be circumcised. In Madagascar, a boy cannot become a man unless he is circumcised. People will come with gifts and we will have a celebration.'

And then Alain said something that stunned me for a moment.

'I will eat my son's foreskin.'

'Eat it?' I asked to make sure I heard him correctly.

'Yes, usually you put it in a piece of bread and eat it.'

The thought of this was unsettling but I did not have to respond because I was saved by a distraction. I heard a noise from behind our boat and when I looked over my shoulder, I saw a haggard woman who was kneeling at the river's edge with a bucket.

'What is she doing,' I asked Alain.

'She is waiting for crabs to walk up on the beach. She will grab them when they come up there.'

Our guide paddled the boat back across the river and returned us to shore. We then returned to the SUV and headed back to Tulear. On the way back, I was thinking once again what it would be like to "eat my son's foreskin" when Alain asked me if I wanted to have dinner at his house that evening. I gratefully accepted and we agreed to meet on the street in front of *Le Blu* restaurant at seven o'clock that evening.

That evening the streets were dark but the air was cool and pleasant. I had been a frequent breakfast guest at *Le Blu*, so when the security guard saw me standing in front of the restaurant, he offered me a chair to sit on while I waited. Two young men wearing white short-sleeved shirts and clip-on ties approached the entrance and said hello to me.

They wondered what I was doing sitting there, so I told them, then I asked them what they were doing.

'It's going to be busy in here tonight; soccer match starts at eight,' one of them said. He was referring to the Euro cup that was being played in Paris. I guess the God bothering ceased when there was a good soccer match on T.V. The restaurant was busy with more than just soccer fans.

In the span of five minutes an ATV and SUV pulled up to the restaurant, the drivers walked in, and a moment later came out with a pizza to take back home. A man, in his sixties, came stumbling drunk out the entrance. The security guard seemed familiar with him and tried to offer him help, but the old man rebuffed this gesture by swatting away his hand. The old man looked down at me and said: 'I better get home or my wife…or she will,' he then slid his index finger across his throat.

'Do you live here?' I asked him.

'I've been coming to Tulear for many years. I live six months in Newcastle and six months here. I'm sixty-nine years old; me wife's twenty-one. Yes, the best things in life are bread, Viagra, and penicillin.' He said this staring slightly off into the distance as though there were depth and wisdom to this statement. He made me imagine his young son asking: 'mommy, why is daddy older than grandpa?'

He then remembered what he was doing and stumbled over to an ATV sitting near the ropeway entrance.

'Who turned on the light?' he complained. The security guard had turned it on so that the man could better see what he was doing.

'The battery will go flat.'

The security guard ignored him. He fired the engine and I watched him disappear down the dark street. An instant later, Alain arrived on a moped. I jumped on and then we too sped off down the dark streets.

We rode to a residential area in the south-east part of the city that had tall wooden fences and muddy roads. To me, in the dark, with the unfamiliar streets with high fences, it felt like moving through a maze. We stopped at a small shop to buy some beer, where the shop owner had a question for me that Alain translated.

'Where are you from?'

'Where is Canada?'

'What do you think of Tulear?'

'Why did you come here?'

I told him to meet people like you.

'Do you like Madagascar women?'

I told him that I thought they sing and dance very well, and then I told him the story of the woman in Tana who came to my hotel room door and what she said to me. This made the shop owner laugh and I think he accepted me.

Less than a minute later, we pulled up to a large wooden fence where Alain beeped his horn twice, and then a teenage boy opened a gate. Alain had a grass yard enclosed in a high fence. His house was a square, concrete, single-story home divided into quadrant rooms. His introduced me to his wife, brother, nephew, two daughters, and young son. Alain told me to have a seat at a table located on a terrace just in front of his home. From my seat, I could see a kitchen through the open door on the right, and a sofa and television through the open door on the left. Bright bulbs illuminated the entire home and offered enough light for us to see well on the terrace.

Alain poured some glasses of rum and the two of us, plus his brother and nephew, made a toast and we drank. In Alain's toast, he thanked me for being a guest at his home and eating with his family. When he poured more drinks, I reciprocated the toast and thanked him for the invitation. The rum burned and had a mild vanilla aftertaste that was tolerably better than the stuff I had tried in Fianarantsoa.

'I want you to try our local rum they brew in villages,' he said, and disappeared into his home for a moment. I saw Alain move from the kitchen to the living room, where he put on American country music.

'Do you recognise this?' he asked. 'Many Malagasy people like American country.'

I told him that I had heard this song at home, but could not tell him who the singer was. He brought the bottle of rum to the table and poured some in our glasses. I drank it, hid the pain it caused, suppressed a gag, and said 'it's strong.' It was a transparent liquid that tasted similar to the kind I had at Tom's house in Fianarantsoa. The next song that came on was Johnny Cash. 'I walk de line,' Alain's brother said, making Alain laugh at his English.

A medium-sized yellow dog squeezed through a portion of the fence made of bamboo.

'Ahh, this is my dog,' Alain said. 'She is very popular in the neighbourhood. I always catch dogs in my yard trying to make with her.' He laughed. 'I think they can smell her in here and they go crazy. Always coming in here.'

Alain's brother got up and went over to a charcoal barbeque where he began cooking a leg of goat. Alain's wife sat down with us and his son sat down on his lap. His son gulped down a glass of soda, prompting Alain to say 'this kid, he loves soda.' Alain put his arms around him and said into his ear 'soon you will have your circumcision. Malagasy boys cannot become men unless they are circumcised.'

I told him a story from Nelson Mandela's book *A Long Walk to Freedom*.

"When I was sixteen, the regent decided that it was time that I became a man. In Xhosa tradition, this is achieved through one means only: circumcision…For the Xhosa people, circumcision represents the formal incorporation of males into society."

On the day of the actual circumcision, Mandela wrote, "…we were clad only in our blankets, and as the ceremony began, with drums pounding, we were ordered to sit on a blanket on the ground with our legs spread out in front of us."

An old man who was a circumcision expert known as an *ingcibi*, knelt down in front of Mandela, pinched and pulled his foreskin, "and then, in a single motion, brought down his assegai. I felt as if fire was shooting through my veins; the pain was so intense that I buried my chin into my chest. Many seconds seemed to pass before I remembered the cry, and then I recovered and called out, *Ndiyindoda!*"

Alain enjoyed this story and his wife wanted to know what I had said to make him laugh. Alain spoke for about ten seconds, then I saw his thumb and index finger pinch the air, pull towards him, then with his left index and middle finger he made a scissor snip through the imaginary foreskin. This story and her reaction made us both laugh, and the sight of each other's laughter made us both erupt.

When Alain regained his composure, he told me 'my wife is from the southeast of Madagascar; from the Antanosy tribe. We each have different tribal customs. In her custom, a man must present a zebu to his father-in-law to show he can provide for his daughter. Other tribes sit down and have a negotiation and meeting with the man and if they are convinced he can provide for his daughter, he will give her to him. Once a father gives his daughter to a husband, she cannot come back to the father. She is with him.'

I asked Alain about divorce and said that I had met other people who had more than one wife.

'Yes, in some tribes it is more common and they have different customs. A woman must follow her husband's traditions and taboos. For example, in my wife's culture, they do not allow dogs. They will kill dogs. But in Betsileo, dogs are ok so in our family we have a dog because she must follow me.' I kept to myself the thought that maybe this was why the taxi-brousse full of passengers did not feel any pain at the death of the dog two weeks ago.

Our goat was ready and served in dishes. For the next few minutes there was only the sound of country music and lips smacking as everyone dug into the succulent meat. Next, we had freshwater eel that I thought tasted similar to the eel I have had in Japan. The next dish we ate was a piece of manioc, which was starchy, stringy, and fibrous with a bland taste. After what Dr Patel had told me about it being toxic, I hadn't eaten it since, but in joining Alain's family, I had several pieces and found it to be plain and edible, but an unremarkable root that provided little more than cheap calories to a poor nation.

The final dish was a plate of rice with small bits of tomato sauce and tuna. Overall, I enjoyed the food very much and thanked Alain and his wife for the time they took to prepare it. Not long after, Alain and I climbed back onto his moped and he drove me back to my hotel. I shook his hand and thanked him for an enjoyable time with his family. With a pledge to keep in touch, he went home, and I went to my room and had a great sleep.

I spent my final evening near a village called Ankilibe, which was less than thirty minutes from downtown Tulear. My hotel was called Bakuba, which was run by a woman and her husband who was absent at the moment. It was elegantly decorated, and had the architectural theme of a cross between a stone castle and an African thatched house. It relied largely on natural light, so the rooms and main guest areas had a shadowy cavernous feeling. The back of the hotel had a lounging pool and a view of the ocean.

That final evening, I sat at a dimly lit back terrace and watched the sun set below the Mozambique Channel. My host walked out to where I was sitting to check on me and ask if everything was alright. Before she left, I asked her why the villagers were walking like that along the beach and singing. This had been going on for the past fifteen minutes or so. There was a steady procession of people walking in loose bunches of three or four people moving along the beach across our line of sight to the ocean. The dusk had made it so I could no longer tell how many were there but I could still make out the shape of people moving, and I could still hear their singing.

'It's a funeral,' she said. 'A man died in the village. Some of our staff didn't come to work today because they had to take part in the ceremony.'

I sat there a little longer listening to the villagers sing as they walked by on the beach. I wondered if their songs mourned the loss of the village man, or if perhaps they somehow celebrated his life. I reflected on the fact that I had come to the island in search of life; in search of the amazing human and natural stories that were part of the history of this island. What will become of Madagascar twenty or thirty years into the future? Will the words in this travel narrative describe things that were part of the past, or will life today still be recognisable several decades into the future?

It seemed that after three months of travel in Madagascar, I still had just as many questions as I did before I had come here, and I resolved there and then to answer them all…slowly.

The End

Ingram Content Group UK Ltd.
Milton Keynes UK
UKHW021834270423
420895UK00002B/10